DATE			

Francis Bacon
and the Politics of Science

MO AITI MELI RA

MEDIO FIRMA GRIA

Hon.^mo Francisc.^o Bacon.^o Baro de Veru=
lam. Vice-Comes S.^cti Albani mortuus 9 Aprilis,
Anno Dñi. 1 6 2 6. Annoq, Aetat 66.

Francis Bacon

and the Politics of Science

JOHN E. LEARY, JR.

IOWA STATE UNIVERSITY PRESS / AMES

John E. Leary, Jr., teaches at the Francis W. Parker School in Chicago and offers courses in early modern science at the Newberry Library. He received his Ph.D. from the University of Chicago in 1988.

Title page portrait of Francis Bacon from an engraving in *Advancement of Learning* (1674), courtesy of Department of Special Collections, University of Chicago Library.

Authorization to photocopy items for internal or personal use, or the internal or personal use of specific clients, is granted by Iowa State University Press, provided that the base fee of $.10 per copy is paid directly to the Copyright Clearance Center, 27 Congress Street, Salem, MA 01970. For those organizations that have been granted a photocopy license by CCC, a separate system of payments has been arranged. The fee code for users of the Transactional Reporting Service is 0-8138-1407-3/94 $.10.

♾ Printed on acid-free paper in the United States of America

First edition, 1994

Library of Congress Cataloging-in-Publication Data
Leary, John E. Jr.
    Francis Bacon and the politics of science / John E. Leary, Jr. — 1st ed.
        p.   cm.
    Includes bibliographical references and index.
    ISBN 0-8138-1407-3 (alk. paper)
    1. Bacon, Francis 1561–1626 — Views on science.   2.   Science — Social aspects.   I.   Title.
Q143.B223L43   1994
509'.2 — dc20
[B]   93-31898

TO MY WIFE AND SONS

this work is lovingly dedicated

Contents

Preface

This book began as something quite different. Many years ago, I began to do research on John Wilkins's proposal for an international, philosophical language. Beyond the narrowly linguistic and philosophical problems implied in Wilkins's bold scheme, I soon discerned a level of intent scarcely hinted at in the existing literature on Wilkins or on the tradition of seventeenth-century language reform. While the proposal to refashion language may have sought to give new powers to communicate, it also had a restrictive and constraining aim — an aim which might legitimately be called political. Wilkins sought to define the lawful limits of discourse and above all to prevent people from saying what was not philosophically permissible by depriving them of the means to do so. Implicit in Wilkins's whole scheme for language reform was the desire — not the only one, but a very important one — to limit the freedom to speak and write, to prevent certain things from being said, to impose an external restraint on the public discourse of science and, ultimately, of social life in general. Alongside or beneath Wilkins's much-discussed latitudinarianism seemed to lurk an unmistakable, if muted, authoritarianism.

Such a reading of Wilkins's proposal led to certain reflections on the fundamentally conservative character of the Royal Society; to an appreciation of the way in which Restoration science must be understood partly as a reaction to the intellectual anarchy of the mid-century decades; and, finally, to the study of Francis Bacon, the man whose thought was in so many ways the fountainhead of the English scientific ethos in England prior to Newton. Bacon, like Wilkins, was quite interested in language as a determinant of thought, and it was this link that initially led me to look backwards from the Restoration bishop to the Stuart

Lord Chancellor. I was soon struck by a deeper affinity between the two men. Both were ardent partisans of order as against anarchy—in the political *and* the intellectual realms.

Closer study of Bacon disclosed what seemed to be a manifest contradiction between his politic, cautious, and deeply conservative character as a man and thinker and the intellectual radicalism that was often imputed to him. I found myself increasingly interested in his scheme for organizing science as a collective, collaborative enterprise—the program to which he gave the name *Great Instauration*—and then in his political ideas more generally. A conviction grew that any attempt to understand the ethos of Baconian science must begin with a careful study of Bacon himself—of his ideas and of his life.

In this way, what began as a study of John Wilkins has ended as a study of Francis Bacon. And yet, though I have shifted my gaze from one historical period to another, from one man to another, many of the problems and interests whose pursuit lies at the heart of the inquiry remain the same. Both men conceived of intellectual reform as a kind of social reform, as the establishment of a legitimate order where there was none before, and, finally, as intimately bound up with questions of power and control. Neither man was willing to treat the predicament of learning merely in terms of ideas or even of individual psychology. Both sought to redirect the way humans, living and working together, behaved, and both were willing to grapple with the imperfections of human nature. Both—but each in a way that expressed his own peculiarities and the distinctiveness of his historical setting—sought a political ascendancy over others in the commonwealth of learning as a way of redirecting and renewing learning itself. So there has been a continuity and enduring center to the meanderings that led from my first conceptions to the present study.

I have found the themes elusive and slippery ones, and, because my topic straddles the division between the political and intellectual realms, I have had to invent the framework within which the connections I seek to make seem viable. The end-product now seems awkward and clumsy, rather than elegant and efficiently spare. I hope, at any rate, that the substance is sound even if the elegance is lacking.

Acknowledgments

Two scholar-teachers of great humanity and wide-ranging intellect taught me when I was an undergraduate at the University of Chicago. I offer my deep and affectionate thanks to Christian Mackauer and Gerhardt Meyer.

Edward Collins, who now practices patent law in Boston, introduced me to the history of science in the late 1960s. Allen Debus taught me to look beyond the "classics" of science for a full historical understanding of the Scientific Revolution, and Keith Baker led me to ponder that early and profoundly important impulse which prompted men to attempt the creation of a "social science." Although I did not come to know Charles Gray until the present study of Bacon was already underway, it is difficult for me to express my full debt to him — as a careful and learned reader and as a friend who seemed miraculously able to understand what I was trying to say even before I had learned quite how to say it myself. These three men — Allen Debus, Keith Baker, and Charles Gray — have each, in his own distinctive way, challenged and broadened me. Each has my utmost thanks.

Along the way, thanks to Allen Debus, the late Robert Rosenthal, and funds provided by the Morris Fishbein Center for the Study of the History of Science and Medicine, I was privileged to work for nearly two years with the fine collections in the history of science which are housed in the Department of Special Collections at the Regenstein Library of the University of Chicago.

Two other libraries have been important to my work. One is the Newberry Library, where the richness of the collections is matched by the warmth and helpfulness of the staff. The other is the Winnetka Public Library, where my wonderful local librarians have shown a remarkable eagerness to bring books to me from far away.

At a crucial time in my life and studies, Julia Meyer became my friend and supporter. Though she read parts of the present work, offering comment and criticism, my true debt to her is more general and more personal. It is certainly no exaggeration to say that without her the present work would not have been completed.

I owe a similar debt to my teaching colleague, Bernard Markwell, whose immediate influence stems from his continuing effort to teach me about the traditions of Anglicanism, but whose importance to me has been much larger. For a decade and a half he has given me a daily dose of wit and a constant sense of intellectual companionship.

When I began this study I was single and naive, and barely understood how completely fitting it is for married scholars to dedicate their works to their spouses and children. In this respect at least I am wiser now. My wife, Jan, has borne with my labors nearly all the years of our marriage, has helped and cheered me, and has made space and time in our life together for me to work. Without her I would never have written this book.

My sons, James and William, have been a daily inspiration. With the joy and freedom that belongs to children alone they are true learners and makers of wonderful things.

Francis Bacon
and the Politics of Science

Fr. Baconis de Verulamio
SYLVA SYLVARVM,
Sive
HIST. NATVRALIS,
Et
NOVA ATLANTIS.

AMSTELODAMI,
Ex Officina Elzeviriana . A.º 1661.

Introduction

I t is common to associate the birth of modern science with a revolt against the authority of "the Ancients." In their enthusiasm for establishing the liberal character of modern science, some commentators have gone so far as to suggest that from its inception science harbored a deeply anti-authoritarian, even democratic animus. Indeed, there are some general arguments which seem to support such a contention. The abandonment of texts long held sacrosanct, the widespread criticism of the standard university curriculum, the formation of new intellectual circles outside the walls of the university, and the new emphasis on "experience" and "the senses" as a basis for knowledge about the natural world, for example, would all seem to signal some profound shift in favor of the free individual mind and against the strictures of established orthodoxies.

Later sixteenth- and early seventeenth-century England, the period and place within which this study is located, was the setting for a pro-

---

DURING the course of the seventeenth century, Baconianism became closely associated with the compiling of natural history. The Sylva Sylvarum, *published posthumously in 1627, was the beginning of what Bacon imagined would be a mammoth undertaking of collecting and organizing the raw materials of science. The* New Atlantis, *Bacon's utopia, is particularly famous in the history of science for its account of Salomon's House, a research institution that forms the scientific and technological heart of the island society. Courtesy of Department of Special Collections, University of Chicago Library.*

longed complex of struggles during the course of which various particular authorities and the principle of authority itself were the subject of fierce contention. In the area of religion, with the authority of the Pope still a recent memory, the emerging Anglican establishment found its own authority challenged by varying kinds of radical Protestantism, known loosely as Puritanism. In the political realm, a host of disagreements over governmental policy were leading England to a constitutional crisis which would eventually take the form of a dispute over the nature, legitimacy, and extent of royal authority. As in the case of religious disputes, it became difficult for those who advocated moderate limitations on royal authority to prevent the emergence of movements advocating more extreme limitations — movements which sometimes seemed to oppose the very principle of political authority.

It was not only a matter of isolated crises in the various subdivisions of the social order, but also of a process in which particular crises of legitimacy reinforced one another. Religious, social, political, and intellectual dissent frequently coalesced to contribute to a deeper and more thoroughgoing quarrel over the foundations of social and institutional life, the nature of authority, and the necessity for obedience. There was what might be called a general crisis of authority.

The most dramatic manifestation of this crisis was the English Revolution, in which the beheading of Charles and the seizure of power by Parliament were symbols of a profound shift taking place. The revolution unleashed a flood of beliefs and movements — political, social, religious, and intellectual — which challenged virtually every aspect of the traditional order. But the English Revolution was neither the origin nor the settlement of the deep tensions and stresses in English society during this period. They went back at least as far as the late years of Elizabeth's reign and would not be settled until the end of the seventeenth century.

It was against the background of this protracted period of disorientation, during which the nature and limits of legitimate authority in virtually every aspect of life were disputed, that early-modern English science began. Discussions of authority and liberty within the scientific realm were shaped in large part by the general crisis. Science had not yet achieved the institutional or ideological closure that might have allowed it to insulate itself from the larger controversies (as it has sometimes been able to do more recently). That is to say that there was not yet a single, unambiguously defined scientific community within the larger community of English society. One cannot yet speak of "a scientific community" or even of "scientists." One can say that men of many outlooks and persuasions were attracted for varying reasons to the planning and doing of what has come to be recognized as *science*. They brought with them varying definitions of what science should be and do, and they had different conceptions of the method, normative system, and institutional arrangements that should govern scientific inquiry. What we should expect under these circumstances — and what was indeed true — is that science during this period was not so much an intellectual position or commitment among other positions and commitments as a new battleground on which the old quarrels could be enacted anew. Modern science, that is to say, experienced at its birth what might justly be called constitutional struggles — struggles over the nature of intellectual authority and the shape of intellectual community, questions of legitimacy and citizenship — which seemed to echo some of the greater quarrels which wracked the political community per se.

It makes as little sense to try to characterize science in seventeenth-century England as "anti-authoritarian" or "democratic" as it does to apply these terms to politics or religion. In fact, there were some versions of science which were more anti-authoritarian, more democratic (though such terms must be redefined for a scientific context), others which were less so. The point is that science was still in the process of forging its self-definition and that in this process science to a degree mimicked the disorientation and conflict of the larger society.

THE ALLEGED LIBERALISM OF FRANCIS BACON

And what of *Baconianism,* that encompassing program which is said to have inspired seventeenth-century English science with a unifying vision and given it a practical agenda? Was not Baconianism the shared ideology that raised men of science above the sectarianism and factionalism of the age and gave them a common sense of purpose? And was not Baconianism a clearly "progressive" ideology, even in the current sense of the word, embodying ideals of anti-authoritarianism, liberty and even the democratization of the intellectual community?

The vicissitudes of Baconianism in the seventeenth century are as complex as the movement of every other aspect of English culture, but it is safe to say that there were many Baconianisms.[1] To call someone Baconian does not adequately specify their position in the great controversies which wracked the English intellectual scene. The mid-century, "revolutionary" versions of Baconianism which Charles Webster has studied in his *Great Instauration,* for example, differ radically from the Restoration Baconianism of the Royal Society.[2]

And what of Bacon himself? However much his writings might have been turned to different uses by different groups during the course of the century, can they now be made to yield some unambiguous general meaning which will clarify their relationship to the great controversies of the age?

The overwhelming opinion of twentieth-century scholars would seem to place Bacon squarely among the "progressive" forces of the age in terms of specifically scientific matters, and also in terms of many of the larger human issues which confronted the English at this point in history. Although there have been no good studies of the manner in which Bacon sought to organize scientific inquiry, many commentators casually impute to him democratic, libertarian, and egalitarian motives.

This "democratizing" tendency can be seen in offhand remarks by both Paolo Rossi[3] and Benjamin Farrington,[4] two of the most influential Bacon commentators of recent decades, and forms the backbone of Christopher Hill's argument in *Intellectual Origins of the English Revolution.*[5] The imputation to Bacon of democratic tendencies, coming from men who know both Bacon and the period well, would seem to be compelling, and yet they pose certain seemingly intractable problems. While the accounts of each of these scholars contain much that is sound and useful to the study of Bacon, all of them do more to obscure than to elucidate Bacon's actual ideas about the social organization of science, just as they confuse the actual relation which existed between science and the broader ideological struggles of seventeenth-century England.

Bacon did propose to organize science as a collective, collaborative enterprise, and it is not inappropriate to characterize his organizational ideas in terms of broad political attitudes and predispositions since his approach to organization was based on his political experiences and beliefs. His lifelong royalism, however, should make us wary of attributing democratic ideals to his vision of organized science. Not that it is impossible for him to have viewed the political commonwealth and the commonwealth of learning as operating according to different sets of principles, but it would be startling — and a fact requiring further explanation — to find such a radical disjuncture of principles between the two spheres. But no such reconciling explanation is required, for if we examine Bacon's ideas about organization dispassionately and without prejudices as to his "modernism" or "progressivism" we find no disjuncture between the ideas which underlay his political and his scientific schemes. On the contrary, there is a close correspondence.

In his schemes for organizing science no less than in his political thought generally, Bacon invoked views of human nature, of social life, and of government which were recognizably Tudor and profoundly conservative. At the same time he attempted to accommodate and capitalize on the changes which had already begun to disturb the familiar political and intellectual landscape by domesticating them and turning them to the advantage of the existing social and political order. Democracy, liberty, equality—these had little to do with Bacon's schemes for science because they were foreign to his whole outlook. If he aimed positively at the improvement of the conditions of human life, his pursuit of this aim was conditioned by the fear of ungoverned change, particularly the kind of change that was likely to be produced by ordinary people in public forms of discussion. If he quarreled with the authority of the Ancients and at times employed an anti-authoritarian rhetoric against the tyranny of traditional learning, it was hardly his belief that people could do without authority in their intellectual lives or that intellectual liberty should be enshrined as a fundamental, constitutional principle in the commonwealth of learning. In the course of developing his views, Bacon expressly condemned intellectual "democratie." He was not a believer in the virtues of the masses or commonality, and one of the most insistently recurring themes in all his writing—intellectual no less than political—concerned the dangers which the "popular" and the "vulgar" posed for progress. He stood squarely for a view of science which emphasized its closed, nonpublic character, just as he consistently sought to insulate the core workings of government from public view and public participation. His vision of science was elitist in its external face and hierarchical in its internal organization. While both government and science aimed at public good and human improvement, in his writings about both Bacon betrayed a pervasive, insistent belief that public benefactors must contend above all against the populace itself. For Bacon, scientific progress would not go hand in hand with public enlightenment but, on the contrary, depended on a dissociation of scientific inquiry from public discourse. Bacon's scheme, finally, did not rest on the liberation of the natural human mind from artificial constraints but on subjecting it to a new set of intellectual constraints which were more stringent than any of those attempted in the past. What Bacon wished, above all, was to introduce intellectual order where before there had only been chaos, government where there had been anarchy. In this he was doing no more than any Tudor statesman might have been expected to do once he turned his attention to the predicament of learning.

Far from demonstrating that science had some privileged place in the cultural storms of seventeenth-century England which lifted it above the time-bound character of the struggles and permitted it to play a prophetic or revolutionary role, a close study of Bacon's ideas about the organization of the scientific enterprise shows precisely the opposite. It demonstrates, in fact, that science was deeply enmeshed in the struggles of the time and conditioned by them. More specifically, the work of Bacon furnishes an opportunity for a case study of the way one particularly influential vision of science was shaped by the social and political outlook of its author and for the exploration of one particularly interesting nexus linking scientific thinking to general social thought in an age of controversy and conflict. Likewise, the study of Bacon offers a powerful caution against seeing science as an innately liberal enterprise (as if it had some intrinsically "modern" spirit of its own) or endowing Bacon with some emotionally appealing but intellectually mystifying prophetic vision. Finally, it offers the possibility of restoring to the study of Bacon particularly, and of seventeenth-century science generally, some sense of historical rootedness and proportion.

THE CENTRAL PLACE OF ORGANIZATION IN BACON'S THOUGHT

B acon's ideas on the organization of science—its government and administration—have not received the attention that they merit. On the one hand, the general case which he made for the new science has cast him in the role of rhetorician, propagandist, *buccinator*. On the other, his narrower efforts at outlining procedures and providing instigative examples have cast him as a methodologist, experimenter, or natural philosopher. To a great extent these two approaches to Bacon have tended to reflect the biases and interests of his "humanistic" and his "scientific" commentators. One of Bacon's principal innovations, however, lay somewhere between his diffuse campaign of literary and rhetorical suasion and his detailed prescriptions for scientific practice. This was his conception of the Great Instauration as a tightly organized and carefully governed enterprise of people working in concert. It is perhaps in his conception of scientific organization that we find a bridge between his humanistic and scientific concerns. Much of Bacon's rhetorical activity on behalf of the new science aimed not so much at persuading people to engage directly in scientific inquiry as at persuading them to enter a new kind of scientific community and to submit to the organizational regimen which alone would make scientific inquiry productive. It is this fact that renders unsatisfying those accounts of Bacon's thought which portray him principally as a general propagandist for certain new conceptions. Bacon sought something more specific and more ambitious than the public presentation of ideas. Beyond publicizing the new scientific ideas, therefore, he sought to found a new community of learning, recruit its members, give it government and laws, provision it, and launch it on a narrowly defined and rigidly controlled set of investigations. Much of his methodological writing and procedural prescriptions presupposed the establishment of such a community of scientists, so that apart from his ideas on organization many of his more detailed prescriptions for the practice of science make little sense. Above all, Bacon seemed to be calling for a new kind of social organization which would bind together, channel, and integrate the labors of people involved in scientific inquiry in a way that was novel and fruitful. It is only as a part of this larger program that the much-discussed prescriptions of method and procedure can be properly understood.

In focusing on Bacon's ideas about scientific organization, therefore, this study seeks to explore a topic which is not only important in its own right (the desirability of collaborative science and the consequent impulse to create new scientific institutions form a dominant and enduring theme in seventeenth-century discussions of science) but also holds a central place in Bacon's thought. It is in his treatment of the problem of organization that Bacon attempts to join satisfactorily the human material of scientific inquiry with the process of inquiry itself. Organization is the missing link which connects his general suasive campaign on behalf of science to his specific procedural prescriptions. And, finally, because Bacon came to do his serious work on science only in mid-life, after he had spent his youth and early middle age in legal and political activities, it represents the distinctive contribution that a man like Bacon—not, after all, really a professional philosopher or scientist but, rather, a man schooled principally in the ways of Tudor politics and law—could make to the world of learning.

Though I would argue that his thought on organization lies at the very heart of Bacon's thinking about science in general and as a consequence has an important bearing on nearly every aspect of his conception of scientific inquiry, the choice of this as a topic has necessitated the imposition of certain limits. It is in the interest of clarity to make some of these limits explicit at the outset. Many matters that have traditionally been of central concern to historians of science will not, or only tangentially, be treated here. For example, I do not treat in any substantial way that aspect of Bacon's methodological thought that deals with the intricacies of either induction or experimentation. Nor do I deal extensively with his philosophy of nature. Both method and philosophy of nature are, indeed, related to Bacon's conception of organization in ways that I try to explain, but my discussion of these matters goes no further than is necessary to specify their bearing on the focus of the study.

Implicit in the approach that I have taken is the conviction that

Bacon is best understood as a man whose fundamental attitudes and outlook were formed in the world of politics and law. The publication of his wide-ranging *Advancement of Learning* in 1605 shows that Bacon must have been a constant and ardent student of learned literature when, to outward appearances, he was wholly committed to professional and political advancement. But when he finally turned to serious writing about the reformation of learning and particularly that of science — the Great Instauration — it was principally as a "statesman" that he offered himself.

This approach has certain novel implications for interpreting Bacon's thought, but it also rests on a distinctive view of his personality and life. Therefore, I have decided to begin with a biographical sketch. Here certain caveats and disclaimers are in order. The reconstruction of Bacon's life is specifically intended to elucidate possible relationships between his political experience and outlook on the one hand and his approach to scientific reform on the other. It is not a full-dress biography, but rather a biographical essay intended to lay a foundation for the interpretation of his writings.

The most embracing definition of Bacon's commitment to learning lies in his desire to establish a new order among the branches of learning and a new order among learners themselves. It is precisely this attempt at reordering that I indicate by the term *organization*. I hope not only to show the central place that the problem of organization occupied in the conceptual order of Bacon's thought but also to suggest the way in which organizational ambitions and convictions might have formed a bridge between Bacon's political career and his activities on behalf of learning.

Bacon's conviction that the investigation of nature must be a collective, collaborative enterprise has not, of course, gone unnoticed by Bacon commentators. Yet there are a number of commonplace assertions about the nature of the collaboration that bear reexamination. It has been suggested, for example, that Bacon rode the crest of a popular scientific wave, that his ideas about organized science were a recognition and legitimation of this groundswell of popular science, and that his idea of collective science was little more than an attempt to draw together and join those forces that had already gained momentum among artisans, mechanics, and empirics. This view ignores Bacon's very serious criticism of popular science as essentially flawed by its lack of direction and discipline.

It is not uncommon for those commentators who interpret Bacon's ideas through the eyes of the Baconian generation which followed to view the Royal Society (a bit too uncritically) as an actualization of Salomon's House and to interpret Bacon's ideas about organization in terms of what came to pass in the century following his death. *Organization,* however, is much broader and more encompassing than the establishment of a scientific society like the Royal Society. Bacon sought to analyze the various stages of scientific inquiry and the strengths and weaknesses of the men who would be responsible for conducting it, to design a comprehensive regimen to govern virtually every aspect of the inquiry, and to plan for the relationship between the new community so constituted and the larger society. The loose arrangements of the Royal Society would, in his eyes, have fallen far short of the requirements of the Great Instauration, no matter how much its members might subscribe to Baconian ends and Baconian slogans. There were aspects of Bacon's thought, moreover, that men like Sprat and Cowley either did not understand or ignored, and a great gulf separates Bacon's conception of organized science from the prevailing conceptions of the Restoration period.

Finally, there have been many who, eager to establish the larger progressive import of Bacon's thought, have attributed to him intimations of libertarianism, egalitarianism, and democracy. Such formulations read into Bacon a modern progressivism which is highly questionable. If Bacon opposed the illicit authority of classical and scholastic philosophy, it was out of a sense that the human mind must be submitted to an authority that was not specious but legitimate. If he spoke of creating a method that would level wits, it was not in the interests of egalitarianism but of unexceptional submission to an externally imposed intellectual rule which would give little leeway to individual judgment. In the few explicit references Bacon made to intellectual democracy, he made it clear that in his view the very idea was tantamount to intellectual anarchy and the debasement of ideas by the vulgar.

Bacon's conception of scientific organization has not, in short, been adequately treated as an separate topic, nor has its central place in his thought as a whole been recognized.

POLITICS AND SCIENCE IN BACON'S THOUGHT

As I began to study the way in which Bacon conceived of collective scientific inquiry, I found myself drawn to his ideas about collective life more generally—that is, to his political thought. I came to believe that Bacon's political outlook formed an important key to his whole approach to science and that much of what he did—or at least intended to do—in the scientific realm amounted to the application

of political analysis, political wisdom, and political solutions to the predicament of scientific inquiry, which, in terms of conventional wisdom
in Bacon's day, should have been far removed from politics. Many in the
sixteenth century still clung to the older classical idea that the contemplative life and the active life were poles apart, and in numerous places
Bacon seems himself to have subscribed to this idea. Yet his treatment of
science as a form of activity — even of labor — requiring the same sort of
administration and government as other collective endeavors does not
confirm the idea that for him the *vita activa* and the *vita contemplativa*
were mutually opposed. Reflections such as these led me to include a
section on Bacon's political outlook as part of my effort to elucidate his
thought on scientific organization.

This decision had the further consequence of leading to biographical inquiries that were far more extensive than I had initially planned.
The juxtaposition of Bacon's political and scientific ideas — which
sounds innocent enough in itself — brought me face to face with the fact
that in the Bacon literature generally, and in the biographical literature
specifically, there has been little attempt to explain the connections between Bacon's political and philosophical sides. Bacon himself frequently spoke of them as if they represented incompatible alternatives,
and many scholars have taken his word for this. The possibility that his
political and philosophical careers might have been substantively related
has not so far been seriously explored.

Let me state what I hope to accomplish in the chapters which follow. In reviewing Bacon's biography, I wish to establish that, far from
being mutually incompatible alternatives, Bacon's political and philosophical careers seem to display a certain parallel development, both
apparently drawing on the same energies, reflecting the same motives,
rising and falling together. From a biographical standpoint there is no
reason to reject a close relationship between Bacon's political outlook
and his schemes for the advancement of natural inquiry. Then I take up
Bacon's political outlook. In addition to a general account of some of
the main themes in his political thinking, I show more specifically that
Bacon was no mere reactionary in politics as has sometimes been
claimed, particularly by those who wish to sharpen the contrast between
his political and scientific careers. I argue, on the contrary, that his
political thought combines deeply conservative social and political principles with a genuine desire for material progress — order and increase
being closely connected in his mind. Finally, I take up Bacon's ideas
about the organization of science and try to show that here, as in his
political ideas, we find a balancing of conservative — even strongly authoritarian — organizational ideas with a desire for intellectual progress.

The similarities between Bacon's political ideas and his ideas about organizing science are striking. Aside from elucidating an important aspect of Bacon's Great Instauration, the exploration of these political dimensions of Bacon's program for learning and the demonstration of a close relationship between the political and scientific dimensions of his thought suggest a unity of thought as a whole, and also a starting point for understanding the intellectual development which carried him from politics to science.

FR. BACONIS
De
VERVLAM.
Angliæ Cancellarii
DE
AVGMENTIS
SCIENTIARVM
Lib. IX.

AMSTELÆDAMI,
Apud Henricum Wetstenium. 1694.

I

Bacon's Life

*B*ACON *planned for the Great Instauration (his scheme for the systematic discovery of natural knowledge) to begin with a review of existing branches of learning and knowledge. Although the* Advancement of Learning, *published first in 1605, constitutes a first version of such a review, the* De Augmentis, *a greatly expanded Latin version of the* Advancement *that was published in 1623, stands as the final and fullest version of Bacon's survey of intellectual culture in his time. Courtesy of Department of Special Collections, University of Chicago Library.*

1

The Formative Period

B acon's life is not well understood. The outward events, of course, are well-enough known, particularly for the later years when he had become a public figure. But of the interior dimensions of his personality and of his most fundamental motivations, we know little with any certainty. Bacon himself wrote much about his high-mindedness and general passion for human improvement, and on the basis of such self-portraiture many scholars have constructed extremely adulatory and unconvincingly idealized accounts of Bacon-the-man. The skepticism recommended by Jonathan Marwil has been too rare. "No man, of course, is an impartial judge of himself," writes Marwil, "and memory invariably serves present interests. But for too long the charm and detached quality of Bacon's style have won him undeserved credibility."[1] Bacon was not a man to indulge in candid outpourings of his heart and mind, and at times his own words seem to confirm Marwil's admonition. It was Bacon himself who wrote in his essay "Of Simulation and Dissimulation" that "nakedness is uncomely, as well in mind as body,"[2] and the suspicion arises that virtually all of what he had to say about himself — even if he sincerely believed it to be true — must be viewed as part of an essentially rhetorical self-presentation that was consciously or unconsciously adapted to the occasion.

Nor is it merely Bacon's continual rhetorizing that should make the student of his life cautious. Bacon was a genuinely complex man whose character and motivation defy one-dimensional formulations. Bacon's ambition — to cite a pertinent element of his personality — was as ambiguous in its directions, aims, and objects of satisfaction as the aspirations and drives of the age in which he lived. At times (as when he outlined grand projects for the reform of the law or the beginning of a new science) he seems to embrace humanity's future welfare with the passion, sincerity, and selflessness of an evangelical reformer and visionary. At others (as when he offered counsel to readers of the *Essays* or to the Crown in numerous letters of advice) he seemed a shrewd and wily *politique* who measured every action, every choice against present and immediate opportunities. At still others (as when, in the years of his success, he indulged his taste for high living and expensively liveried servants or allowed his household and staff to become involved in bribe taking) he seems just another self-seeker motivated by the most ordinary and uninteresting of human pretensions and desires, capable of the most venal compromises.

Bacon frequently presented himself as a selfless benefactor of humanity at large, but he was singularly unsuccessful in his relationships with the men and women among whom he lived and worked and on whose support the accomplishment of his grand purposes depended. He was thin-skinned and oversensitive to those around and above him, and his capacity for taking offense was apparently equalled by his capacity for giving it. Bacon never inspired among those around him the confidence, trust, affection, or true respect which he desired, nor does he seem ever to have succeeded in trusting them. Toward those whom he considered beneath him, he sometimes exhibited an offensive and alienating sense of his own superiority, while to those who figured as his superiors he showed a deference which was often interpreted as fawning subservience. "There is little friendship in the world," he wrote in one of his essays, "and least of all between equals, which was wont to be magnified. That that is, is between superior and inferior, whose fortunes may comprehend the one the other."[3] His philanthropy and plans for collaborative enterprise were thus joined to a keen attentiveness to his own status, an oversensitivity to the slights he believed to be inflicted on him, and an almost perpetual feeling of being undervalued and misunderstood. Many of his contemporaries seem to have seen him as a climber and manipulator.

Bacon always justified his quest for political position on the grounds that power would enable him to do good, but in some respects his years in power were the least inspired and least productive period in his mature life. This has given his ambition an ambiguous quality and raises questions about his true — as distinct from his stated — ends. It is in his writings rather than his life that we can see the grand and orderly sweep of Bacon's mind and vision, and it is principally on the basis of his literary self-presentation that scholars have interpreted him as a man driven by simple altruistic passion and well in control of himself. But when we look at his life—at his actions and choices—we see a man torn by competing desires. He spent much of his energy in petty and meaningless affairs and his failures, in the end, stemmed much more from his own self-defeating foibles and psychological divisions than from the insensitivity, indifference, or shortsightedness of his contemporaries. It is thus with a character whose deep motivations are obscure and ambiguous that we must deal. Bacon's personality was genuinely and deeply complex in a way that has not been sufficiently emphasized.

Bacon sometimes schematized his life ambitions by reference to the classical topoi of *vita activa* and *vita contemplativa,* and many biographers have followed him in this. In this view, Bacon was engaged in two distinct and potentially incompatible careers—those of politics and philosophy. Such a separation at the biographical level has made it possible to treat Bacon's ideas and motivations in each domain as mutually isolable and indeed has sometimes given rise to portraits of virtually different men.

Despite Bacon's occasional use of them, these motifs suggest misleading characterizations of Bacon's commitments to both politics and philosophy. In politics Bacon represented himself as a peculiarly "contemplative" statesman, believing that policy should grow out of the broadest, most far-sighted kind of reflection. In philosophy, on the other hand, Bacon argued that the end of true knowledge must be use, and also that the scientist must be active in the acquisition of knowledge. Bacon's construction of political and philosophical wisdom, in other words, seems to conflate the active and the contemplative in a new way which precludes any simple opposition.

At the biographical level, the opposition of *vita activa* and *vita contemplativa* fails to help schematize Bacon's actual activities. Even given the difficulty he claimed to have had in choosing between politics and philosophy, one might expect to find in Bacon's life an alternation between philosophical and political activity. An examination of the broad contours of his life, however, yields a different and suggestive pattern. The years of political waiting and thwarted ambition were also a period during which the kernels of certain new philosophical ideas were enunciated in the most rudimentary way but not developed into their historically consequential form. Yet the years of political rise, with the attendant heightening of demands on Bacon's time and energy, were precisely the period during which the earlier seeds grew into their recognizably Baconian form and were given literary embodiment. The years of political success, in turn, were a time of philosophical consolidation though perhaps of waning creativity; the years of political disgrace, a time of renewed ambitions in both politics and philosophy followed by discouragement and weariness in both areas. The reconstruction of Bacon's life that is presented in this and the following chapter suggests that in Bacon's case politics and philosophy may have been mutually supportive and mutually stimulating activities, rather than opposites that pulled him in two different directions.

If Bacon's political and philosophical careers unfolded in tandem, rather than by way of mutual opposition and alternation, two important consequences follow. First, we might understand his life differently — not as that of a man torn between two incompatible vocations but as a single biographical development manifesting itself in different domains. Such a possibility might lead us to speculate on what sort of protean aptitudes, orientations, and ambitions could have expressed themselves simultaneously in such apparently different ways and on whether, at a psychological level, there was some cross-stimulation and -fertilization at work. Second, we might entertain the possibility that Bacon's political and philosophical ideas and activities are substantively and intrinsically related in ways that are not yet recognized. In this light, his works on the reformation of natural science might come to seem not merely the writings of a man who happened also to be pursuing a political career, but rather as precisely the sort of reform scheme that would be proposed by a man with Bacon's political outlook and experience.

In fact, much of what Bacon had to say about science — and particularly his desire to organize scientific inquiry as a collective and collaborative enterprise — reflects the political outlook he developed prior to his serious work on behalf of science. The more immediate aim of the following biographical sketch is to show that within the context of his life Bacon's political and scientific pursuits can be understood as developing along parallel trajectories and to suggest that the relation between these two apparently disparate activities was not one of opposition and alternation but something much more close and complex.

CHILDHOOD AND YOUTH, 1561–1579

Francis Bacon was the youngest son of Nicholas Bacon (1509/10–1578/79), who by the time of Francis's birth in 1561 had become the Lord Keeper of the Great Seal of England. Nicholas Bacon was most certainly one of those men who had risen in the first half of the sixteenth century and he embodied many of the most characteristic virtues of the "new men" who played such a central role in later Tudor administration. According to his recent biographer, Robert Tittler, he was more than the mere representative of a type.

He brought to his political endeavours a distinct philosophical outlook well grounded in the literary and ideological trends of the Renaissance; he championed progressive reforms in education and government administration as well as in his proper *metier* of the law; he served as an ardent and enlightened supporter of Puritanism whenever he could; and he played a crucial role in determining the course of politics in East Anglia following the demise of Thomas Howard. In short . . . Bacon's life fully epitomizes many of the central themes of the Tudor era.[4]

Educated at Corpus Christi College, Cambridge, and at Gray's Inn, Nicholas began his career under Henry VIII, building his advancing fortunes on a foundation of legal practice and shrewd investment but moving surely and deliberately toward politics by way of Parliament and the courts. Already an important figure by the time Mary acceded to the throne, the cautious and tactful elder Bacon weathered the trying interim period and, with the help of his friend and brother-in-law, William Cecil, emerged upon the accession of Elizabeth as the Lord Keeper of the Great Seal. By 1559 he was exercising the full powers of the office of Lord Chancellor. Nicholas Bacon's success during these years owed much to his unostentatious practicality and preference for moderation, his motto being *Mediocria Firma* (Safety in Moderation).

Francis Bacon undoubtedly owed much of his outlook, ambition, and success to his father, eventually rising to his father's position in government, but it would be a mistake to let the continuities overshadow the discontinuities. If father and son shared many of the same aspirations, they were nonetheless very different in the early experiences which formed and seasoned them. Nicholas Bacon had spent his early life building his private fortunes and learning the kind of stolid, self-restraining patience which would see him through the vexed Marian period and make him a desirable servant to Elizabeth. Unlike his father, Francis Bacon, having grown up in the lap of his family's recently acquired wealth and political success, turned out to be burdened with a sense of entitlement. Overeager for achievement and overneedful of recognition, he was thin-skinned and quick to take offense, forever feeling unappreciated, impatient of delay, and never quite in full control of his financial and personal life. In Nicholas one sees a man who was seasoned and matured before he entered the heady circles of political power and whose style and personal fortunes were largely set before his political ambitions were aroused; in Francis, on the contrary, one who had been raised from childhood in the artificial, perhaps overstimulating, society of the court by important and busy parents. In Francis there seems to have been a precocity of talent but none of the solidly grounded ego of the father.

It was probably to his mother that Bacon owed much of his personal fragility and impatient zeal. Nicholas Bacon's professional rise had brought him into contact with the humanist court circle of Anthony Cooke, and following the death of his first wife, Jane Ferneley, probably in 1552, Nicholas Bacon married Anne Cooke, the second daughter of Anthony. All of Anthony Cooke's daughters married well, and the marriage of Anne's older sister, Mildred, to William Cecil, Lord Burghley, was to hold a special significance for Francis Bacon's life. Anne herself was born in 1528 and was said to have served as governess to Edward VI while her father was his tutor. Like her sisters, Anne received a broad, humanist education and was reported to read Latin, Greek, Italian, and French fluently. She gained some repute as a Latin translator, well-versed in theology, and as an ardent Puritan. She bore Nicholas two sons, Anthony and Francis.

Most of what we know of Anne as a mother comes from later correspondence in which she appears as an over-anxious and over-bearing parent, meddlesome and opinionated, confident that she and not her two sons (then in middle-age) knew what was best for them. It is not uncommon for biographers to credit her with giving Francis his taste for learning and his zeal for reform, but it seems unlikely that she was an easy mother for small children, already made unnaturally precocious by the artificiality of court life.

We do not really know much about Bacon's childhood. There are a few stories, part of the standard repertoire of biographers who are eager to find something to fill up the chapter recounting his childhood and youth. These stories, told by Bacon himself as a man and therefore naturally suspect, emphasize his intellectual precocity and artful charm. Much more telling are Bacon's general references to family such as appear in the *Essays,* and, though always framed in terms of detached wisdom, these are almost uniformly negative, emphasizing the burdensomeness of family life and the likelihood that its emotional demands would interfere with the accomplishment of great things. Except with his brother Anthony there is no evidence that Bacon formed deep emotional ties with others, and it is possible that this was due to a certain emotional void in his early years. We know that between the birth of Anthony and that of Francis (1559), Nicholas Bacon took on the duties of Lord Chancellor and that from that time until his death in 1579 his official responsibilities must have consumed the great bulk of his time and energies. We know also that in 1564, when Francis was three and Anthony five, Anne Bacon was heavily involved in preparing her translation from the Latin of Bishop Jewel's *Apology for the Church of England.* It is possible that this youngest child of two preoccupied parents simply suffered from a kind of emotional neglect.

When Anthony left for Cambridge in 1573 at the age of fifteen, Francis was sent along at the age of twelve. Spedding noted that this was particularly young for a boy to be sent to university, and we might wonder whether this also was an indication that Francis was being left to his own emotional devices too early.

We know little about Bacon at Cambridge. In Rawley's account we hear of an early aversion to Aristotle.

> Whilst he was commorant in the university, about sixteen years of age (as his lordship hath been pleased to impart unto myself), he first fell into the dislike of the philosophy of Aristotle; not for the worthlessness of the author, to whom he would ever ascribe all high attributes, but for the unfruitfulness of the way; being a philosophy (as his lordship used to say) only strong for disputations and contentions, but barren of the production of works for the benefit of the life of man; in which mind he continued to his dying day.[5]

Spedding and many other biographers since have made this brief statement by Rawley the basis for their contention that Bacon's passionate commitment to intellectual reform dates from his youth at Cambridge. Spedding writes:

> From that moment he had a vocation which employed and stimulated all the energies of his mind, gave a value to every vacant interval of time, an interest and significance to every random thought and casual accession of knowledge; an object to live for as wide as humanity, as immortal as the human race; an idea to live in vast and lofty enough to fill the soul for ever with religious and heroic aspirations.[6]

The evidence for this statement, however, is scant. What we know for certain is that when he left Cambridge Bacon pursued a course that seemed exclusively directed toward a career in law and politics and that it was another quarter century before he would begin to write seriously about philosophical matters.

In 1576 Bacon was admitted to Gray's Inn, but shortly after he began his legal studies he was sent along with his brother, Anthony, to accompany Sir Amyas Paulet on a diplomatic mission to France. The experience was presumably to prepare both boys for a political career. Bacon travelled around France as part of Sir Amyas's entourage — Paris, Blois, Tours, and Poitiers — and seems to have had ample opportunities for acquainting himself with continental affairs. While in Paris, Bacon later wrote, he had a dream that his father's house was plastered over with black mortar, and a few days later he learned of his father's death. Nicholas Bacon had died after falling asleep at an open window and, according to Rawley, contracting a fatal illness.

Beyond its psychological impact, at which one can only guess, the death of Sir Nicholas has always been taken as an event which shaped Francis's life in a specific practical way. The youngest son had by a mischance been left without the provision of an income. As Rawley recounted the situation:

> In [Francis's] absence in France his father the lord-keeper died, having collected (as I have heard of knowing persons) a considerable sum of money, which he had separated, with intention to have made a competent purchase of land for the livelihood of this his youngest so (who was only unprovided for; and though he was the youngest in years, yet he was not the lowest in his father's affection); but the said purchase being unaccomplished at his father's death, there came no greater share to him than his single part and portion of the money dividable amongst five brethren; which means he lived in some straits and necessities in his younger years.[7]

While most biographers have accepted this account as straightforward, Epstein has said that "the reasons Bacon was not left comfortable and secure remain unclear."[8] Tittler tells us that Nicholas Bacon, ill long before he was finally taken by pneumonia, "faced the prospect [of death] with confidence and characteristic forethought. His preparations were as methodical as his speeches in parliament."[9] As early as August 1576, Nicholas Bacon had begun the construction of his tomb and funerary monument in St. Paul's, and these were apparently completed about a year later, at which time Nicholas made arrangements for their perpetual care. It is hard to reconcile the foresight and methodical planning which Tittler calls "characteristic" with Sir Nicholas's apparent lapse in the matter of providing for his youngest son. Perhaps it is part of a larger pattern of early experience, and perhaps it contributed to Bacon's life-long sense of being unappreciated and unrecognized. There is no way to be certain. It is clear, however, that Francis Bacon entered upon his adulthood with considerably less financial security than his upbringing had led him to expect. Financial problems would plague him throughout life even after his own income had become quite substantial, and it is highly questionable whether a larger estate at the outset would have changed any of this. The real problems later were Bacon's uncontrollable prodigality and addiction to the lavish accoutrements of court life, which were a function of his personality more than of anything else.

One biographer has pictured Bacon's childhood and youth as an "Elizabethan Eden," lost upon the sudden death of his father.[10] Given what we know about Bacon as an adult, there is little reason to believe that he had a particularly happy childhood however splendid its physical setting and however illustrious the attainments of his parents.

Despite his lack of personal financial fortune, Bacon entered young adulthood with many advantages: a background of wealth and power which made him unmistakably a member of the politically important upper class, the beginnings of an education, and court connections which he would use to the fullest.

DEBUT IN THE PUBLIC WORLD, 1579–1591

When Francis Bacon returned to England from France following Nicholas's death, he moved into his father's rooms at Gray's Inn and resumed his legal studies. He also immediately set about launching his political career by applying to his uncle, Lord Burghley, for a position in the Crown's legal service. He failed in this initial bid.

Bacon was eager to get ahead. Impatient for advancement and apparently convinced that he was entitled to special treatment by virtue of his late father's position, he seems to have alienated certain older men who saw him as impatient and forward. Bacon had been admitted to the bar as "utter barrister" in 1582. Normally there was a five-year waiting period following admission before a barrister could practice (as a "bencher") in the Westminster courts. Bacon used the influence of his uncle, Lord Burghley, to have this waiting period shortened and in so doing seems to have elicited some negative comment.

While continuing at Gray's Inn, Bacon began his parliamentary career in the 1580s, and here, too, his desire for rapid progress seems to have alienated at least one of his older colleagues. Probably through Burghley's influence, Bacon was returned in a by-election for a seat in Parliament early in 1581. Later, in the session of 1584–85, he is known to have taken on committee work, but nothing substantial is known about the nature or extent of his participation. We know from an entry in his journal that William Fleetwood, a member for London and an old parliamentary hand, found Bacon irritating. Although the entry is cryptic, it seems that Bacon included in a speech some reference to his father and that Fleetwood found this inappropriate, as if Bacon was calling attention to his parentage to bolster his own position. Epstein suggests that perhaps "Bacon's age and familial connections did cause resentment among his colleagues."[11] Evidence from a later period in his life suggests that Bacon could treat those whom he regarded as his social inferiors (no matter how great their abilities) with open contempt. Perhaps he conveyed some sense of social superiority in his manner even at the beginning of his career.[12] These are only hints of a certain brashness on Bacon's part, however, and Epstein cautions that although "arrogance is a characteristic that many would find appropriate in describing Bacon throughout his life, we know too little about him, this early in his career, to determine whether he had earned such a label."[13]

Bacon appears more prominently in the Parliament of 1586–87. Here he is recorded as having spoken in favor of the execution of Mary Stuart and as having favored a grant to the government. Opposing the view that Bacon's position during this Parliament was one of wholehearted advocacy of royal leadership in foreign policy and that Bacon was already fully committed to a defense of the royal prerogative, Epstein argues for a more subtle interpretation of Bacon's position and motives at this time. "Bacon was still a political novice, constantly observing, occasionally participating, and always seeking an opening that might lead to political power."[14] Epstein supports his view of this as an experimental phase in Bacon's parliamentary career by reference to Bacon's advocacy of a bill which would have reformed purveyance (the right of the government to purchase its provisions on the market at an advantageous fixed price), a bill which the Crown staunchly opposed. Epstein suggests that here Bacon may have been motivated by "the hope of winning the trust of his colleagues."[15] This session was important in Bacon's career in any case, according to Epstein, for it "marked Bacon's emergence as an active participant in the Commons."[16]

In addition to his legal pursuits and his involvement in these parliamentary sessions, Bacon began to write on political issues during the 1580s. In a letter of advice to Queen Elizabeth which Gardiner attributes to late 1584 or early 1585, for example, Bacon urged the Crown to follow a generally moderate and conciliatory course in framing its religious policies. In a fuller piece, "An Advertisement Touching the Controversies of the Church of England," written in 1589, Bacon advised moderation in dealing with radical Protestants. Epstein believes that the "Advertisement" is somewhat naive but a good indication of the direction of Bacon's political thought in this period:

> His efforts in the 1580s to advise on religious affairs should perhaps be seen as the thoughtful attempts of a concerned man, a gifted writer, and a developing philosopher. It remains questionable, however, whether he ever fully grasped the character of radical Protestantism.[17]

I shall discuss the substance of this piece in greater detail when we come to examine Bacon's political ideas. Here it is sufficient to note that Bacon began early to write and think with an eye to cultivating an image of himself as a policymaker, using his pen (as he would do to the end of his life) to recommend himself for political advancement.

If Bacon was naive about the nature of Puritanism, as Epstein suggests, he was perhaps even more naive about the nature of political advancement under Elizabeth. His father's office and his uncle's continuing status in the government undoubtedly opened many doors for the young Bacon. But they guaranteed nothing. He would have done well to cultivate his father's stolid patience and dependability. Also, it ill befitted a young man beginning his career, no matter how distinguished his background or how powerful his connections, to alienate those with whom he would have to work—in Parliament or the law. A pleasing manner, the ability to get along well with colleagues, and the capacity for give and take, all these counted for a good deal in the professional, political, and court life of the time—perhaps more than a quick mind and talented pen. So far as its governing circles were concerned, England was a surprisingly small community where personal reputation played an important role. But Bacon would never have ease with people. Nor would he ever make any real political progress under Elizabeth. It is hard to believe that his social ineptitude was not at least part of the cause.

Epstein suggests that Bacon was naive in yet one other way. Although he had gained entrance to the legal and political world, he had not yet had to deal with the cold ruthlessness which could rule the inner circles of real power and had not yet learned "how brutal the struggle for power could be." Epstein adds that "the 1590s were to provide him with that lesson."[18]

A DECADE OF FRUSTRATION, 1591–1603

I f the 1580s were a decade of political and professional initiation for Bacon, the 1590s were a time of deepening experience during which he found himself drawn close to the seats of real power but, at the same time, repeatedly denied the appointments he desperately sought. The decade was overshadowed by his association with Essex, the dazzling favorite to whom Bacon pledged his service and on whom he counted to further his career. In the end, however, his association with Essex did not secure the position he wanted. At the close of the decade, Essex was in disgrace and facing trial, and Bacon was still without advancement.

Before recounting the events of this period we must examine Bacon's own account of his position at the age of thirty-one. A letter written to his uncle, Lord Burghley, is particularly interesting for the

light it sheds on our problem: the relationship between Bacon's political
and philosophical ambitions. Bacon here presented himself for the first
(time as poised between a life of politics and a life of philosophy — the
traditional dichotomy between the *vita activa* and the *vita contemplativa* — and the letter is a key document for those who interpret Bacon's
life by way of these classical topoi. But the letter was above all a request
for help in furthering his political career; this was the context for the
references to philosophy.

Near the beginning of the letter Bacon praised Burghley as "the atlas
of this commonwealth, the honour of my house, and the second founder
of my poor estate." He assured his uncle that political advancement
would not threaten his fragile health, "because I account my ordinary
course of study and meditation to be more painful than most parts of
/ action are."[19] The account which Bacon gave in the remainder of the
letter of his philosophical ambitions was couched in the form of a statement of what he would do if he did not succeed in politics.

> *I confess that I have as vast contemplative ends, as I have moderate
> civil ends: for I have taken all knowledge to be my province; and if I
> could purge it of two sorts of rovers, whereof the one with frivolous
> disputations, confutations, and verbosities, the other with blind experi-
> ments and auricular traditions and impostures, hath committed so
> many spoils, I hope I should bring in industrious observations,
> grounded conclusions, and profitable inventions and discoveries; the
> best state of that province. This, whether it be curiosity, or vain glory,
> or nature, or (if one take it favourably)* philanthropia, *is so fixed in my
> mind as it cannot be removed. And I do easily see, that place of any
> reasonable countenance doth bring commandment of more wits than of
> a man's own; which is the thing I greatly affect. And for your Lordship,
> perhaps you shall not find more strength and less encounter in any
> other. And if your Lordship shall find now, or at any time, that I do
> seek or affect any place whereunto any that is nearer unto your Lord-
> ship shall be concurrent, say then that I am a most dishonest man. And
> if your Lordship will not carry me on, I will not do as Anaxagoras did,
> who reduced himself with contemplation unto voluntary poverty: but
> this I will do; I will sell the inheritance that I have, and purchase some
> lease of quick revenue, or some office of gain that shall be executed by
> deputy, and so give over all care of service, and become some sorry
> book-maker, or a true pioner in that mine of truth, which (he said) lay
> so deep.*[20]

Extracts from Bacon's own writings are set in *italic.*

The letter is interesting but ambiguous.

In the first place, many of the ideas and phrases in the letter seem clearly to prefigure the outlook and program that Bacon would develop seriously after 1603. His reference to "two sorts of rovers," Aristotelian academics and popular experimenters, looks forward to his fully developed critique of the commonwealth of learning. His mention of "industrious observations" and "grounded conclusions" anticipates his central interest in method. His linking of "profitable inventions and discoveries" to *philanthropia* foreshadows the practical and humanitarian ends of Baconian science. His desire for a "commandment of more wits than [his] own," finally, indicates that he already thinks of learning as a potentially collective enterprise in which he might play a directing role. It is thus clear that certain key ideas were seminally present already in the early 1590s. Bacon's statement that he has "taken all knowledge to be [my] province," however, calls for a final comment. Though this is an idea that is central to a work like the *Advancement of Learning,* it was precisely such an all-embracing commitment that he would have to put behind him before he could develop the idea of science as a *special* kind of learning, whose progress would depend on segregating it from the world of learning at large. There is no indication, in other words, that Bacon had yet begun seriously to distinguish the project issued in the *Advancement* from that which yielded the *Novum Organum.*

Secondly, the exact relation between Bacon's political and his philosophical ambitions was still unclear. Bacon seems to be saying here that he wished for a political post so that he would be in a position to carry out his philosophical schemes. It was on the basis of such a reading that Spedding could conclude:

> His main object still was to find ways and means for prosecuting his great philosophical enterprise; his hope and wish still was to obtain these by some office under the Government, from which he might derive both position in the world which would carry influence, employment in the State which would enable him to serve his country in her need, and income sufficient for his purposes, — without spending all his time in professional drudgery.[21]

The idea that Bacon sought political power only in order to further his philosophical schemes has prevailed among many of Spedding's successors, but it has not gone unchallenged. Jonathan Marwil, principally interested in Bacon's political career, has treated Spedding's interpretation with some skepticism. Bacon often presented his philosophical commitments as primary, it is true, but Bacon was not "a reasonably dependable observer of himself." Bacon's statements "habitually, if not always intentionally, solicit the world to see him as he would have liked, at the moment, to be seen."[22] Marwil thinks that this letter is "more plausibly construed as an attempt by Bacon to justify himself and press his uncle to live up to the title of being 'the second founder of my poor estate.' "

> He claims to want only "some middle place that I could discharge" and dismisses the often heard objections — age, health, arrogance — to his advancement. It is not really for himself, however, that he makes his suit. Instead, he would use the leisure office would give him, as well as the "wits" it might enable him to employ, to advance his "vast contemplative" projects. . . . If Burghley ignores his suit, he will become "some sorry bookmaker, or a true pioner" in the search for truth. Periodically in his life Bacon made the same threat: if civil advancement did not come soon, he would retire to his books.[23]

Marwil goes on to observe that "it is odd, considering that his bluff was often called, how later writers should so readily swallow this convenient assessment of himself."[24] Marwil suggests that Bacon's political ambition ("the consuming desire to put his mark upon life") was so deep-rooted psychologically that Bacon was virtually unable to withdraw from political life, "the only place where a man might become the center of his world."[25]

Finally, it is worth noting that Bacon had one obvious motive for emphasizing the moderation of his political ambitions when applying to his uncle for help. Robert Cecil, Burghley's son and Bacon's cousin, was being groomed for a political career at the same time that Bacon was trying to make his way. The two cousins were roughly the same age and, in effect, rivals in the struggle for advancement. Any appeal for help that Bacon made to his uncle would certainly have to be framed in a way that would not make Francis seem a threat to his cousin's chances. While this consideration does not, of course, prove that Bacon's stated commitment to philosophy was disingenuous, it does lend credibility to Marwil's skeptical contention that we should take Bacon's protestations and disclaimers with a large grain of salt.

Around the time that Bacon wrote this letter to his uncle, and perhaps as a result of his uncle's failure to advance his interests, Francis along with his brother, Anthony, newly returned to England after thirteen years on the continent, moved into the orbit of the Earl of Essex. As Gardiner recognized, Bacon's association with Essex was hardly a friendship. What Gardiner refers to as the "so-called friendship" of these two men, was in fact a kind of partnership in which Bacon provided advice to Essex and Essex, by virtue of his position at court, provided influence and the possibility of Bacon's advancement.[26] Two opportunities for such advancement presented themselves in the course of the decade. First, in 1593, there opened the possibility of the Attorney-Generalship, for which Bacon (with the backing of Essex) and Edward Coke (with the backing of Burghley) competed. Coke was ultimately chosen. Shortly after losing this office, Bacon sought the Solicitor-Generalship, which he likewise failed to attain. The facts of Bacon's failure in these two attempts are clear and simple, though it is hard to convey their impact on Bacon's state of mind without recounting the lengthy, tormented correspondence that surrounded them. Both were long drawn-out affairs and a continuing source of anxious fretting for Bacon. They must have constituted a major drain on his intellectual and emotional energies.

Some commentators are incensed that Bacon should have been denied these posts, as if somehow Bacon was entitled to advancement by the (only subsequently demonstrated) greatness of his intellect. But it should be remembered that Bacon was still a young man with little experience in the practice of law and that in the case of the Attorney-Generalship he was pitted again Coke, perhaps the great legal mind of the age, who had the backing of Burghley.

The standard explanation for Bacon's failure to receive government jobs is the petty anger of Elizabeth over Bacon's behavior in the Parliament of 1593, where Bacon spoke in opposition to the Crown on a subsidy bill, and it is to Bacon's parliamentary career during this decade that we must now turn.

The Parliament of 1593 was tense with the discovery of a new Spanish plot against England, and in response to pressures from the government a committee of the Commons recommended an enlarged subsidy for the defense of the realm. Bacon opposed the government, first on a procedural question and then subsequently on the length of time over which an increased subsidy should be collected. In the first instance, his opposition seems to have been a defense of the privileges of the lower house; in the second, a plea on behalf of the populace on whom the increased tax burden would fall. Bacon lost his point and also apparently seriously damaged his chances for advancement under Elizabeth.

The episode has attracted much attention: first because it is supposed to have cost Bacon the Attorney-Generalship and second because it is seen as offering insight into Bacon's political character. None of the existing interpretations, however, does a satisfactory job of squaring Bacon's behavior in the Parliament of 1593 with his patent desire for royal favor and advancement. Gardiner takes the view that Bacon's opposition on this bill demonstrates Bacon's capacity for principled action even when he ran the risk of damaging his personal career. "It settles in his favour the question whether he was the fawning sycophant which he has been represented as being," writes Gardiner.[27] Neale, however, saw Bacon's opposition to the Crown as a blunder and suggests that Bacon might have taken a different position had he known what the consequences would be for his political career. Neale also suggests that Bacon might have been carried away by the desire for popularity.[28]

Epstein sees in the speech evidence that Bacon passed through a stage of parliamentary "idealism" and "naivete."

> He was still politically naive enough to believe that he could speak his conscience on important matters without damaging his governmental ambitions. He may have been somewhat "intoxicated by popularity," but he was primarily inspired by his own convictions. He would always believe in utilizing power constructively, and in this case he felt it was wrong to overburden the people with a highly concentrated tax. The year 1593 marks the high water mark of Bacon's idealism in Parliament.[29]

Epstein bolsters his contention that Bacon was a parliamentary idealist at this time by pointing to his other recorded participation in the Parliament of 1593. Bacon proved, according to Epstein, "something of an obstructionist voice during this Parliament. While he can never be categorized as a 'rebel' against government policy, his stubborn independence during this session . . . represents a curious twist in the pattern of his political behavior."[30] Bacon was on several committees during this Parliament and was a significant speaker. He served on a committee whose basic aim was to safeguard parliamentary liberties and privileges; he wished to see Parliament undertake law reform; he expressed, according to Epstein, an earnest belief in Parliament's role as a "lawmaking body."

It is difficult to square parliamentary idealism with indications that Bacon was deliberately cultivating in himself a ministerial outlook even at the beginning of the decade. Even in his parliamentary speech Bacon was taking the role of an outspoken royal counsellor, cautioning the government against a course of action which might arouse popular indignation and unrest. I think it probable that Bacon regarded his opposition to the Crown in this instance not so much as a defense of popular interests against the excessive demands of the government or of parliamentary privilege against procedural usurpation but as a piece of wise counsel, delivered by one who did not differ from the government on fundamentals but only on the safest, most effective means for attaining the ends the government sought. Such an interpretation would explain Bacon's injured, sulky behavior when he learned of the Queen's wrath as well as his self-righteousness and difficulty in apologizing.

But if, indeed, Bacon was motivated by some sort of parliamentary idealism in 1593, it had disappeared by the Parliament of 1597, perhaps because Bacon had been chastened by the Queen's displeasure over his opposition to the subsidy bill. In this latter Parliament, Bacon played a more prominent role, strongly advocating government positions to the extent that some have portrayed him as the Crown's virtual representative. Epstein points out that one of the Crown's main concerns at this time was the growing unrest among the poor, that the government let the Commons take the lead, and that Bacon "served as [the Crown's] chief manager of this business."[31] Epstein seems to suggest that Bacon's parliamentary "idealism" had by this time been replaced by another idealism, more in line with the aims of the Crown. Commenting on Bacon's opposition to "enclosures, depopulation of towns, and houses of husbandry, and for the maintenance of tillage."

> Such a view reflected the general opinion of both government and membership of this subject. Bacon's stated belief in the importance of social peace and order in the commonwealth can hardly be called unique. While his concern for basic social harmony was shared by those with vested interests in political and economic power, Bacon's motivations were infinitely more profound and idealistic than those of his colleagues. Having already shown a concern for religious peace, he now spoke on the importance of general order in society.[32]

Epstein concedes to Neale that there may have been an element of expediency in Bacon's having moved to strong advocacy of the Crown position in this Parliament but holds to the idea that Bacon's stands reflected a sincere conviction, tempered with increased "political realism." More to the point in terms of the overall evolution of Bacon's political views, is a kind of emerging paternalism joined to a view of the constitution which gave primacy to the Crown in the making of governmental policy. Looking ahead to the views which would characterize Bacon's outlook in his political prime, Epstein writes:

> A Parliament tactfully led by the Crown, in which the membership cooperated and contributed as a "junior partner," would be Bacon's ideal in the future. He was in the process of developing this view as the Elizabethan period approached its finale.[33]

It was the Parliament of 1601 that would solidify many of Bacon's political views and provide a lifelong paradigm for a successful working relationship between Crown and Parliament. The crucial issue was that of monopolies. Parliamentary opposition to monopolies had mounted, and a bill was introduced which would have forced the hand of the Crown by declaring many of them illegal. By this time, according to Epstein, Bacon had emerged "even more significantly as an 'unofficial' government spokesman in the Commons" and was playing "a leading role as a Crown supporter."[34] In this capacity Bacon opposed Commons taking a legislative lead on the monopolies issue and favored instead a plan to petition the Crown for relief. In the course of arguments, Bacon defended the granting of monopolies as part of the royal prerogative and asserted that by outlawing monopolies Parliament would be committing a breach of the constitution. As Epstein remarks, "Bacon's political conservatism was emerging. Tradition was to be upheld and relief was to be sought without disrupting governmental harmony."[35] In the end Elizabeth behaved precisely as Bacon thought a monarch should. Without either compromising the prerogative or precipitating a constitutional crisis, she stepped in to resolve the impasse by promising royal relief from the unpopular monopolies. The Crown's success – a combination of tact, realism, compromise, and protection of the prerogative – would form the model to which Bacon would look back repeatedly during the years of growing tension under James I.

Bacon's writings during this period were mostly occasional pieces connected to his professional or political interests. One of the most interesting of these is surely Bacon's "Certain Observations Made upon a Libel Published This Present Year, 1592,"[36] whose immediate object was a defense of Elizabeth from the attack of Roman Catholic polemicists eager to discredit her regime by taking special aim at the influence of Burghley. As in his earlier writing on the "Controversies of the Church of England," Bacon used the piece to demonstrate his capacity for what might be called a "ministerial" approach to public issues – that is, an approach resting on expert knowledge and showing a capacity for grasping policy issues from the vantage point of government. Neither the "Observations" nor the earlier works on religious dissent were detached analyses; on the contrary, they were designed to recommend Bacon as a policymaker and thus to serve as self-recommendations for royal service. Bacon sought to show his knowledge of current affairs and to demonstrate his capacity for rising above the partiality of sect and faction to see issues as a complex totality. Such a combination, Bacon thought, was required of royal policymakers, and this piece was to serve as a sample of the vision he would bring to government.

The most lasting literary production of the decade was the first edition of the *Essays,* published in 1597.[37] This collection grew during Bacon's lifetime, going through two more editions, each with new essays added. Crane has argued that the expansions of the *Essays* seem directed to supplying gaps in learning which Bacon had identified in the *Advancement* (1605),[38] and this may well be the case. But the initial collection contained in the first edition does not seem related to any overarching plan.

In the later 1590s Essex was growing restless. In the summer of 1597 he failed in an attempt to capture the Spanish treasure fleet. Then in 1599 he undertook a campaign to subdue Ireland, which likewise failed. Eager to vindicate himself in the eyes of Elizabeth, Essex impetuously rushed back to England in September and presented himself to the Queen. Apparently with a desire to humble and chasten Essex, Elizabeth had him brought before the Star Chamber, and this seems to have greatly increased his popularity with the London populace. Bacon was caught between his loyalty to his patron and his awareness that Essex would have to give some unmistakable sign of submission if he were to be restored to royal favor. Incapable of the patient and compromising political tact which was now required of him, Essex was drawn to wilder schemes to regain the Queen's favor, eventually attempting to reestablish himself in her good graces by using force to remove the counsellors he believed stood between him and Elizabeth. In February of 1601 Essex went to London with an armed retinue. When he failed to arouse support, he retired to Essex House where he was subsequently arrested. It was following this desperate attempt that Essex was put on trial for treason.

It is ironic that in the end and after so many failures, Essex should at last have been the occasion of Bacon's being called to the service of the Crown, for Elizabeth appointed Bacon one of the prosecutors. Having counselled Essex to be cautious when such counsel might have done some good, Bacon now turned his energies to proving his former patron's treason.

In his own time and subsequently, Bacon's reputation suffered from participation in the Essex trial, though few political commentators now hold it against him. Bacon's loyalties formed a hierarchy in which his commitment to the Queen and the state took precedence over his commitment to his patron. He had said as much to Essex when he began to see trouble brewing. Such an ordering of loyalties was perfectly consistent with Bacon's larger political outlook. "To Bacon," writes Gardiner, "the maintenance of the authority of the state was a sacred work, and in the sixteenth century the authority of the queen was the equivalent of the authority of the state."[39]

The trial and execution of Essex brought the decade to a close for Bacon. Only at the end and in a way that must have been extremely painful to Bacon did Essex afford him the opportunity of entering the service of the Queen and state. But the years around the turn of the century were important for Bacon in more ways than this. Regarding his public doings, it may be, as Gardiner suggests, that "the two years which succeeded the trial of Essex were not years of great importance in Bacon's life,"[40] but it is difficult to believe that these were not years of anguished readjustment.

The loss of Essex, whom Bacon had served for a decade and on whom he had staked his hopes, must itself have required a profound reorientation of his quest for political advancement. On top of this, Anthony died early in 1601. The two brothers had been together in their childhood, had gone together to Cambridge and then to Gray's Inn, had travelled to France together before the death of their father. They had been reunited upon Anthony's return from the Continent and had both served Essex through the decade of the 1590s. There was probably no one, throughout his life, with whom Bacon was closer than his brother.

It may also have been around this time that his mother, Anne Bacon, became increasingly deranged. She had always been a religious zealot, and her zeal is said to have increased in her later years. While her incessant meddling in her sons' lives was sometimes charitably portrayed as maternal solicitude by nineteenth-century biographers, there is something unmistakably neurotic and over-involved in her mothering. Alexander Ballock Grossart, Anne Bacon's *Dictionary of National Biography* biographer, notes that she maintained "her authority over [her sons] long after they had reached manhood," always rebuking them for disregarding her wishes, attempting to pry into every detail of their lives, trying to steer them away from the secular entertainments that she believed to be corrupting. "Her mind gave way in the later years of her protracted life," writes this biographer, quoting Bishop Goodman's claim that "she was but little better than frantic in her age."[41] We hear little of her from the end of the 1590s until her death in 1610, and may suppose that it was sometime around the turn of the century that "her mind gave way."

On top of the loss of Anthony and what might have been the loss of his mother to mental illness, Bacon's money problems had grown acute. Following his loss of the Solicitor-Generalship, Bacon had received Twickenham Park from Essex as a compensatory gift, which Bacon was subsequently forced to mortgage. There were some other rewards during the 1590s that might have eased his financial situation, but he spent far beyond his means and was continually indebted. Prior to Essex taking command of the Irish expedition, Bacon was arrested for debt and, for a short time, imprisoned. There is evidence that both Anne Bacon and Anthony were called upon at times to relieve Bacon's indebtedness. That Bacon's money problems were chronic and common knowledge is suggested by Chamberlain's uncharitable but revealing remark (quoted by

Spedding), "Anthony Bacon died not long since, but so far in debt that I think his brother is little the better by him."[42]

Then in 1603 came the death of Elizabeth. Though this event and the accession of a king reputed to be a man of learning are usually taken as renewing Bacon's hopes for political advancement, the death of Elizabeth must have constituted a psychological loss of some kind. It was, after all, Elizabeth whom Bacon's father had served and whom Bacon had entered public life hoping to serve. During his early years in politics he rested his claim to political preferment on his father's services to Elizabeth. Though she had (in his eyes) misunderstood him and refused to advance him, Bacon must have felt some deep, if ambivalent, attachment to her and to the world whose continuity her queenship had symbolized.

It is difficult to assess the psychological effect of being subject to two women as imperious as Anne Bacon and Elizabeth Tudor, each holding over Bacon a different sort of power and each perfectly willing to use that power to manipulate his behavior. Little wonder, with these two looming as dominant figures during his youth and early manhood, that Bacon should have had so little use for women. It is hard to know what to make of the oft-repeated suggestion of Bacon's homosexuality. It is not difficult to see, however, that Bacon's later marriage left much to be desired and brought him little but trouble.

If Bacon's feelings about his mother and Elizabeth were ambivalent, the loss of one to madness and the other to death must have had a powerfully disturbing and disorienting impact on Bacon's inner life, and feelings of loss must have mingled closely with a sense of relief and release.

We do not know enough about Bacon's inner life to be able to trace the outlines of what may have been a serious personal and psychological crisis, but we know enough to doubt Gardiner's assertion that "these were not years of great importance." In the space of three years—from Essex's attempt to restore himself to favor by force to the death of Elizabeth—the entire interpersonal constellation of Bacon's life changed. That this was a watershed in Bacon's life seems almost certain. There is a clear sense of release in the years immediately following and also the fact that a period of long-awaited political success and intensified literary production begin with the accession of James.

2

The Productive Years

T he first decade of the reign of James I offered new opportunities to Bacon, who in turn, seemed more ready to take advantage of them. The main task was to distinguish himself in the eyes of the new king, and this he attempted to do by writing the *Advancement* and by demonstrating his political value as a representative of the Crown in the House of Commons. As he embarked on this new phase, Bacon displayed a remarkable burst of creative energy. There is no indication of real conflict between politicking and philosophizing. Indeed, a surviving notebook of personal memoranda, the *Commentarius Solutus,* shows him briskly allocating his time and energy among a host of schemes and projects, some political, others philosophical, but all crammed together—the work of a busy man with a busy mind. During the 1590s much of Bacon's correspondence with those whose patronage he sought was petulant, impatient, and self-pitying in tone, clearly expressing the agony of his enforced waiting and anxious inactivity. Now, however, the mood of his writings and correspondence changes. One senses in the *Commentarius Solutus* the exhilaration of a man with too little time and too much to do. Bacon might have complained at times about having to divide his energies between politics and philosophy, but he also seems pleased to have been so fully engaged. Far from suffering from his active involvement in affairs of state, his philosophical projects seem to have drawn energy from his rising sense of self-esteem and growing self-confidence as a political actor. In the 1590s Bacon's pronouncements regarding the ills and cures of learning had been meager and thin, actually no more than a few suggestive lines, important only retrospectively as the seeds of what later would grow. In the first decade of the seventeenth century Bacon would develop these ideas into a fully elaborated position and a program—not (as he so often threatened) by withdrawing from politics but as he began to get a taste of the political power that he had so long craved.

It was during this period that Bacon seems definitively to have split his plans for intellectual reform into two very different projects. The "survey of all knowledge," which he had mentioned in his letter to Burghley more than a decade before, appeared now in the *Advancement*. But even as he was writing this remarkable work, he began to sketch the outlines of a program for the renewal of natural science, which would culminate nearly two decades later in the plan for a "Great Instauration." The *Advancement* was an offering to the King and kingdom intended to redirect and revivify traditional learning in its traditional institutional setting, the university. By contrast, the Great Instauration was an attempt to create a new kind of learning and to lay the foundations for a new learned community—Bacon's own commonwealth of learning devoted to the investigation of nature. It was a project shaped decisively by Bacon's political experiences and ideas.

Spedding suggests that Bacon began to write *The Two Bookes of Francis Bacon of the Proficience and Advancement of Learning Divine and Humane* immediately upon the accession of James, that he worked on it intensively until the meeting of Parliament in March 1604, and that he picked it up again after Parliament was prorogued.[1] The work was dedicated to James, whom Bacon praised as "invested of that triplicity which in great veneration was ascribed to the ancient Hermes; the power and fortune of a King, the knowledge and illumination of a Priest, and the learning and universality of a Philosopher."[2] The first book of the *Advancement* is an extended vindication of learning from various charges which had been brought against it and an attempt to analyze various distempers which had corrupted it from within. The second book was a survey of the arts and sciences, organized by Bacon into three divisions, history, poetry, and philosophy, corresponding to the three faculties, memory, imagination, and reason.

The *Advancement* is a rich work and a virtuoso performance by Bacon, summing up what must have been several decades of private reading and reflection, but in its practical face the *Advancement* was a call for reformation of the educational system along civic lines. That a reform of the universities was a principal object of the *Advancement* is clear from Bacon's concrete recommendations at the beginning of the second book. (Solicitude for science is expressed in Bacon's proposal for laboratories and scientific equipment, but this suggestion is one of several, which makes it only one phase of a larger, principally educational reform.) Bacon wanted to see less emphasis placed on the professions—

law and medicine — and more on "fundamental knowledges," because he thought that a liberal arts program, "education collegiate which is free," would allow the study of "histories, modern languages, books of policy and civil discourse, and other like enablements unto service of estate."[3] He wanted an educational program that would train statesmen and civil servants. To such an end, he proposed higher salaries for teachers. Also, he wished to see more frequent visitations to the universities by those in positions of civil authority, "princes or superior persons," and a thorough review of curriculum to insure that it was fit to meet the current educational needs of the kingdom, "inasmuch as most of the usages and orders of the universities were derived from more obscure times." Finally, he expressed a hope that there might be greater communication and cooperation among the various universities of Europe, "a fraternity in learning and illumination." All of these things Bacon called *opera basilica,* works that must be undertaken by the prince. The bulk of the second book of the *Advancement* represented the contribution that a private individual might make to this ultimately princely work: "a view and examination of what parts of learning have been prosecuted, and what omitted" with the particular aim of identifying areas for future cultivation.[4]

While Bacon does not consistently distinguish in the *Advancement* between the acquisition of new knowledge and the effective teaching of existing knowledge, i.e., between research and educational matters, his introduction to the second book makes it clear that university reform is the practical framework within which he was undertaking his survey of the arts and sciences. This is important to note, because the character of the work as a self-recommendation to James hinges not only on Bacon's ability to demonstrate his wide learning but, more importantly, on his argument that the political life of England might depend on the creation of an educational system adequate to educate men for government service.

In 1603 Bacon was, according to Epstein, a "frustrated political man who would still have to prove his value" to the new monarch. His opportunity to give such proof would come in Parliament.[5] Bacon wrote to James early, offering his services. In his *Apology* he tried to vindicate his role in the Essex affair so that James would not hold this against him. The same year he wrote "A Brief Discourse Touching the Happy Union of the Kingdoms of England and Scotland" and "Certain Considerations Touching the Better Pacification and Edification of the Church of England." Both pieces offer advice on matters that were sure to be of special concern to the new monarch. The publication of the *Advancement* in 1605 seems not to have affected his political prospects markedly.

Part of the problem in these years stemmed from the fact that the Cecil family continued to block Bacon's attaining high office. Bacon's uncle, William Cecil, Lord Burghley, had given Bacon his entrée into politics in the 1580s, but had used his influence principally to advance his own son. Burghley had died at the time of Essex's Irish expedition; his "skill and policy" as well as his influence, according to Spedding, fell to his son, Robert Cecil, subsequently the Earl of Salisbury.[6] Like his father, however, Robert Cecil seemed wary of Bacon and determined to keep his cousin safely away from the centers of power.[7]

It was thus neither his writings nor family connections, but rather his work as "the Crown's leading servant"[8] in the House of Commons that laid the groundwork for Bacon's political advancement under James. His position in Parliament was not easy. Bacon had placed himself in the service of a monarch who was neither tactful nor prudent in his dealings with Parliament and who lacked Elizabeth's capacity for skilled maneuvering and effective management. Parliament, too, was becoming more fractious. These years witnessed the emergence of a genuine political opposition which did not willingly accept James's expansive concept of the prerogative. In the five sessions of James's first Parliament, which took place between 1604 and 1610, Bacon seems to have hoped to become the instrument for the sort of reconciliation which Elizabeth had effected in 1601 over the monopolies issue, but this was not to be.

Epstein, who has chronicled Bacon's parliamentary activities during this period, summarizes Bacon's overall position in this way:

> Bacon saw his role as one committed to a governmental harmony in which Parliament remained the junior partner. Balance in government was necessary, but that balance must remain in favor of the Crown.[9]

To the extent that Bacon may be said to have taken a general position on the constitution of England it was certainly royalist. The principal responsibility for making policy should, in his eyes, belong to the Crown and its ministers. Parliament should follow, raising questions perhaps and representing the immediate, short-term interests and desires of the populace, but in the end Parliament should leave the initiatives of government and the stewardship of the long-range interests of the kingdom to the monarch. As he had done in 1601, Bacon would try to dissuade the Commons from passing bills which would force questions of constitutional jurisdiction or pose in any radical way those questions which were destined to become increasingly divisive over the next few decades. He hoped instead for harmonious cooperation, provided that it was the sort of cooperation which left not only the prerogative but even more importantly the principle of royal initiative and leadership undamaged.

Bacon feared the effects that an imbalancing of the relationship between Crown and Parliament would entail:

> The King's Sovereignty and the Liberty of Parliament are as the two elements and principles of this estate; which, though the one be more active, the other more passive, yet they do not cross or destroy the one or the other, but they strengthen and maintain the one the other. Take away the liberty of Parliament, the griefs of the subject will bleed inwards: sharp and eager humors will not evaporate, and then they must exulcerate, and so may endanger the sovereignty itself. On the other side, if the King's sovereignty receive diminution or any degree of contempt with us that are born under an hereditary monarchy (so as the motions of our state cannot work in any other frame or engine) it must follow that we shall be a meteor or corpus imperfecte mistum; which kind of bodies come speedily to confusion or dissolution.[10]

The passive function of Parliament, in short, was to act as a safety valve in preventing the "griefs of subjects" from flaring into open rebellion, whereas the active function of the sovereign monarch was to give form to the state. A wise monarch, therefore, would not run the risk of shutting up the safety valve, but neither would he surrender any vital part of sovereignty.

It was Bacon's misfortune during these years to serve a monarch who did not share his own subtle and flexible view of the means for preserving the prerogative and to be faced with a parliamentary opposition that pushed more and more determinedly for a clarification of its own role. The principal actors in the political drama that was unfolding were not playing the parts that Bacon, in his mind, had assigned them.

In James's first Parliament, whose sessions extended over the years from 1604 to 1610, Bacon consistently played the role of Crown representative, always working to avoid harsh confrontations while at the same time trying to defend essential royal interests. At the outset an issue arose between Commons and Chancery about the election returns. Chancery had voided the election of Francis Goodwin on the grounds that he was an outlaw, while Parliament decided that Goodwin should be seated. Bacon characteristically wanted to avoid confrontation and urged a conference between Parliament and the Chancery judges as a means of settling the matter, but Parliament rejected this approach as a violation of its privilege. In the end, the case was settled by voiding the return of Goodwin and ordering new elections.[11] In the issue of purveyance, Bacon favored the position of the House of Commons, but when he framed the issue in a speech, he did it in such a way as to avoid a direct challenge to the royal prerogative.[12] When the issue of monopolies arose, Bacon favored an appeal to the Crown rather than the outlawing of patents, apparently hoping that the issue could be settled (or at least avoided) as it had been by Elizabeth in 1601. Between 1604 and 1607 Bacon worked tirelessly on the union of England and Scotland, despite the growing opposition of the Commons. In the end he failed.

Epstein suggests that Bacon's efforts on behalf of the Crown in the matter of union may have been something of a turning point for his work in Parliament:

> It is perhaps questionable whether he fully understood the intensity of the opposition to this controversial question. Although he had long been aware of the complex problems involved in union, he had convinced James to proceed moderately, hoping that Parliament would support a cautious approach to the issue. He appears to have been startled by the wholly obstructive attitude he encountered.[13]

Epstein goes on to say that Bacon was becoming "disgusted with the persistent obstructiveness of the House" and to speculate that by 1607 he was also losing the trust of that body.[14] Bacon's position in 1607, according to Epstein, was one of growing frustration with Parliament and deepening commitment to the Crown. Bacon's service to the new king had, at long last, won him an official position. In 1607 Bacon became Solicitor-General.

Thus when James's first Parliament reconvened in 1610, Bacon sat as a royal official, and Epstein suggests that "while such a position might have given him more prestige with the House in 1604, it would now prove a liability."[15] Bacon found himself charged with the responsibility of representing the position of the Crown at precisely the time when hostility to the royal prerogative was growing and was forced — at least in the case of Salisbury's "Great Contract" — to work for a settlement with which he did not fully agree. What Salisbury proposed was to put the government's finances on a new footing by striking a deal with the House of Commons: the Crown would relinquish its remaining feudal sources of income in return for an equal amount to be raised by taxation. According to Gardiner, the Great Contract represented "the method which Bacon thoroughly distrusted,"[16] and Epstein says that "the entire concept of the contract was contrary to his basic political thinking."[17] Nonetheless, it was Bacon whom Salisbury charged with pushing the Great Contract in the House of Commons and in general with representing the Crown's demands for money.

As the session dragged on, the clash between the Crown and the opposition in Parliament over money and, therefore, over the lawful extent of the prerogative became more open and more harsh. Precisely what Bacon had hoped to avoid was happening. By the end, according to Epstein, "governmental harmony in Jacobean England was farther from reality than ever before."[18]

Commentators disagree as to whether Bacon fully understood what was happening. Epstein takes issue with the claim that Bacon "had little conception of the slow but steady accretion of influence and power by Parliament,"[19] and argues instead that Bacon knew precisely what was happening and did his best to avoid it. Epstein portrays Bacon's situation at this time in tragic terms.

> In a very real sense, Bacon was an unfortunate victim of the tragedy of the session. Having reached officialdom, he would have wanted to use the prestige of his office to help James deal more effectively with Parliament. Whether Bacon could have helped the Crown in 1610 had he not merely been Salisbury's functionary is, of course, questionable. There are, however, degrees of failure. While the atmosphere of 1610 was not conducive to solving major problems, it is conceivable that the kind of open confrontation that so badly estranged Crown-Parliament relations might have been prevented.[20]

Epstein's point is to portray Bacon as "a political man," in opposition to the idealized portraits that have been drawn by Bacon's philosophical admirers, and therefore he is led repeatedly to portray Bacon as a canny and adaptable "realist." But political men may be the captives of ideology, and, indeed, realism itself connotes a certain ideological stance.

Bacon entered the political world at birth, and his first forty years coincided with the reign of Elizabeth Tudor. His whole way of conceptualizing political life was Tudor.[21] The question would seem to be less one of how realistically he grasped the power of the parliamentary opposition than of how adequate his political-ideological framework was to the rapidly changing conditions of English political life. Bacon's conception of the optimal relationship between Crown and Commons (and therefore his idea of what would constitute his own success as the Crown's representative) was being rendered obsolete as both parties to the struggle were changing their political terms of reference. What James wanted was not quite what Bacon, with his Tudor outlook, wanted for his King, nor was Parliament ready to play the passive role it was assigned in Bacon's scheme of things. If there is something tragic in Bacon's position during these years, it is the tragedy of a man who perceives the growth of major tensions but can only conceptualize them in the old way and, therefore, is doomed to apply old remedies and watch them fail.

Epstein summarizes Bacon's position at the end of James's first Parliament in the following way:

> With the failure of 1610, Francis Bacon completed his first "tour of duty" as a servant of James I. He had worked diligently and often brilliantly in efforts that had dealt him continual frustration. Although he was Solicitor-General of England, there was cold comfort in that office as an end in itself. There was still the perennial rivalry with Coke and the twisted shadow of his cousin to plague him as he tried to look at the future. Although he was not without hope, as a man approaching fifty, he could only be uncertain about his political future.[22]

Bacon had carried into this period of intense activity a conception of politics which was deeply royalist. Corresponding to the active role of the King and his ministers, Bacon outlined an essentially passive role for the King's subjects, including those subjects who sat in Parliament. For Bacon, political order necessarily involved central direction which rationalized and coordinated the action of the whole body politic. The maintenance of such central direction precluded a sovereignty which was in any real sense divided between Crown and Parliament. Yet alongside this ideal state of things which Bacon strove to realize was the fact that Parliament was increasingly a fractious and unruly body, impatient with the passive, responsive role that it was assigned in Bacon's scheme. Bacon was thus in the position of having to persuade people to accept a royalist regimen which he deeply believed to be in their own long-term interests, but which he likewise understood ran counter to their inclinations and desires.

Bacon's political position was not altogether different from his emerging position as a would-be reformer of science. These were the years when Bacon began seriously to work on developing his ideas about science as an organized activity. Though the dating is in some cases uncertain, the following works during this period were devoted to elaborating one or another aspect of the ideas that appeared in seed-form in the 1590s:

ca. 1603	*De Interpretatione Naturae Proemium* (On the Interpretation of Nature. Proem.)
ca. 1603	*Valerius Terminus on the Interpretation of Nature*
ca. 1603	*Temporis Partus Masculus* (The Masculine Birth of Time; or the Great Instauration of the Dominion of Man over the Universe)
ca. 1604	*Cogitationes de Natura Rerum* (Thoughts on the Nature of Things)

ca. 1604   *Cogitationes de Scientia Humana*
    1606   *Partis Instaurationis Secundae Delineato et Argumentum*
    1607   *Cogitata et Visa de Interpretatione Naturae* (Thoughts and Conclusions on the Interpretation of Nature or a Science Productive of Works)
    1608   *Redargutio Philosophiarum* (The Refutation of Philosophies)

In addition to these works, there are certain writings on the interpretation of ancient mythology, principally *De Sapientia Veterum* (Of the Wisdom of the Ancients; 1609) and *De Principiis atque Originibus* (Of Principles and Origins, According to the Fables of Cupid and Coelum; *ca.* 1610) which contain much material directly relevant to Bacon's scientific thought.

Though the detailed examination of some of these works will be left to later chapters, a few remarks on Bacon's developing scientific program are appropriate here. Already in 1603, when he had begun to write the *Advancement,* directed principally toward a reformation of the universities, Bacon began to reflect on a different kind of intellectual project, more narrowly aimed at the investigation of nature. From the beginning the aim was two-fold: knowledge which was certain and knowledge which was useful. The attainment of such knowledge, in Bacon's view, required that some body of scholars withdraw in two senses from the existing intellectual community. First they must withdraw their minds, shedding old methods, attitudes, and habits of thinking in order to submit to a new intellectual regimen which was much more strict and demanding than that demanded by the existing intellectual traditions. Second, they must withdraw their labor and become part of an organized effort—a new community of work—in which their individual labors would be regulated and coordinated as part of a single, disciplined inquiry. As many of Bacon's comments make quite clear, the people who joined this project would have to submit to a new kind of intellectual *government.*

While Bacon never tired of praising the benefits that might flow from an organized inquiry into nature, he also recognized that humans, by nature and custom, were predisposed—in the intellectual no less than the political realm—to resist constraint, even in the interest of some long-range improvement. Bacon's actual situation as a would-be intellectual reformer during these years was similar to his situation as a political actor: he had a vision of the well-ordered community but no real authority. The means at his disposal were principally suasive and rhetorical.

Many of Bacon's scientific writings during these years were concerned with persuading people to do what (in his view) was in their own long-term interests but which also ran counter to their spontaneous inclinations since it entailed submitting themselves to an external intellectual authority. Put this way, the task which Bacon set himself in the commonwealth of learning was conceptualized in a way that echoed the task he faced as the Crown's representative in Parliament. People must be persuaded to give up the kind of liberty that was destructive in favor of a regimen that would maintain order and lay the foundation for future progress. Bacon's writings, which aimed at organizing a new scientific community, were informed by a political sense and relied regularly on political language. It is difficult to imagine that they did not owe something to the ideas and experiences of Bacon's contemporaneous political activities.

All the major elements of what would become the Great Instauration were, in any case, present in Bacon's writings of this decade, though still embedded in scattered, tentative works which for the most part he left unpublished. The full-scale and systematic presentation of his scheme for natural inquiry would wait until the publication of the *Novum Organum* in 1620. As Farrington has noted in his edition of some of these early works,[23] however, it is in these writings more than in the later, more systematic work that one can see most clearly Bacon's efforts to develop his ideas and to discover the right tactics for implementing them. Each writing is thus something of an experiment in presentation and a tentative solution to the range of problems with which he grappled. Though the *Novum Organum* manages to incorporate many of the main ideas of these writings, it does not preserve the tone or serve as a good indicator of the process by which Bacon arrived at his conception nor does it register Bacon's intellectual position in the first decade of James's reign.

It is evidence of Bacon's literary vitality that alongside his demanding political activities and his efforts on behalf of natural inquiry he was able to write in other areas as well. Much of what survives is closely connected to his legal and political activities: pieces, for example, on the union with Scotland, on the "pacification" of the English church, and on "plantation in Ireland." Bacon also projected and outlined parts of a history of England, which would bear lasting fruit only after his fall, when he wrote an account of the reign of Henry VII. Beyond these writings, he was probably at work on the enlarged edition of *Essays* which would appear in 1612.

While Bacon must have struggled to carve out time for all this philosophical writing from his busy schedule of political and legal activities, it is almost certain that the relationship between his political-legal commitments and his literary-philosophical production was not one of antagonism. During the decade of the 1590s, when Bacon was intensely frustrated by his political *inactivity,* he wrote next to nothing—at least next to nothing which survives. During the first decade of James's reign, on the other hand, as the burdens of political and legal work mounted, he enjoyed a great burst of literary productivity.

In a synoptic account of his life which he wrote during this period Bacon continued to invoke the distinction between *vita activa* and *vita contemplativa.* Spedding places the writing of *De Interpretatione Naturae Proemium* around 1603. Here Bacon wrote that he believed himself "born for the service of mankind" and set about to consider "in what way mankind might be best served, and what service I was myself best fitted by nature to perform."[24] Though he had been early drawn to the "discovery of new arts, endowments, and commodities for the bettering of man's life," nonetheless he had followed a political career—"because my birth and education had seasoned me in business of state; and because opinions (so young as I was) would sometimes stagger me; and because I thought that a man's country has some special claims upon him more than the rest of the world; and because I hoped that, if I rose to any place of honour in the state, I should have a larger command of industry and ability to help me in my work—for these reasons I both applied myself to acquire the arts of civil life, and commended my service, so far as in modesty and honesty I might, to the favour of such friends as had any influence."[25] When he found, however, that his "zeal was mistaken for ambition" and his "life had already reached the turning-point," he put thoughts of political advancement aside and turned wholly to his philosophical work.

These remarks were part of a preface to an intended work on natural philosophy and therefore must be judged against the rhetorical demands of that work. There is the obvious fact that Bacon did *not* (as he promised) set aside his political ambitions in 1603. Still, this account of Bacon's first forty years is frequently cited as a key to understanding the actual structure of motives that governed and related his political and philosophical activities. Thus Spedding writes: "It retains a peculiar interest for us on account of the passage in which he explains the plans and purposes of his life. . . . It is the only piece of autobiography in which he ever indulged."[26] Whether Bacon actually believed this simple schematization of his first forty years and actually did resolve to leave politics or had only intended it as a dramatic introduction to some work on science that he would write in the event of political failure, I cannot say. What is clear, however, is that Bacon maintained both commitments and that in the years that followed they seemed to flourish together.

Nowhere is the coexistence and compatibility of the political and philosophical impulses more clearly exemplified than in a notebook that survives from the year 1608—the *Commentarius Solutus*. About this piece Gardiner writes:

> It is full of hints as to the advancement of his great schemes in science and politics as well as to the advancement of his own fortunes. Great ideas jostle with small ones, and the thought of a restoration of philosophy and of laying the foundations of a showy and attractive foreign policy is found side by side with a place for flattering the lord chamberlain who might be helpful, or exposing the demerits of an attorney-general who is a rival. Altogether Bacon's character is nowhere else depicted so completely as a whole as in these loose jottings.[27]

The *Commentarius Solutus* suggests that for Bacon science, politics, and his own fortunes had become closely linked by 1608. It shows as well that at a certain level Bacon conceptualized his political and philosophical projects in similar terms. Here, quite clearly, the prosecution of what would come to be called the Great Instauration was not essentially contemplative but eminently active, and required (like politics proper) the persuasion, manipulation, and organized direction of groups of people.

The *Commentarius Solutus* must be of great interest to anyone seeking to understand Bacon's personal life and mind. There is much attention given to money, a constant problem and preoccupation for Bacon. There are entries which show Bacon scheming to bring himself to the attention of James and the court. There are pettinesses regarding Bacon's rival, Coke. There are plans for his estate at Gorhambury alongside recipes for medical cures and evidences of Bacon's moodiness and hypochondria. If the impression from reading the *Commentarius Solutus* is that of an ambitious yet moody man whose mind is preoccupied with calculations of his own public image and of his advantage in the struggle for political advancement, one also senses a man who seems well-suited to the *vita activa*. It is quite clear from the *Commentarius Solutus* that Bacon relished the many matters—some large, some small—that his busy life put in his way and that he enjoyed thinking of himself as a man balancing many enterprises and harboring many ambitions, and the role of planner, projector, even schemer, seems to have been congenial to Bacon's image of himself. It seems likely that Bacon was stimulated and energized by what might have been for others an overabundance of distracting concerns and calculations.

The style, tone, and sense of energy which show themselves in Bacon's jottings about finances, estate management, and political maneuvering also appear in the entries concerning his plans at this time for

scientific reform. The notes on science seem continuous with (and certainly not opposed to) those on other matters, displaying the same restless, ambitious, and manipulative spirit. They show, among other
things, that Bacon's schemes for science were by no means limited to his
literary efforts but encompassed a broad range of practical plans and
calculations of public image and advantage.

Like the other entries in the *Commentarius Solutus,* these on science
are often enigmatic, but a sampling will show the way Bacon conceived
his efforts at scientific reform around the year 1608. Some of them, for
example, suggest the way in which his schemes for science involved the
enlistment of the rich and powerful — men likely to lend prestige to the
enterprise, to endow it financially, to lend it support from positions of
established power:

> *Making much of Russell that depends upon Sr Dav. Murry and by that
> means drawing Sr Dav. and by him Sr. Th. Chal. in tyme the
> prince.*
>
> *Getting from Russel a collection of Phainomena, or surgery, destilla-
> tions, Minerall tryalls.*
>
> *The setting on wo. my L of North. and Ralegh, and therefore Haryott,
> themselves being already inclined to experimts.*
>
> *Acquainting my self with Poe as for my health and by him learnyng ye
> experimts wch he hath of phisike and gayning entrance into the
> inner of some great persons.*
>
> *Seing and tryeng wr the B. of Canterb. may not be affected in it, being
> single, rych, sickly, a professor to some experimts. this after the
> table of Mocion or some other in part sett in forwardness.*
>
> *Qu. of phisicions to be gayned. The Lykest is Paddy, D. Hamond.*
>
> *Q. of learned men beyond the seas to be made, and harkenyng who
> they be that may be so inclined.*[28]

Far from representing a withdrawal from the world of affairs, Bacon's
program for the reformation of science clearly involved him in the same
kind of canvassing, the same kind of calculations, the same attentiveness
to personal image and advantageous connections as his struggle for political advancement.

Other entries in the *Commentarius Solutus* suggest the way in which
Bacon's literary works on behalf of science were conceived in terms of
possible audiences and specific rhetorical effects:

> *The finishing of the 3 Tables of Motu, de Calore et frigore, de sono.*
>
> *The finishing of the Aphorismes, Clavis interpretationis, and then set-*

*ting foorth ye book. qu. to begynne first in france to print it; yf
hear then wt dedication of advantage to ye woork.*

*Proceeding wth ye translation of my book of Advancemt of learnyng;
harkenyng to some other yf playfere should faile.*

Imparting Cogitat et Visa wth choyse, et videbitr.

*Ordinary discours of plus ultra in Sciences, as well the intellectuall
globe as the materiall, illustrated by discouery in or Age.*

*Discoursing skornfully of the philosophy of the graecians wth some
better respect to ye Aegyptians, Persians, Caldes, and the utmost
antiquity and the mysteries of the poets.*[29]

There are some entries, finally, which reveal Bacon's desire to establish some community of scientific workers under his immediate control. He frequently referred to such workers as the true *filii* or sons of science, and among the entries that follow it is interesting to note that Bacon might prefer a community of young men (*postnati*) as being less burdened by the past, more malleable, more manageable, more open to the new.

*Qu. of an oration ad filios, delightfull, sublime, and mixt wth elegancy,
affection,* novelty of conceyt and yet sensible, *and Supersition . . .*

*Layeng for a place to command wytts and pennes. Westminster, Eton,
Wynchester, Spec. Trinity College in Cambridg, St Jhons in Camb.
Maudlin College in Oxford. and bespeaking this betymes, wth ye
K. my L. Archb. my L Treasorer. . . .*

Qu. of you schollars in ye Universities. It must be the postnati.

*Gyving pensions to 4 for search to compile the 2 Histories ut supra.
Foundac. of a college for Inventors past and spaces or Bases for
Inventors to come. And a Library and an Inginary.*

*Qu. of the Order and Dscipline, to be mixt wth some poynts popular to
invite many to contribute and joyne.*

Qu. of the rules and prscripts of their studyes and inquyries.

Allowance for travailing; Allowance for experimts.

Intelligence and correspondence wth ye universities abroad.

Qu. of the Maner and prescripts touching Secrecy, tradition, and publication.

*Qu. of Remooves and Expulsions in case wthin a tyme some Invention
woorthy be not produced. And likewise qu. of the honors and
Rewards for Inventions.*

Vaults fornaces, Tarraces for Insolacion; woork houses of all sorts.

Endevor to abase the price of professory sciences and to bring in aestimation Philosophy or Universality — name and thing.[30]

We see here—present in outline as early as 1608—not only features of the later Salomon's House, but indeed a suggestion of Bacon's entire approach to organized science. By literary, but also by other means, Bacon wished to found a new kind of community, composed of young, pliable workers subject to a demanding regimen and committed to the investigation of nature. He was concerned with the institutionalization of the process of inquiry and with such mundane matters as procedural rules, funding, and the creation of a system of incentives and disincentives to shape the behavior of members. He was, finally, keenly concerned about the prudent differentiation and management of the public and secret activities of the new community.

In the *Commentarius Solutus* Bacon's notes on his scientific projects bear a clear and telling resemblance to those on political and practical concerns and are put side-by-side with them in a way that makes all seem part of a single manifold agenda. In the context of this notebook of memoranda, both political advancement and scientific reform are patently conceived to be works undertaken in the world of power, the world of money, the world of affairs. Both require the enlistment of the sympathies of the great. Both require the same attention to provisioning. Both call upon Bacon to be a manipulator and something of a schemer. No line of demarcation appears here between the *vita activa* and *vita contemplativa,* for the promotion of science is not principally a contemplative affair. Nor are Bacon's literary efforts on behalf of science adequately characterized as the dissemination of new ideas or a campaign to publicize a new approach to nature. Although publicity plays a part in the campaign, much of the writing is directed to ends that are more specific and practical—the recruitment, for example, of a body of followers.

Gardiner wrote that "Bacon's character is nowhere else depicted so completely as a whole as in these loose jottings,"[31] and he is probably correct. These notes suggest that Bacon's schemes for advancing himself and his various projects—political or scientific—were of a single piece. His ambitions in both politics and the world of learning had been simultaneously aroused in the first decade of James's reign and so too his capacity for projecting, calculating, and scheming. The *Commentarius Solutus* shows us Bacon in an active period when both his political ambitions and his designs for science were fueled by heightened ambition and led on by a sense of open possibility.

AMBITION FULFILLED, 1612–1621

The period following the death of Salisbury in 1612 amply rewarded Bacon's years of impatient waiting and restless toiling in the antechambers of power. With his cousin removed as an obstacle to his own advancement, Bacon became Attorney-General in 1613 and Lord Chancellor in 1617. He attached himself to the rising star of George Villiers — later Duke of Buckingham — the new favorite of James, and became part of the inner circle of the conciliar government. At the height of his career, Bacon was created first Baron of Verulam, then, just before his fall, Viscount St. Alban's.

All of his life, Bacon had justified his ambition on the grounds that political power would afford him the opportunity to do good works, including the furthering of his philosophical designs. One of the most revealing aspects of this period of his life was the extent to which his behavior failed to bear out his high-minded statement of motive. Bacon had virtually always been in financial trouble and never in real control of his taste for extravagance. Now he seems to have indulged himself to the full. He spent lavishly, lived in luxury, and prompted the gossips to comment on the pomp and display with which he surrounded himself. Epstein characterizes his use of power in the following way:

> His behavior in this period hardly exemplified the philosophic statesman using "power to do good." His main concern seemed to lie in utilizing the intricacies of court politics to his own advantage, and in buttressing his status and financial condition.[32]

Such a judgment must cast serious doubt on the contention of some of Bacon's philosophical admirers (and on his own stated claim) that he had entered politics in order to put himself in a position to realize his philosophical schemes. Having already come to the conclusion that a renovated science would need an institutional base and ample material support, Bacon conspicuously neglected to use his position to create this base or supply the support.

This is not to say, however, that these years were wasted from the standpoint of Bacon's scientific ambitions. They saw the completion of his great work of organization and method, the *Novum Organum,* published in 1620. Bacon was no longer preoccupied (as he had been in the scientific writings of the preceding decade) with the problems of recruiting the personnel of the new science and leading them to an initial acceptance of the demands which scientific inquiry must inevitably impose. Although the community which he desired did not yet exist, Bacon moved on to outlining the way the investigation of nature might be administered. The tone and rhetorical stance of the *Novum Organum* are quite different from the earlier writings. It is not so much a work of suasion as of direction and assumes a kind of authority which its author did not possess a decade earlier. If the earlier works reflected the outlook and preoccupations of a parliamentarian trying to cajole his colleagues into accepting a rational program, the *Novum Organum* reflects Bacon's new self-assurance as a high-placed royal official, finally able (in theory at least) to deploy and direct a staff of subordinates. In this sense the work seems to have been shaped by Bacon's new political status.

It was Bacon himself who, upon the death of the Chief Justice in 1613, suggested a reshuffling of offices which would open the Attorney-Generalship for himself by removing Coke to the Chief-Justiceship. Characteristically the scheme aimed at what Bacon believed to be a political good at the same time that it served his personal ambitions: Coke's power to obstruct the prerogative would be diminished and he would be made more amenable to royal influence. With Bacon's elevation to the Attorney-Generalship, Epstein says, "a new phase of his political career was beginning."[33] For the first time, Bacon would be involved in the highest levels of government.

Spurred by an increasingly dire financial need, James called a Parliament in 1614. Bacon held to what Epstein calls "his Tudor approach to Parliament, still hoping that such practices might be reinvigorated,"[34] but was undercut in his desire for Crown-Commons reconciliation by James's extravagant claims on the one hand and by Parliament's hostile response on the other. As a royal official, Bacon himself very nearly failed to be seated. He worked tirelessly through the session, pleading for money on behalf of his King, but his efforts were overwhelmed by the growing division and the Parliament was a failure.

Of Bacon's participation in the Parliament of 1614, Gardiner writes:

> Perhaps if any date can be fixed as that on which Bacon's chance of serving the nation politically was at an end, it is that of the dissolution which took place on 7 June 1614; James then deliberately took one way, and the nation took another. Yet it does not follow that Bacon was likely to see that this was the case.[35]

In explaining why Bacon did not see the futile destructiveness of James's course at this time, Gardiner mentions both Bacon's inborn habit of placing himself on the side of authority" and "his disinclination, after tasting the allurements of competency and station, to choose, in advanced middle age, obscure poverty as his bride."[36]

At this point in his political career, the characterization of Bacon as a political realist is severely strained, since his continuing tendency to interpret his political experiences and offer political advice on the basis of "the Tudor approach to Parliament" marks him as a conservative ideologue. As Gardiner points out, Bacon's ideology was in part self-serving. He continued to serve James since it was James and no other who dispensed the rewards that Bacon craved. But Bacon's inability to see that the drift of events were changing the rules of the political game was also, as Gardiner notes, a result of his habit of looking to royal authority for the maintenance of political order.

As Attorney-General, Bacon made himself the legal champion of the royal prerogative, aligning himself squarely against the common-law outlook of his archrival, Coke. Besides representing the Crown in a series of cases, Bacon argued for a rational codification of the laws under the sponsorship of the Crown. Bacon set forth his scheme in his "Proposition to his Majesty . . . Touching the Compiling and Amending of the Laws of England," written sometime in 1616 or 1617. Bacon's legal views are of a piece with his political outlook, stressing the need for the Crown to take control of the law and make it a fit instrument of policy. Though Epstein praises Bacon's proposal for legal reform ("His plans might have become the basis for a badly needed reform of a cumbersome system," had he "been retained as Attorney General and been given the backing to carry out his ideas"),[37] it is important to note that at this point in English political history, the hope of such a reform, requiring as it would a high degree of political harmony, had as little chance of success as Bacon's hoped-for reconciliation of King and Commons. It must also be admitted that Bacon was temperamentally better suited to proposing and framing grand schemes than to actually carrying them out. It is almost certainly a mistake to see this proposal as a great lost opportunity.

When Lord Ellesmere was taken sick in 1616, Bacon made a bid for the office of Lord Chancellor and was immediately given the job following Ellesmere's death in 1617. He held the post for four years until his disgrace in 1621. At the outset characteristically Bacon expressed a desire to clean up Chancery — to deal with the backlog of cases and make it a more efficient court. Epstein writes:

> Potentially, Bacon could have brought greatness to his office. His record of service would never approach such potential. Bacon soon showed that status and power mattered more to him than did any commitment to principles.[38]

Bacon was drawn into the circle of court favorites, which was dominated

by George Villiers, later Duke of Buckingham. Bacon's political inde-
pendent-mindedness had not been great when he was an ambitious aspi-
rant to political office; now it was nil. Having attached himself to Buckingham, according to Epstein, Bacon used his power over the courts to
help his patron outmaneuver political rivals. He supported the revenue-
raising policies of Cranfield, and he strongly defended the prerogative.

Bacon did not handle his success in a way that was particularly high-
minded or philanthropic. He enjoyed his new status and wealth, sur-
rounding himself with well-liveried attendants and maintaining several
lavish establishments. He was a man, as Epstein puts it, "who felt that
luxury was his birthright; he now enjoyed it uncontrollably."[39] His new
status, moreover, seems to have allowed full play to old and deep-rooted
attitudes of social superiority. Writing of Bacon's working relationship
with Lionel Cranfield, Robert Johnson emphasizes how thoroughly Bacon's attitude toward his colleague was shaped by the fact of their differing social backgrounds. Cranfield was, after all, from the family of a
London merchant and largely self-taught. Commenting on Bacon's
haughty bearing during these years, Johnson writes: "The main defect in
[Bacon's] personality was his arrogant manner, which he frequently displayed toward his social and intellectual inferiors. By Bacon's standards,
Cranfield fitted into that inferior category."[40]

On his sixtieth birthday, January 22, 1621, Bacon enjoyed a lavish
party at York House, the place where he had been born and now his
official residence as Lord Chancellor. He seemed to have done what in
some conscious or unconscious way he had set out to do: he had returned to the status of his father. His glory was to be short-lived, however, for Parliament was preparing to convene, and this was to be the
Parliament which destroyed Bacon's political career.

In his opening address to both houses of Parliament, Bacon firmly
defended the royal prerogative and asserted that "the King is the master
of this assembly."[41] Thus not merely his official position but also his
stated opinions put him in the path of the storm which was brewing.
Shortly into the session, Parliament turned to the question of monopolies, a long-standing grievance, and in the course of its proceedings lit
upon Bacon as one of the royal officials responsible for granting and
regulating the despised patents. While the monopoly issue was under
review, the Commons turned to another issue which would prove even
more serious to Bacon—the question of judicial corruption. In the
course of its inquiries, several witnesses came forth to charge Bacon with
having taken bribes.

Most modern scholars are fairly lenient in judging Bacon's judicial
misconduct, arguing that judicial standards were not so clearly defined

then as now and that what Bacon did was common practice. Epstein also makes the point that Bacon's trial should be seen principally in political terms, "a political act against the royal prerogative. . . . He fell from power because he stood as an ideal scapegoat, sacrificed to a Parliament looking for the vulnerability of royal power."[42] His office placed Bacon high enough to serve as a fitting symbol of royal authority but not so high (like Buckingham, for example) as to be out of reach. It would be wrong, however, to believe that Bacon had not contributed to his fall. Coke and Cranfield, both men whom Bacon had given ample cause for dislike, were arrayed against him. For years he had stood as a representative of the prerogative. His personal style must have contributed as well. Nor had Bacon succeeded in making himself so valuable or so loved by his King as to bring James fully and forthrightly to his defense. The House of Commons sent the case to the Lords for trial. Initially Bacon planned to make a defense, but as he learned the nature and strength of the evidence against him, his health began to fail (as it frequently did in time of trouble) and he resigned himself to submitting to the Lords' decision, apparently hoping for a simple, straightforward proceeding which would allow him to escape with minimal penalties. Bacon was willing to make what amounted to a general and pro forma confession of wrongdoing, but the upper house was not satisfied. Eventually he was forced to make a fuller and more pointed confession in writing to each of the charges against him, which he did while still maintaining that he had no intention of misusing his office. In the end, his sentence was much harsher than he had expected. He was fined forty thousand pounds, imprisoned in the Tower for the King's pleasure, disqualified from holding office or sitting in the House of Lords, and prohibited from coming within the verge of the court. Though he did not yet realize it, Bacon's political life was virtually over.

Following the many false starts and tentative strategies of the decade following 1603, Bacon seems to have become much more focused and disciplined in his efforts to launch a new science during the period from 1612 until his fall from power. Although he wrote *Descriptio Globi Intellectualis* (Description of the Intellectual Globe) and *Thema Coeli* (Theory of the Heavens) in 1612, the great fruit of this period was the *Novum Organum,* which was published in 1620.

Although the *Novum Organum* is generally taken as the fullest statement Bacon ever made of the inductive method, it is perhaps more accurately viewed as the first installment of a well worked-out program for an organized inquiry into the natural world, method narrowly considered being only one component of this program. Prefaced to the

Novum Organum in the 1620 publication was a short separate piece which outlined the whole scheme of what Bacon called "The Great Instauration," a program for conducting a collectively organized, rigidly disciplined inquiry into nature which would culminate in "The New Philosophy, or Active Science." The aim of the piece entitled "The Great Instauration" is not simply philosophical—it is the blueprint for a massive research project, a grand effort to organize scientific inquiry in a new way.

While working on the overall plan of "The Great Instauration" and the crucial statement of method in the *Novum Organum,* Bacon was able to conceptualize the whole program in practical terms as a project that could be broken into concrete phases, each requiring a different and appropriate kind of labor, each calling for its own configuration of personnel, and all together taking place under the authority and guiding direction of a mastermind like himself.

The year following the publication of this plan, Bacon fell from power. Possibly this prevented Bacon from organizing and insuring support for the kind of project he had outlined in 1620. There is little evidence, however, that Bacon possessed the temperament and talent that launching such a project would have required. His aptitude was for the bold envisioning of projects and even the detailed working-out of plans, but not implementation. Bacon used his four years as Lord Chancellor on petty politicking and there is no reason to believe that if he had had another four years he would have done anything different. It is also worth noting that while the vision of science which Bacon embodied in "The Great Instauration" and the *Novum Organum* resonated with many of the dominant intellectual themes of the day, his prescription for a tight organization, in which every aspect of the inquiry would be subject to a single all-embracing, peremptory regimen, was as out-of-step with most thinking as were his ideas about a rationalized legal system or a well-disciplined Parliament. In that age, science was destined to grow not in the tightly organized, well-disciplined, and efficient way that he prescribed but rather in the helter-skelter way he condemned. In the end the authoritarian aspiration of "The Great Instauration," like his royalist vision of government, was doomed.

LAST YEARS, 1621–1626

"**B**acon was not a man who could allow himself to remain idle," wrote Gardiner,[43] and, indeed, the last years of his life — from his release from the Tower at the beginning of June 1621, until his death on Easter Day, April 9, 1626, — are a period of almost unrelenting literary activity. During these years he wrote or published the following works:

> *Advertisement Touching a Holy War* (1622)
> *History of the Reign of King Henry the Seventh* (1622)
> *Historia Naturalis et Experimentalis* (1622)
> *Historia Vitae et Mortis* (1623)
> *Historia Densi et Rari (1623)*
> *The Beginning of the Reign of King Henry the Eighth* (1623)
> *De Dignitate et Augmentis Scientiarum* (a Latin translation of the
>   1605 *Advancement of Learning* with much new material added,
>   1623)
> *Novis Orbis Scientiarum, sive Desiderata* (1623)
> *Considerations Touching a War With Spain* (1624)
> *New Atlantis* (1624)
> *Magnalia Naturae, Praecipue Quoad Usus Humanos* (1624)
> *Apophthegms New and Old. Collected by the Right Honourable
>   Francis Lo. Verulam, Viscount St. Alban* (1624)
> *Translation of Certain Psalms into English Verse* (1624)
> *Essays or Counsels, Civil and Moral* (the 3d edition of the
>   *Essays* with additions, 1625)
> *Sylva Sylvarum: or a Natural History in Ten Centuries* (1626)

Spedding suggested that "the true history of Bacon's remaining years is to be looked for in his books."[44]

Biographers who see Bacon's life principally as a pursuit of intellectual goals tend to portray these last years as a time when Bacon was happily freed from politics and thus finally able to devote himself completely to the accomplishment of intellectual work. Taking this idea as her keynote, Catherine Drinker Bowen titled her last chapter "A Noble Five Years,"[45] and Benjamin Farrington begins his essay, "Francis Bacon after His Fall," with the contention that "in the midst of his troubles, some public, some private, he seems to have been a happy man."[46] Farrington argues that these last years are characterized by the same singleness of purpose that (in Farrington's view) directed the whole of his life.

Farrington's assertion notwithstanding, Bacon never seems to have
achieved the calmness of mind and reconciliation to his fate that one
might wish for the old age of a great man. He struggled to the end,
maintaining so far as he could an outward demeanor of contrition, dignity, and Christian forbearance, but likewise displaying at every turn a
desperate desire to mend his fortunes and rehabilitate his reputation,
reenter the service of the King and Buckingham either publicly or pri-
vately, sit again in the House of Lords, retain his estates, especially York
House and Gorhambury, and, in short, put this time of "misery" (the
word is his and was used repeatedly to describe his condition) behind
him. During these five years he complained with increasing insistence
that he had suffered enough for the crimes which he had admittedly done
and now deserved to be relieved of further suffering.

Throughout these years Bacon was plagued with money problems.
He had always overspent and had never managed money well. Now his
creditors flocked around and harried him ceaselessly. But Bowen has
cast doubt on the notion that Bacon was poor in any absolute sense,
suggesting that many of his money worries may have been due to his
inability to scale down his expenditures. It is possible, according to
Bowen, that Bacon enjoyed an income of as much as two thousand
pounds a year, "more than most noblemen could count on."[47] But (as
one can see from the will he drew up in this period) he kept a large
household staff, and he refused to sell off various pieces of property that
might have relieved his financial situation.

Bacon seems to have hoped desperately that James would see fit to
take him back into royal service or, when that prospect became dim, at
least to provide him with income sufficient to continue his lavish living.
Immediately following his release from the Tower, in June 1621, Bacon
was writing to Buckingham, "My mind nevertheless will be still in
prison, till I may be on my feet to do his Majesty and your Lordship
faithful service,"[48] and to the King, "Let me live to serve you, else life is
but a shadow of death."[49] Apparently, some time shortly after Bacon's
fall, the King did invite his comment on the matter of judicial reform;
Bacon answered in the old way — as a royal counsellor. During the
months following his release from prison, Bacon wrote his *History of
the Reign of King Henry VII,* published in 1622 and dedicated to Prince
Charles. In one of his many letters to James, Bacon describes Henry VII
as one "who was in a sort your forerunner, and whose spirit, as well as
his blood, is doubled upon your Majesty,"[50] and there can be little doubt
that the timing of this piece of writing was determined in large part by
Bacon's desire to reestablish himself in royal favor and possibly royal
service. It is interesting to note that among the passages which James

wished to have deleted from the final version of the *History,* was one in which Bacon alluded to the restoration of attainted men. "Of persons attainted," wrote Meautys to Bacon, "enabled to serve in Parliament by a bare reversal of their attainder without issuing any new writs, the King by all means will have left out."[51]

In March of 1622, Bacon was pleading with Buckingham to arrange a meeting between himself and James and, in expectation of such a meeting, was preparing notes on how to present his case and offer his services:

> *I am like ground fresh. If I be left to myself I will graze and bear natural philosophy: but if the King will plough me up again, and sow me with anything, I hope to give him some yield.*[52]

Bacon seems to say that he will use his free time in philosophical writing but will gladly put this work away if he is called back to the King's service. He also appears to have recognized that it would be impossible at this time, with the scandal of his fall so recently passed, for the King to act vigorously and openly on his behalf, but he thought that some commission to undertake a literary project might be managed. There is no record that the meeting which Bacon desired took place, but Bacon pursued the matter in letters to the King and Buckingham in which he offered his "service, for bringing into better order and frame the laws of England."[53] The offer to undertake a "digest of your laws," alluded to in this letter, was expanded into a short essay in which Bacon argued for the nobility and worth of such a project. The project came to naught, however, and realizing that it would be a major undertaking which could be completed only with a large organized effort (such as the King was unwilling to support) Bacon gave it up.

It was probably in the summer of 1622 that Bacon wrote *Advertisement Touching a Holy War,* an unfinished piece in which Bacon urged a European war against the Ottoman Turks. Spedding viewed the idea of such a war as a device for bringing together King and Parliament at home and Protestant and Catholic within Europe as a whole against a common external enemy. To the extent that this is the case the piece must be viewed as an effort of Bacon's part to make himself a counsellor on current political matters.

Sometime after this Bacon drafted another letter to the King. Though, according to Spedding it was not sent, it is revealing of Bacon's state of mind and continuing ambitions. "As I have often said to your Majesty, I was towards you but as a bucket, and a cistern; to draw forth and conserve; whereas yourself was the fountain."[54] Bacon reminded the

King that the crimes for which he was disgraced were not crimes against James himself and went on to appeal to the King's sense of compassion and mercy. Interestingly, Bacon acknowledged here that his present financial straits were the result of his own improvidence.

When the Provost of Eton died in April of 1623, Bacon made a bid for the position. Letters were sent to those Bacon believed might help his suit, and, as had happened so many times before in his life, Bacon waited, inquired, and waited. It came to nothing.

In the autumn of 1623, Bacon was planning conferences with Buckingham. He thought of offering himself to undertake a mission to France on behalf of the government but under the guise of a private traveller. He wrote a letter to Buckingham on the best policy for the government to follow towards Puritans, on the treatment of Catholics in England, and on the Spanish match.

In the winter of 1623–24, anticipating that James would soon have to call a Parliament, Bacon undertook a campaign to lift the part of his sentence which forbade him from sitting in the House of Lords. He hoped that the sentence might be reversed by the Lords themselves, without the intervention of the King. That, he thought, would ruffle fewest feathers among his peers. The campaign failed, and Bacon did not sit in the Parliament that met in February 1624.

Early in 1624, when the negotiations for the Spanish match had been broken off, Bacon wrote a long piece titled "Considerations Touching a War with Spain," in which he argued the justification for such a war and the likelihood of its success. Though it was dedicated to the Prince, Spedding did not know what use, if any, Bacon made of this piece. Its main interest is that it shows Bacon to have been intent on serving as an advisor to the Crown on great affairs just two years before his death.

Though Spedding notes that this piece was "Bacon's last contribution to the political business of his day,"[55] it did not end Bacon's pleadings with the government and with highly placed persons. By the spring of 1624, Bacon seems to have abandoned any hope of government service. He was anxious, however, to win "a complete and total remission of the sentence" against him. In a petition to the King, he wrote:

> *I prostrate myself at your Majesty's feet; I, your ancient servant, now sixty-four years old in age, and three years five months old in misery. I desire not from your Majesty means, nor place, nor employment, but only, after so long a time of expiation, a complete and total remission of the sentence of the Upper House, to the end that blot of ignominy*

may be removed from me, and from my memory with posterity; that I
die not a condemned man, but may be to your Majesty, as I am to God,
nova creatura.[56]

The period from the spring of 1624 until the winter of 1624–25
seems to have marked a kind of turning point for Bacon. Abandoning
his bid to reenter the service of the King, Bacon now became more
modest in his appeals. He suffered recurring bouts of illness which kept
him confined to Gorhambury and interrupted his correspondence and
writing. Spedding noted a six-month period during which next to nothing is known of Bacon's activities. During the winter, he published only
two works, *Apophthegms New and Old* and *Translation of Certain
Psalms,* neither one related to politics or to the Instauration. When
James died in March 1625, and was succeeded by Charles, Bacon's hopes
appear to have been temporarily rekindled, but the general impression
he gives at this point in his life is one of defeat and resignation.

This brief review of Bacon's political involvements and pleadings in
the last years of his life does not support the notion that his renunciation
of political place was a welcome relief as some have suggested, or that he
was now able to devote himself single-mindedly to his philosophical
pursuits. Bacon struggled desperately to resurrect his political life, continually pruning back his expectations and requests in the face of repeated disappointment, until at last he gave up hope for a return to the
king's service and pled only for "a complete and total remission of the
sentence of the Upper House." (It should be noted, however, that such a
"remission" would have allowed him to sit in the House of Lords, and
there are signs that Bacon intended to exercise that right if he were able.)
It remains to look at Bacon's philosophical activities and the fate of the
Great Instauration during these years.

Farrington has suggested that Bacon's writings in these last years of
his life can nearly all be understood as part of a single effort to round out
the great plan that dominated his life — the Great Instauration.[57] In view
of Bacon's own pronouncements about his writing — and particularly his
willingness to undertake whatever writing projects the King might suggest — this contention seems to overestimate the element of design in
Bacon's literary activities of his last years and to underestimate the element of contingency. More importantly for an understanding of the man
himself, Farrington seems to neglect Bacon's desperation and to depict
him as feeling more in control of his life than was in fact the case. There
is one area, however, in which Farrington's idea has some plausibility
and that is with respect to those of Bacon's writings which were narrowly

connected to the Great Instauration. Bacon had laid out the plan for this
project along with all the component parts in 1620 when he published the
Novum Organum so that there was, in a manner of speaking, a clear
agenda.

In part, Bacon's philosophical activities during these last years can
be understood in terms of this agenda. His expansion of the *Advancement* into the Latin *De Augmentis* and his work on the natural history,
specifically, seem to fit the agenda. But Bacon's philosophical work was
complicated by other developments, realizations, and feelings during
this time, and it will be helpful to point a few of these out before we turn
to our narrative. In the first place, Bacon came to believe that translation of his works into Latin must be given a high priority and this, in
turn, was connected to the growing realization that his project was not
attracting the following that he had hoped for within England itself.
Second, and connected with this, was a growing sense that he was now
writing for the future rather than for the present and that his works were
not fully appreciated by his contemporaries. Third, one senses in Bacon
a growing resentment that he should be forced to do the kind of work
that he would rather have delegated to a staff of helpers had such a staff
been available. Fourth, one finds him breaking off projects and turning
to others; that is, an increasing inability to follow plans that he himself
had laid down. And, finally, one finds Bacon's efforts toward the completion of his philosophical design succumbing to the same set of disrupting influences — ill-health, discouragement, pressing personal problems — so that, the oft-retold story of his death notwithstanding, there is
little evidence of fruitful work on the Great Instauration in the last year
or so of his life.

During the winter of 1621–22 and the spring of 1622, Bacon worked
on the expanded Latin translation of the *Advancement of Learning,* a
project which resulted in the publication of the *De Augmentis* sometime
around October of 1623. Two letters, probably both from the summer of
1622, show Bacon taking stock of his life and his writing. In a letter to
Lancelot Andrewes, Bishop of Winchester, Bacon compared his plight to
that of Demosthenes, Cicero, and Seneca:

> *All three, persons that had held chief place of authority in their coun-
> tries; all three ruined, not by war, or by any other disaster, but by
> justice and sentence, as delinquents and criminals; all three famous
> writers, insomuch as the remembrance of their calamity is now as to
> posterity but as a little picture of night-work, remaining amongst the
> fair and excellent tables of their acts and works: and all three (if that
> were any thing to the matter) fit examples to quench any man's ambi-*

tion of rising again; for that they were every one of them restored with great glory, but to their further ruin and destruction, ending in a violent death.[58]

Finding consolations in the examples of these three, Bacon went on to announce that they

Confirmed me much in a resolution (whereunto I was otherwise inclined) to spend my time wholly in writing; and to put forth that poor talent, or half talent, or what it is, that God hath given me, not as heretofore to particular exchanges, but to banks or mounts of perpetuity, which will not break.[59]

Bacon's resolution to write was not in and of itself a decision to abandon the political realm. Later in the letter, when he tells Andrewes of his project to compile the laws of England, he admits that he "cannot altogether desert the civil person that I have borne, which if I should forget, enough would remember."[60] He had not in fact given up the desire for a return to political life, and he continued to prepare pieces of advice on specific matters of policy, to bid for royal service, and to prepare speeches for Parliament should he ever be able to sit again in the House of Lords. With these qualifications, we may accept Bacon's claim that his fall had directed him principally toward writing and turn to his remarks on the progress of the Great Instauration.

Having not long since set forth a part of my Instauration; *which is the work that in mine own judgment (*si nunquam fallit imago*) I do most esteem; I think to proceed in some new parts thereof. And although I have received from many parts beyond the seas, testimonies touching that work, such as beyond which I could not expect at the first in so abstruse an argument; yet nevertheless I have just cause to doubt that it flies too high over men's heads. I have a purpose therefore (though I break the order of time) to draw it down to the sense, by some patterns of a* Natural Story *and* Inquisition. *And again, for that my book of* Advancement of Learning *may be some preparative, or key, for the better opening of the* Instauration; *because it exhibits a mixture of new conceits and old; whereas the* Instauration *gives the new unmixed, otherwise than with some little aspersion of the old for taste's sake; I have thought good to procure a translation of that book, which handleth the* Partition of Sciences; *in such sort, as I hold it may serve in lieu of the first part of the* Instauration, *and acquit my promise in that part.*[61]

To judge from this passage, Bacon is determined to return to the plan of the Great Instauration but does not feel bound to complete it systematically. The *Novum Organum,* published in 1620, had left Bacon's explication of his new method far from complete. It was not to this, however, that he returned in the spring and summer of 1622, but rather to the expansion and translation of the *Advancement* so that it might do duty as the first part of the Instauration and to the compiling of natural history. The reason he gives here for turning from method to natural history is interesting for it sheds light on his understanding of the way his work was being received by the public. We don't know the extent of the positive reactions Bacon claims to have received "from many parts beyond the seas," but it is clear that he is not satisfied with the overall response to his plans for a Great Instauration and that he believed he would be more successful in winning public support if he presented his ideas less abstractly. Here he mentions this tactical resolve in connection with his turn to natural history, but it might also explain his subsequent preparation of the *New Atlantis* for publication. We can say, in any case, that Bacon seems torn between adhering to the systematic agenda published for the Great Instauration in 1620 and departing from it. At least part of his ambivalence was a reaction to the lack of public response to his ideas.

At about this time, Bacon received a letter from Father Redemptus Baranzan, professor of philosophy and mathematics at Anneci, raising questions about the method explicated in the *Novum Organum*. Baranzan apparently had doubts on a number of points: reluctance to relinquish the syllogism as a philosophical tool, concern for the place of metaphysics in the new philosophy, and worry over the magnitude of the task Bacon had set for science, especially the natural histories. Bacon sought to reassure him on each of these points. The syllogism would continue to be useful in mathematical reasoning and might be used in physics as well, once true axioms had been established by induction. Metaphysics would disappear. "When true Physics have been discovered," wrote Bacon, "there will be no Metaphysics. Beyond the true Physics is divinity only." As for the labor involved in compiling natural histories, Bacon's answer was simple: there was no alternative. "What need to dissemble?" asked Bacon. "Either store of Instances must be procured or the business must be given up. All other ways, however enticing, are impassable." Bacon asked, "What matter if the description of the Instances should fill six times as many volumes as Pliny's history?" If one wished to build a new kind of philosophy, which would lead to certain and useful truths about nature, one had no choice.[62]

These reassurances notwithstanding, Bacon himself elsewhere expressed concern about the labor that would be required to complete the natural histories. "A Natural History out of which philosophy may be built is (as you also observe) what I desire before anything else; nor shall I be wanting to the work, so far as in me lies. I wish I may have fit assistants."[63] It was here that Bacon invited Baranzan himself to take on part of the work,

> *by composing a history of the Heavens, in which only the phenomena themselves, and the different astronomical instruments, with their uses, and then the principal and most celebrated hypotheses, both ancient and modern, and at the same time the exact calculations of the periodic returns, and other things of that kind, shall be set forth plainly and simply, without any doctrine or theory whatever.*[64]

At the end of the letter, Bacon tried to make plain the kind of choice he thought Baranzan would need to make: either he must "submit" or be condemned to the sterility that had characterized all past philosophy. Baranzan seems to have inquired whether Bacon had read Patricius, Telesius, and other *"novatores,"* as Bacon called them. Bacon said he had read them, but then dismissed them by lumping them together with others "of the kind," Anaximenes, Anaxagoras, Democritus, and Parmenides. None of these, ancient or modern, differed in their failure to attain truth. "The sum of the matter is this — if men will submit themselves to things, something will be done; if not, those wits will come round again in the circle."[65]

In these letters Bacon's commitment to the Great Instauration seems unshaken, but there is some anxiety about the practical implementation of the plan. Specifically, he seems to struggle with two issues. First, how to get "fit assistants" (*adjutores idoneos*) without whom such vast projects as the natural history would be impossible. Second, how to present his ideas in a sufficiently concrete and appealing way that the influential public would be won over to his program and persuaded to support it. The pursuit of the Great Instauration could be no solitary business if it were to succeed. Perhaps it was partly this pressing realization that prompted his bid for the Provostship of Eton.

Bacon's decision to move on from the completion of the *Novum Organum* to the natural histories, his distress at the lack of support for his work and his concern to enlist such support, and a certain resentment at having to do the menial work of the Great Instauration himself — all these show up in Rawley's preface, "To the Reader," to the *Sylva Sylvarum,* published in 1627 following Bacon's death. Rawley's comments confirm much of what we have already seen in Bacon's letter to

Lancelot Andrewes. Although Bacon understood (according to Rawley) that natural history was unlikely to serve the "glory of his own name . . . for it may seem an indigested heap of particulars, and cannot have that lustre which books cast into methods have," still he was resolved to turn to the compilation of such history because he knew that "there was no other way open to unloose men's minds, being bound and, as it were, maleficiate by the charms of deceiving notions and theories." But if part of Bacon's aim continued to be didactic and propaedeutic, he also intended his histories to serve as an actual foundation on which inductive science might be built—a reservoir of empirical data from which true general axioms might be derived. It was this that distinguished his history from all existing natural histories which had been "gathered for delight and use, [and were] full of pleasant descriptions and pictures, and affect and seek after admiration, rarities, and secrets."[66]

Bacon is often credited with having dignified the menial and manual side of scientific research by making himself an example of the high-minded scientist who was not too proud actually to perform experiments and humbly gather data. While there is some truth to this idea, particularly as regards the image which posterity held of Bacon, it also misrepresents to a degree how Bacon viewed his work and the work of others engaged in organized scientific inquiry. Bacon seems to have been ambivalent about the menial work of science, defending it as noble to the outside world, but more candidly complaining that it was a misuse of his talents. Thus Rawley wrote:

> I have heard his lordship speak complainingly, that his lordship (who thinketh he deserveth to be an architect in this building) should be forced to be a workman and a labourer, and to dig the clay and burn the brick; and more than that (according to the hard condition of the Israelites at the latter end) to gather the straw and stubble over all the fields to burn the bricks withal.[67]

His own resentment seriously qualifies the notion that it was one of Bacon's aims to ennoble the menial labor of science or that his approach harbors a deliberately egalitarian animus. If Rawley's report is accurate, Bacon retained to the end a strong sense of the difference between architect and brick-maker and an unambiguous desire for an elevated position in the hierarchy of the Great Instauration. It was not entirely with a sense of release from the cares of high political office, therefore, that Bacon turned to the compiling of natural history in 1622, and there seems to have been more than a hint of bitterness in being forced to do the drudge-work of science.

In November 1622, Bacon published his *Natural and Experimental*

History, comprising the "History of Winds" and introductions for the particular histories which he promised to complete at a rate of one a month over the succeeding six months. During the winter of 1622–23, Bacon appears to have occupied himself principally with the "History of Life and Death," which was published in 1623.

Bacon's health was apparently bad during the spring and summer of 1623, and it is to this circumstance that Spedding attributed Bacon's decision to give up the publication of new parts of the natural history at regular intervals. But it is possible that his resentment at having to do this work alone entered, consciously or unconsciously, into the decision as well. Work on the preparation of the *De Augmentis* continued through the autumn of 1623. When he began this project, his motive seems to have been primarily the completion of the Great Instauration according to plan, the *De Augmentis* doing duty as the first part of the program. Now, however, a new element entered Bacon's considerations, and this was the need to have his works systematically translated into Latin so they might appeal to an audience which was wider in space and time.

There is evidence that Bacon was despairing of his countrymen and his age as likely vehicles for the accomplishment of the Great Instauration. In his "Life," Rawley almost certainly echoed Bacon's own frustration when he wrote, "His fame is greater and sounds louder in foreign parts abroad, than at home in his own nation; thereby verifying that divine sentence, *A prophet is not without honour, save in his own country, and in his own house.*"[68] In the letter which accompanied the copy of the *De Augmentis* which he presented to the King, Bacon wrote that he had deleted certain parts of the work which might make it offensive to a continental (and, therefore, a largely Roman Catholic) audience. "I have been also mine own *Index Expurgatorius,* that it may be read in all places. For since my end of putting it into Latin was to have it read everywhere, it had been an absurd contradiction to free it in the language and to pen it up in the matter." In a similar letter to Prince Charles, he wrote, "It is a book I think will live, and be a citizen of the world, as English books are not."[69] There is poignancy in these lines, coming as they do from a man whose lifelong outlook was intensely nationalistic and who, up until this point in his life, had directed virtually all his appeals for support to the English public and the English Crown.

The commendation of his program to posterity, put forth again with some poignancy in his letter to Father Fulgentio in the autumn of 1625, would seem to denote a similar shift in Bacon's thinking. Bacon had been ill in the summer of 1624, had published nothing in the winter of 1624–25 but *Apophthegms New and Old* and the *Translation of Certain*

Psalms, and was ill again in the summer of 1625. His letter to Fulgentius seems to have followed his recovery from this last illness. This is Bacon's last full statement on his philosophical enterprises.

> *I wish to make known to your Reverence my intentions with regard to the writings which I meditate and have in hand; not hoping to perfect them, but desiring to try; and because I work for posterity; these things requiring ages for their accomplishment. I have thought it best, then, to have all of them translated into Latin and divided into volumes. The first volume consists of the books concerning the "Advancement of Learning"; and this, as you know, is already finished and published, and includes the partitions of the sciences; which is the first part of my "Instauration." The "Novum Organum" should have followed: but I interposed my moral and political writings, as being nearer ready. These are: First, the "History of the Reign of Henry the Seventh King of England"; after which will follow the little book which in your language you have called* Saggi Morali. *But I give it a weightier name; entitling it "Faithful Discourses — on the Inwards of Things." But these discourses will be both increased in number and much enlarged in the treatment. The same volume is (as I said) interposed, not being a part of the "Instauration." After this will follow the "Novum Organum," to which there is still a second part to be added — but I have already compassed and planned it out in my mind. And in this manner the second part of the "Instauration" will be completed. As for the third part, namely, the "Natural History," that is plainly a work for a King or a Pope, or some college or order: and cannot be done as it should by a private man's industry. And those portions which I have published, concerning "Winds," and concerning "Life and Death," are not history pure: because of the axioms and greater observations that are interposed: but a kind of writing mixed of natural history and a rude and imperfect intellectual machinery; which is the fourth part of the "Instauration." Next therefore will come the fourth part itself; wherein will be shown many examples of this machine, more exact and more applied to the rules of induction. In the fifth place will follow the book which I have entitled the "Precursors of the Second Philosophy," which will contain my discoveries concerning new axioms, suggested by the experiments themselves: that they may be raised as it were and set up like pillars that were on the ground. And this I have set down as the fifth part of my "Instauration." Last comes the "Second Philosophy" itself — the sixth part of the "Instauration": of which I have given up all hope; but it may be that the ages and posterity will make it flourish. Never-*

theless in the "Precursors"—those I mean which touch upon the univer-
salities of nature—no slight foundations of this will be laid.[70]

In this letter Bacon still clings to the overall plan of the Great Instauration that he had laid down in 1620 but is less hopeful about its quick
completion. Bacon had always said that he was working for posterity, of
course, but generally this had been offered as an argument for patient
scientific toil and the avoidance of attempts to reap the fruits of inquiry
prematurely. Now, however, his commendation of the work to posterity
seems to carry a different message, and his admission that the great body
of work requisite to the Great Instauration "is plainly a work for a King
or a Pope, or some college or order" implies a recognition that neither
the establishment nor the direction of such an organization would belong to him. If, indeed, Bacon's bid for the Provostship of Eton had
been made partly with an eye to gaining an institutional setting for his
work, the failure of this bid might have marked the end of Bacon's
dream of having "commandment of more wits than [his] own," as he had
written to Burghley more that three decades earlier.

One might ponder also Bacon's allusion to the Pope as a possible
patron of science. When he began his career in the 1580s, Bacon shared
the anti-Roman feelings of his generation. Now, in his old age, he had
come to look to Gondomar, the Spanish ambassador, for help in mend-
ing his political fortunes, to continental Catholic correspondents for
intellectual understanding and support, and to Tobie Matthew, an English convert to Catholicism and thenceforward an important Catholic on
the political scene, for friendship. In his letter to King James, Bacon had
written of toning down parts of the *De Augmentis* to make them more
acceptable to a continental audience. And Rawley notes that Bacon
came to regard himself as a prophet without honor in his own land. All
this suggests again a deep and painful disillusionment and loss of hope
that the Great Instauration might be a grand English and Protestant
undertaking.

By the autumn of 1625, Bacon's health seems to have been improving, allowing him to return to literary work. A third, enlarged edition of
the *Essays* appeared in this year and he was apparently working on the
Sylva Sylvarum. It is uncertain whether the writing of the *New Atlantis,*
Bacon's utopia in which the famous Salomon's House figures so prominently, dates from this time or whether it was written earlier.

In addition to his recurring illness, Bacon suffered another personal
trouble at the very end of his life having to do with his wife. While
Spedding narrates the episode with nineteenth-century tact, it seems that

Alice Bacon became involved in an illicit relationship with one of her servants. The affair was sufficiently serious to have aroused public comment by the gossips of the day and led Bacon to cut her out of his will.

By the beginning of 1626, Bacon was still hoping for some relief in his financial plight, probably through the help of Buckingham. We know little about Bacon from this time except the circumstances of his death. While the familiar anecdote about Bacon's last illness does, indeed, indicate that he was "doing science" up to the last, it tells us little about the way in which he regarded the Great Instauration as a whole on the eve of his death. Toward the end of March, Bacon was out driving and, as it was snowing, decided to make an experiment concerning the power of snow to retard the spoilage of food. He stopped at a cottage and procured a chicken, which he then proceeded to kill and fill with snow. Once back in the carriage and on his way, Bacon was taken ill. He stopped at a house of Lord Arundel and went to bed, where he died on April 9, 1626, Easter Sunday.

Thus ended the life of Francis Bacon, fallen Lord Chancellor and designer of the Great Instauration. The last five years show him to have been troubled and restless. He clung to the schemes which he had formulated when he was younger, but his hopes of carrying through seem to have been progressively eroded. He had to face the truth that James was not going to call him back into public service, or commission him to undertake the literary or legal projects he proposed, or even take any decisive action to mend his personal fortunes. At the same time, he came to realize that support was not going to be forthcoming during his lifetime or in his native land and, consequently, to become more measured in his projections of what he could hope to accomplish. Both his scheme for compiling the laws of England and his plan for completing the natural history foundered on the same shoal — both had been projected as large, organized undertakings which would require the combined labors of many intellects. This kind of *organized* intellectual activity lay at the heart of Bacon's vision, and midway through the last phase of his life Bacon had to give up hopes of completing either project. Much of his life Bacon had spent in elaborating vast schemes in which he himself figured as a leader and director of other men, and now he found himself working essentially alone. He had imagined that these enterprises would bring him status and recognition, and now he was in disgrace politically with his philosophical schemes largely ignored by his English contemporaries. He did not accept this situation with the kind of calm and Stoic forbearance that some have claimed for him. Rather, he complained bitterly to the King that he had suffered enough for his judicial misconduct and deserved to suffer no more and to Rawley that he should not be forced to labor alone at the menial work of science which, by rights, he should have been directing others to do.

Toward his death Bacon exhibited the same mixture of bold imagination and self-pity that had marked his whole life. He remained to the end the projector of great designs which would have required for their success that he win the hearts and minds of those around him, just as he remained one who was little capable of making true human contact with those he sought to influence. This, if anything, was the tragedy of his life, but it was not a tragedy in which his high ideals were thwarted by the baseness of his age, but rather one in which his desire to organize and lead men was continually undercut by his perpetual capacity for inspiring in them mistrust and, at times, even derision.

CONCLUSIONS

The view of Spedding and many of his successors that Bacon's life can be understood as having been guided by a single dominating intellectual ambition dating from his early adolescence is untenable. Political biographers have come nearer the mark in viewing Bacon's character and life as fraught with contingency.

The common view (apparently supported by some of Bacon's own remarks) which insists that Bacon's commitments to both philosophy and politics were activities so different in kind that they pulled him in two different directions throughout his life is mistaken. Accounts which portray Bacon as having lived two different kinds of life—the *vita activa* and the *vita contemplativa*—attempt to render an integrated interpretation of the whole field of biographical data yet lack psychological plausibility. Moreover, they fail to account for the specific ways in which his various activities conditioned one another.

In the final analysis, Bacon's life and personality are more complex than is generally recognized. This biographical sketch shows that an impulse toward both public service and private advancement played a part in Bacon's ambition. This ambition sought satisfaction in both political and philosophical enterprises. Until he was about forty, Bacon seems to have been almost completely driven by a desire for "place." So powerful was this desire, that Bacon seemed capable of the most distasteful sort of climbing and self-abasement in the pursuit of office. There is little evidence before 1603 of a serious effort to serve the world through reforming learning or founding a new science. During the first decade of James's reign, Bacon's political ambitions were stimulated

through being partially satisfied, and this is the period of his most creative philosophical work. As we have seen from the *Commentarius Solutus,* the bold and sometimes enigmatic writings of this period were only
one side of his philosophical campaign. The other side was the courting
of powerful and wealthy men, the manipulation of opportunities, and
the cultivation of his own image — the same kind of activity which characterized his political campaigning. Once he defined science as a collective and collaborative enterprise, the attainment of his philosophical
goals in some measure came to involve the same sort of quest for place —
now a place which might provide ample material resources and allow
him to direct "wits" — as did his political ambition. When, in the following decade, he attained the highest political office in the kingdom there is
little evidence of any real and effective resolve to use his power (as he
had so often claimed he would do) to further his high-minded projects
for a new science. Rather, he seemed delighted to bask in the glory of his
long-sought office and to enjoy the perquisites that it made possible,
often extravagantly indulging his taste for the various symbols of status
and power. Though the psychological dimensions of Bacon's ambition
await a skillful and sensitive interpretation, I have at least tried to show
that his life cannot be understood by assuming that some unalloyed
altruism or disinterested desire for human improvement stood as its
guiding center.

The point of all this is not to pass moral judgments. It is, rather, to
displaying the nobility of mind freed from worldly cares,
the last years of Bacon's life seem to confirm our picture of him as a
rather fragile, brittle man, excessively needful of external confirmation
to go on with his work. After his fall, Bacon lost his philosophical
impetus. Though for a time he clung desperately to his hopes for political rehabilitation, when this failed to materialize, he became increasingly
preoccupied with the thought that his countrymen would never awaken
to his philosophical call. Although he continued to project and to
scheme, there is an increasing sense that he was beset by disorganization
and demoralized by despair in all his activities — philosophical and political — as his death approached.

The point of all this is not to pass moral judgments. It is, rather, to
attempt a portrait which, unlike so many that have been drawn of him,
possesses some psychological plausibility and, at the same time, allows
us to interpret the fruits of his apparently divergent activities as the work
of a single mind and soul. A more realistic portrait, will allow us to
attempt new assessments of his writings and deeds. Specifically, an appreciation of Bacon's psychological complexity and of the mutually
stimulating character of his philosophical and political activities may
allow us to discern new orders of both intellectual complexity and intel-

lectual unity in the various parts of Bacon's disparate body of writings.

Far from displaying the alternation we have been led to expect between the *vita activa* and the *vita contemplativa,* Bacon's life presents a pattern in which literary and philosophical concerns proceed apace with engagement in worldly affairs. Indeed, if anything, Bacon's project for a new science would seem to have been stimulated by his political success in the first decade of James's reign and, in the last phase of his life, to have suffered a discouragement which paralleled his political disgrace. A possible key to the parallelism is suggested by the recognition that the Great Instauration was more than a plan to propagate new ideas. In Bacon's mind it necessarily involved an active campaign to enlist support, to recruit followers, and to establish a new community. It was this practical side of the campaign to organize a new science (no less that his frequently recognized desire that science be for the betterment of man's estate) that gave the Great Instauration a quasi-political character and rendered it yet another manifestation of Bacon's "active life."

If a simple division of Bacon's pursuits into "active" and "contemplative" phases seems untenable at a biographical level, there arises the possibility that the substance of Bacon's political and scientific conceptions are related to one another in ways that have not been well explored. The long-standing tendency to compartmentalize and segregate Bacon's ideas about politics and science has perhaps deprived us of the means for understanding not only the connection between these two domains in Bacon's work but also the full extent to which his version of organized science reflected a general and encompassing social vision.

Suggestive as it may be for new avenues of inquiry, biography can take the intellectual historian only so far. It is highly suggestive, for example, that by the time Bacon turned to serious and sustained work on what came to be called the "Great Instauration," he was already over forty years of age and that — so far as the evidence allows us to draw conclusions — most of his concerted effort up to that time and much of the experience which must have formed his character and outlook had been in the areas of politics and law. This chronology suggests the possibility that as Bacon took up the question of intellectual and, more specifically, scientific reform in the first decade of James's reign, his ideas about science might have been shaped to a great extent by the outlook he had formed in politics. But to test such a hypothesis we must turn to Bacon's writings about politics and science.

Franc. Baconi
DE VERULAMIO
HISTORIA REGNI
HENRICI SEPTIMI
Angliæ Regis
OPUS VERE POLITICUM

Amstelodami,
Apud H. WETSTENIUM.
1695

I I

The Well-Ordered Commonwealth

*B*ACON's History of the Reign of Henry VII, *written shortly after Bacon's fall from political office and first published in 1622, recounted the career of the first Tudor monarch but was more than simple narrative. In such "civil" history Bacon sought to exhibit the principles of prudent government and his generally laudatory account of Henrician rule has led some to consider Bacon to be an English Machiavelli. Courtesy of Department of Special Collections, University of Chicago.*

3

Order and Productivity
in the Larger Commonwealth

THE CONTEXT OF BACON'S POLITICAL THOUGHT

Recently some writers have portrayed Bacon as a political prophet of modernity, though the more common view, expressed long ago by G. P. Gooch, has been that "whereas in philosophy he was a pioneer, in politics he was a conservative if not a reactionary."[1] Concerned largely with constitutional issues and viewing Bacon as a champion of "enlightened absolutism,"[2] Gooch argued that the weakness of Bacon's political system was that "it depended for its success on the character and capacity of the ruler, and that it overlooked the educative influence of self-government."[3] According to Gooch, it "never occurred" to Bacon "that the instinct of common men might sometimes be wiser than the wisdom of kings and philosophers."[4]

> His system, in a word, was suited to a state of society that had already passed away. If in science and speculation his face was turned towards the dawn, as a political thinker his horizon was bounded by the autocratic monarchies of the century of the Reformation. He had no insight into the strength and value of the newer currents that were bearing his countrymen in the direction of a wider and more assured liberty.[5]

Aside from the underlying assumption that the superiority of popular government is self-evident, there is a good deal of truth in Gooch's characterization of Bacon's political thinking. Bacon did not merely "overlook" the possibilities of popular government, however; he expressly rejected them. The assumptions on which this rejection is based lead us to an appreciation of the deep gulf that separates Bacon's political thought from the modern ideologies of popular government if not, perhaps, from the practices of modern states.

The fact that Bacon was a constitutional conservative, however, must not be taken to imply that he was a conservative in the matter of political policy. Bacon was acutely aware that the transformations of his age had revealed previously unimagined possibilities for social, economic, and cultural improvement, just as they had raised the specter of anarchy and dissolution. The task of government was to check the forces of disorder and to channel the emerging energy and creativity of society for the betterment of the commonwealth. There was no incompatibility in Bacon's mind between authoritarian constitutional arrangements and progressive governmental policies. On the contrary, in his view the improvement of the commonwealth could be achieved only by holding popular depravity in check. Bacon stood resolutely for a policy which, in his view, would benefit the populace by making the commonwealth well-ordered and productive, but equally he believed that such a policy would often need to be pursued against the volatile and irrational will of the people.

Though Bacon's political and scientific projects can easily be distinguished in the way suggested by Gooch, it is important to recognize that his approach to science bears certain striking similarities to his approach to politics — particularly in that he consistently combines constitutional "conservatism" with a "progressive" conception of policy. The premises and arguments whereby he sought to organize a new beginning for the commonwealth of learning closely parallel those of his political thought. Bacon's organization of his scientific enterprise reflected the same conservative assumptions about human nature, about the need for regulating and rationalizing authority, and about the dangers of unrestrained freedom and public discussion that we find in his political writing. Both display the same impetus toward human improvement and material progress.

Bacon's political thought may be understood against a number of backgrounds, the most general of which has been explored by Quentin Skinner in his discussion of political humanism in the Renaissance. Skinner attempts to show how a certain configuration of political ideas and attitudes began to grow in the later Middle Ages, flowered in the fifteenth and early sixteenth centuries among the republican writers of Italy, and subsequently spread northward to France, Germany, the Low Countries, and England.[6] He begins with an analysis of the ideal of liberty as it began in the city republics of northern Italy in opposition to the pretensions of both Emperor and Pope. It was fed by two learned traditions: that of rhetorical studies and that of later scholasticism. Republican thought flowered with the Florentine Renaissance, was threatened and briefly checked by the rise of princely regimes, but revived in the late fifteenth and early sixteenth centuries when it seemed for a moment that princely rule in Rome and Florence might crumble. It was this last efflorescence of Italian republican thought that produced the writings of Guicciardini and Machiavelli.

Although Skinner does not believe that the spread of Italian humanism offers a complete explanation for the northern European Renaissance, he does believe that it played a crucial role. As Italian scholars came to teach at northern universities and northern students went to study in Italy, certain texts, ideas, formulations of problems, characteristic attitudes, and approaches to solutions migrated northward. One of the most important of the political convictions of these northern humanists (and one which is of obvious relevance to Bacon's approach to politics) was the "well-established humanist belief that the links between sound learning and sound government were extremely close."[7] From this belief sprang the various educational treatises for princes and courtiers, the "mirror-for-princes" treatises, and the books of advice addressed to the whole body of citizens. Among English examples of this genre Skinner includes Sir Thomas More's *Utopia* (1516) and Thomas Starkey's *Dialogue between Reginald Pole and Thomas Lupset* (1535). Beyond writing works of advice, many northern humanists were actually drawn into responsible positions of government. Though such work offered a practical expression of the idea that political life would benefit from the influence of "learning," it also seemed to threaten the detachment which some humanists regarded as essential for intellectual pursuits. So they engaged in an ongoing discussion about "the rival merits of *otium* and *negotium*—the life of quiet and contemplation versus the life of activity and business."[8] This choice presents itself (rhetorically at least) as a constant dilemma for Bacon. In the end, most northern humanists chose *negotium* if given the opportunity, and their reasons for doing so were twofold. First, there was the "familiar humanist (and later Puritan) claim that all knowledge ought to be 'for use' ";[9] second, assuming as they did that a "well-ordered" monarchy was the most nearly perfect form of government, they concluded that service to the monarch was the highest form of civic involvement.

Like their Italian predecessors, the northern humanists (and Bacon with them) devoted a good deal of attention to the ills of their various societies and represented themselves as "physicians to the body politic."[10] Principal among social ills, they believed, was tendency of either the Prince or some portion of the population to choose "individual or factional interests" over the good of the community as a whole. Princes were admonished to govern for the general good. Lawyers, clerics, and nobles were variously castigated for selfishness. Enclosing landlords and forestalling merchants were arraigned for threatening the public order.

The fundamental purpose of government, according to most of these humanist writers was "to maintain good order, harmony, and peace."[11] In so defining the ends of government, the northern humanists owed much to the Italians, who had likewise decried faction and corruption, but Skinner also points out an important change that occurred as humanism moved northward. Whereas Italian political humanism had been closely aligned with republicanism and the defense of virtue and had thus harbored a potentially radical animus, northern humanism was considerably more conservative. With the important exception of More, Skinner argues, most of the northern humanists committed themselves to the deeply conservative idea that "in order to maintain the best-ordered form of political society, [they] ought not to tamper with any existing social distinctions, but ought on the contrary to preserve them as far as possible."[12]

The English writers introduced by Skinner to exemplify one or another aspect of this conservative northern humanism are Thomas Elyot, Thomas Starkey, and Thomas More. At many crucial points, however, it is easy to see Bacon's debt to the tradition as well, not only in his conception of the close links which should exist between learning and government, but in his conception of the overarching aims of government as well.

In his study of sixteenth-century commonwealth ideas Whitney R. D. Jones provides a framework which allows us to specify a little more closely Bacon's relation to political thought in Tudor England.[13] Focusing on the period from 1529 to 1559 — a period which he calls "a crisis period" for Tudor England and, incidentally, the crucial period for Nicholas Bacon's generation — and on several groups of men — the More Group, the Cromwell Group, what came to be called the Commonwealth Party, and certain of the radical Protestants — Jones shows that certain essentially medieval but certainly traditional social and economic ideals were adapted to the changed circumstances of the sixteenth century.

The crisis through which England was passing, according to Jones, was profound and multifaceted, entailing at the most general level the passing of an organic medieval society and the birth of fragmented modernity. On the economic and social side, it involved the "loss of communal society" in economic relationships[14] and the growth of the market,[15] the enclosure movement, the decline of guilds, the debasement of money, the dissolution of the monasteries, the boom in woolen exports, and the growing sense that medieval remedies — including traditional means for dealing with poverty — were no longer workable. Politically it entailed a growing sense of the fragility of the established order and a fear of sedition and rebellion. The Church in its new, Henrician form, was deemed by many incapable of exercising the old regulatory power over social and economic life and of curbing human avarice or of enforcing the traditional standards of justice. Commonwealth political thought, according to Jones, must be understood as a political response to the growing perception of crisis.

Although the commonwealth thinkers generally championed some version of social and economic justice, according to Jones, they were not political radicals. Indeed, "good order and obedience" in the populace were, for them, among the cardinal virtues of political society and the sine qua non of all social good. It was, indeed, to the Crown that they generally looked to curb the aggressions of particular interests and to oversee the well-being and harmony of the whole as against the pretensions of the parts. Yet alongside their almost unexceptional insistence on obedience most did argue that the government had an equally unconditional responsibility to manage society in such a way that the weak would not be ground under the heel of the strong, and this idea produced certain radical undercurrents in what was generally a conservative movement of thought.

In his discussion of the body of commonwealth literature, Jones shows the manner in which these mid-century political thinkers and propagandists looked to the state to remedy a wide variety of contemporary issues. They were concerned to promote policies, for example, to overcome religious division and ensure that standards of Christian justice and charity found expression in the social life of the realm; to maintain the "due degree and order" upon which the stability of society and government inevitably (in their view) rested; to address the linked problems of enclosure, price fluctuations, unemployment, and poverty; to curb avarice and curtail the pernicious economic influence of middlemen; to prevent the extension of private liberties that threatened the public good; and to strengthen the means by which the ordinary citizen might find protection and justice from the state.

Toward the end of his study, Jones suggests the way in which the political thought of Bacon relates to that of the commonwealth propagandists. Bacon's indebtedness to the mid–sixteenth-century thinkers is clear. But there had also been an important shift, according to Jones, by the time we get to Bacon and others of the late sixteenth and seventeenth centuries. "General governmental supervision was still desired, but maximum production tended to replace optimum distribution as the primary objective."[16] During the Middle Ages economic and technological changes had been sufficiently gradual, according to Jones, to convince people that the best chance for social improvement lay in redistributing wealth that already existed. It was this outlook—still essentially medieval—that informed the commonwealth emphasis on social justice. Bacon and others after him, however, were beginning to respond to social, economic, and political problems on the assumption that the production of wealth could itself be dramatically increased. This meant that the redistributive—and potentially radical—elements in the commonwealth vision tended to fall away by the end of the century and be replaced by a growing emphasis on social efficiency leading to increasing production.

If Bacon was steeped in the learning of his times, he was also a man of affairs. His outlook on politics bears the unmistakable mark of the practical political milieu in which he was involved by his birth and to which he committed himself by choice: the world of Tudor politics, centered on the court of Elizabeth.

While a lengthy excursus on Tudor political ideology would be out of place, J. H. Hexter has provided a brief sketch of the governing ideas of Tudor policy that highlights the salient features of Bacon's political culture. The Tudors, according to Hexter, adopted as the basis for their vision of government the "hierarchical organic conception of society" that they inherited from the Middle Ages, and if they added something new to this older idea it was the "magnification of the active regulatory role of the royal government as a means by which society might approximate its own ideal."[17] In order to preserve "social peace and harmony" it was Tudor policy "relentlessly to repress violent breaches of order, riot, sedition, and rebellion, and to subject the unregulated desires and particular interests of individuals and groups to the good order and harmony of the commonwealth."[18] The threat of disorder was perpetually posed by powerful and unruly nobles, on the one hand, and the mass of the poor and discontented on the other, but, as Hexter points out, these two were, in the Tudor view, "but heads and tails of the same coin—a disordered commonwealth."[19] Given their pervasive fear of social disorder, the Tudors tended to view change—even such change as might swell the wealth of England—as something requiring great caution on the part of rulers. Thus Tudor policy "sought to establish itself in a regulatory position vis à vis the whole range of commercial and industrial life."[20] Such regulation was designed, as Hexter points out, to insure that change would work to the advantage of the established regime and the established order and not against them.

> It was not the policy of the Tudors either to stand mulishly athwart the path of change, or to allow it free rein, but to guide, to bring it as they said to some good rule conformable with good order. The vast mass of Tudor legis-

lation on economic activities rests solidly on three principles—privilege, regulation, supervision. The purpose was to prevent the unchecked greed and ambition of any group—middle-class or other—from dislocating the social order.[21]

This view of government and social order supposed a conception of human nature as fundamentally erratic, egoistic, and unreliable, so that the work of government might seem a monumental holding action against anarchy and dissolution.

Throughout the life of the Tudor dynasty the awareness of the origins of Tudor rule in war and civil chaos never vanished, nor did the belief that if government weakened all of England might be thrown back into the era of destructive feudal competition or laid open to plundering and dissolution by some elemental rising of the vast sea of poor. Fear played a major role in the rhetoric by which the regime legitimized itself. When Tudor apologists spoke of social disorder, it was social war that they had in mind, so that their historical memories made the stakes of government seem inestimably high.

Tudor ideology, in short, combined an acute sensitivity to the potentially disruptive, potentially enriching forces of change with a steadfast determination to ensure that change would be contained within the old social and political framework. Since the social order was perceived as fragile, change would have to be carefully managed, old and new forces balanced and rationalized, and all classes subordinated to the overarching authority of the Crown. To the extent that the forces of change were expressed in new and potentially disruptive ideological movements like Puritanism, the government must attempt the management of ideas, for close and potentially dangerous links were perceived to exist between people's opinions and their behavior as subjects.

Bacon was thoroughly imbued with the beliefs and attitudes of the Tudor administrative apparatus to which he attached himself. General tendencies in Bacon's political and intellectual milieu were worked out concretely and given individual expression in his writings. A selective account may demonstrate the affinities between Bacon's political conceptions and the way he went about organizing the smaller commonwealth of scientists. I shall focus on two phases of Bacon's political concern. For Bacon, "policy" (that catchall phrase for what a particular government does with its authority short of war) was Janus-faced and sought two different sorts of political goods. One face of policy had to be directed to the maintenance of political and social order, without which no other social goods could even be imagined. The other, once order was secured, was directed to the attainment of a host of positive social goods. I call these two aspects "order" and "productivity." In Bacon's view these two tasks of government were not to be conceived as sequential. It was not as if any government could settle the question of order and then move on confidently to the problem of productivity. Bacon was not of the opinion that political order, once secured, could be perpetuated indefinitely by material well-being. People were not so rational as to be rendered obedient by the rational benevolence of their government. Hunger and human suffering might produce disorder, but their absence would not ensure peace. The sources of disorder lay in the most deep-rooted irrationalities of human nature, and therefore government must be ever vigilant. This was most true of progressive governments, i.e., governments which deliberately innovated in order to improve their subjects' estate, for innovation itself could loosen the bonds of political authority and open the gates of "tumult."

THE IDEOLOGICAL DIMENSIONS OF DISORDER

T hough every political outlook may embody some positive conception of the well-ordered society, it is a preoccupation with disorder which presents itself most saliently in the writings of Bacon. He wrote continually of the dangers which threatened the stability of the commonwealth, and his regular resort to terms like "faction," "sect," "sedition," "tumult," "distemper," and "swelling humours" serves to remind us that in Bacon's writings the ideal of order was to a great extent a latent one, never fully articulated and usually overshadowed by his preoccupation with its violation. Thus, while it may be convenient to speak as Hexter does of a "hierarchical organic conception of society," this conception is negatively defined in Bacon's writings by his stereotyped denunciations of uncivil behavior.

Christopher Morris has written that Tudor political writers adopted "an almost hysterical attitude toward rebellion."[22] There was, he suggests, some basis in reality for the fear and a practical political reason for these writers to emphasize the horrors that might stem from political disobedience:

> Fear of disputed succession and of civil strife was very real in Tudor England. Probably the alleged horrors of the Wars of the Roses were much exaggerated by Tudor propagandists but men had before their eyes the terrible examples of the German and French wars of religion. . . . There had in fact been several rebellions in Tudor England, and the government, with no

police or regular army, was very ill-equipped to meet them. All the more reliance had to be placed on propaganda. Law and order were still precarious and could not yet be taken for granted; and therefore their praises were sung by Tudor writers to an extent that must now seem redundant and forced.[23]

Morris's use of the term "hysterical" suggests that perhaps there was an irrational and exaggerated component to the fear, and in the case of Bacon one suspects that regular references to "tumult" and "rebellion" have come to serve something of an ideological function. It is clear, at any rate, that in Bacon's writings political disorder was handled in a highly schematic and stereotyped way which could be applied easily to phenomena that were not strictly political. Certain interpretive schemata appear over and over again in Bacon's treatment of human collective life — now in relation to politics, now to religion, now to learning. An understanding of these is essential to grasping his positive conception of order and to understanding his analysis of disorder in the commonwealth of learning.

Bacon's writings on religious conflict in the 1580s serve as an introduction to his analysis of disorder. Though they are early works, they display habits of mind that would remain with Bacon throughout his life. For the Tudors after Henry VIII religion was quite clearly and explicitly a political matter. The monarch headed the Church of England. The government of Elizabeth, however, was confronted with a dangerous religious situation: the established Church seemed threatened on one side by unreformed and unreconciled Roman Catholics and on the other by a growing Puritan opposition. The survival of Roman Catholicism and the growth of Puritanism were more than an embarrassment to the Crown; they were a threat to the unity of the national religious community and to the firm control which the state aspired to exercise over the activities of its subjects.

The decade during which Bacon entered political life saw a heightening of the religious threat. In the years prior to 1588 England was moving toward the symbolic climax of its long quarrel (religious, political, economic) with Roman Catholic Spain. The fear that Spain would attempt to reimpose Roman Catholicism on England by force was very real and formed a chronic preoccupation of English political life. Fear of Spain coalesced with and reinforced fear of Roman Catholics in England, who were frequently viewed as subversives and a potential fifth column. If Roman Catholicism loomed as a religious-political threat from the right, Puritanism seemed to pose a corresponding threat from the left. During most of the 1580s, according to M. M. Knappen, English Puritans had worked for reform in the Church of England under the disciplining leadership of John Field, who served (in Knappen's words) as "organizer, propagandist, and party secretary all in one."[24] After Field's death in 1588, however, "the extremist element, left to its own devices, soon ruined all remaining chances by the violence of their tactics."[25] Toward the end of the decade, under the pen name of "Martin Marprelate," one of these extremists launched a harsh and abusive attack on the established Church and was answered in kind by the defenders of the existing ecclesiastical government.[26]

It was to this situation that Bacon addressed himself in two of his earliest pieces of political analysis and advice on policy matters, the "Letter of Advice" to Elizabeth, written in late 1584 or early 1585, and the "Advertisement Touching the Controversies of the Church of England" written in 1589 in the wake of the Martin Marprelate furor. In the case of both English Catholicism and an increasingly aggressive Puritanism, Bacon was responding to disruptive threats from below. The rhetorical and analytic stance that he adopted in both pieces showed him identifying himself with the government as a would-be counsellor and royal policymaker. It is striking throughout that Bacon avoided dealing with any of these issues in religious terms, choosing instead a decidedly secular standpoint from which religious conflict was merely a species of social disorder generally.

The "Letter of Advice" began with the assertion that Elizabeth's "present estate can no way be encumbered but by . . . strong factious subjects and . . . foreign enemies" and proceeded to deal with these two evils in turn. By "strong factious subjects" Bacon meant the English Roman Catholics, strong, he wrote, both in numbers and in their ability to unite; factious, because they are deeply discontented. Either their strength or discontent must be removed, Bacon argued, if they were to be eliminated as a political danger. Bacon did not believe that Elizabeth, a Protestant queen, could ever content the Catholics. Nor did he think that the English Catholics themselves would respond *rationally* to the policies of a Protestant government. "To suffer them to be strong, with hope that with reason they will be contented, carries with it in my opinion but a fair enamelling of a terrible danger."[27] The best the government could do, Bacon argued, was avoid policies that would transform discontent into despair. Most immediately this might mean that the oath of loyalty, which was being deliberated, might be drawn up in a way that was not unnecessarily provocative.

Bacon turned next to the question of how the government might lessen the power of Roman Catholics to harm the state. In this context he broached the other major issue facing the established church and the government: that of the Puritans. Ever wary of zeal in any form, Bacon expressed personal distaste for what he called the "preciseness" of Puritans. They were "over-squeamish and nice, and more scrupulous than they need."[28] But he also disagreed with the bishops' persecution of Puritan preachers, first because such open conflict would bring the English Church into ill-repute abroad, then, more importantly, because these preachers "bring forth that fruit which your most excellent Majesty is to wish and desire; namely, the lessening and diminishing of the papistical number."[29] Bacon recommended the Puritans as ideal weapons against the Papists and suggested that they be used by the Crown as Frederick II had employed Saracen soldiers against the Pope "because he was well assured and certainly knew that they would not spare his Sanctity."[30] So long as the Puritans could be made instruments of royal policy, the very excesses of these zealots might be turned to the benefit of the government. Bacon explicitly rejected a policy of violent persecution of Roman Catholics, not for moral reasons but because he believed that such a policy would only make martyrs of them and have the opposite of the intended result.[31]

Recognizing, however, that not all Roman Catholics would be won over to Protestantism even by the zeal of the Puritan preachers, Bacon suggested, finally, that Catholics be scrupulously excluded from all positions of influence in the nation. They should be kept from the ranks of officialdom; royal policies should minimize the influence of Catholic landlords over their tenants; and, finally, they should be excluded from military ranks and military training.

The "Letter of Advice" points to a number of habits which would characterize Bacon's analysis of disorder throughout his life. First is the notion that, besides foreign threats, "factious subjects" pose the most serious danger to the "estate" of Elizabeth. As his analysis develops, it turns out that the factiousness of Roman Catholics was not to be stilled by concessions, since they were not likely to respond rationally. The connection between disorder and irrationality is one that occurs again and again in Bacon's writing. Bacon suggests that the zeal of the Puritans also carries a large dose of distasteful irrationality, but hopes to use their fervor to neutralize the threat of Catholicism. As a would-be royal counsellor, Bacon evinced a self-conscious indifference to the religious issues involved in these religious controversies and a determination to view the conflicts in purely secular terms as one who was above all responsible for the maintenance of civil peace and the security of the state. Refusing to be drawn into a discussion of the substance or merits of the religious quarrels, he offered himself to the Crown as one who could stand above the factional divisions and look to the well-being of the commonweal.

Many of the same themes and much the same kind of analysis emerge again in Bacon's "Advertisement Touching the Controversies of the Church of England," written at the height of the Martin Marprelate furor. Here, however, the right and left are the bishops and the Puritan opposition respectively—a different configuration, to be sure, but one that was susceptible to the same kind of analysis. Both right and left, in any case, have gone astray: "Some have sought the truth in the conventicles and conciliables of heretics and sectaries, and others in the extern face and representation of the church; and both sorts been seduced."[32]

At the outset, Bacon invokes the concept of *adiaphora* to deny importance to the substance of the quarrel and open the way for treating only as another instance of faction. "The controversies themselves," he said, "I will not enter into, as judging that the disease requireth rather rest than any other cure."[33] He was able to do this because, in his view, the disagreements do not touch the high mysteries of faith or the "great parts of the worship of God." "We contend about ceremonies and things indifferent; about the extern policy and the government of the church."[34] As always Bacon claimed to rise above the fray, arguing that the point was "not to enter into assertions and positions, but to deliver counsels and advices."[35]

Bacon chastised the radical Puritans for what he called their "immodest and deformed manner of writing" and the bishops for having imitated the Puritan pamphleteers whom they sought to condemn. "The second blow maketh the fray," he reminded them. But he did not accept the view that this religious conflict was the forerunner of a more general political upheaval "as if the civil government itself of this estate had near lost the force of her sinews, and were ready to enter into some convulsion, all things being full of faction and disorder."[36] (And even if this were the case, he added ambiguously, it would be unwise to acknowledge the danger.)

Having denied the Church quarrels and substance of merit, Bacon went on to discuss the causes of these controversies. Here he analyzed disorder by way of certain schemata which would recur in both his political and philosophical writings. At root, Bacon seems to suggest, these quarrels were not religious at all, or, better said, they stemmed from deep-rooted human tendencies toward disorderly conduct and had merely donned a religious garb. Bacon invoked three schemata to organize his characterization of the events he treats: first, the relation of masters and followers; second, the tendency of people to array themselves into mutually opposing positions; and, third, the contrast between the failings of the vulgar and the virtues of the select. These schemata are not, of course, new with Bacon. Since he used them over and over again, however, in a variety of ways, it will be useful to examine their application to the case at hand.

Bacon believed that some people were bound by their natures to fall into the leader-follower relationship with one another. The Puritan opposition was only a particular case of this general phenomenon:

> *The Church never wanted a kind of persons which love* the salutation of Rabbi, master; *not in ceremony or compliment, but in an inward authority which they seek over men's minds, in drawing them to depend upon their opinion, and* to seek knowledge at their lips. *These men are the true successors of* Diotrephes, the lover of pre-eminence, *and not lords bishops. Such spirits do light upon another sort of natures, which do adhere to them; men* quorum gloria in obsequio; stiff followers, and such as zeal marvelously for those whom they have chosen for their masters. *This latter sort, for the most part, are men of young years and superficial understanding, carried away with partial respect of persons, or with the enticing appearance of goodly names and pretences.*[37]

The leaders of the dissenting religious factions, thus, not only use the crowds of followers to attain their larger ends, but have a psychological need to be followed and to exercise authority over other minds. If some glory in leadership, others crave to follow. This predisposition is as much a result of intellectual inadequacy as anything else; such fellows are superficial in their understanding and likely to be carried away by language.

If this schema accounts for a dynamic which holds a faction together (and it is the only explanation Bacon gives for this phenomenon) there is another schema which rationalizes the way factions seem to move naturally toward a relationship of extreme mutual opposition. Again, Bacon's language suggests that in this respect, the disorder under discussion is just a particular case of a general phenomenon. "I know, some persons," Bacon wrote of the Puritan attackers, "(being of the nature, not only to love extremities, but also to fall to them without degrees) were at the highest strain at the first."[38] On the other side, the defenders of the episcopacy delivered themselves into an opposing extremism. "They grew to a more absolute defense and maintenance of all the orders of the Church, and stiffly to hold that nothing was to be innovated; partly because it needed not, partly because it would make a breach upon the rest."[39] The natural tendency of factions, in other words, seemed to be to move farther apart and to become more hostile, differences becoming exaggerated and positions entrenched. In opposition to those who would change everything and those who would change nothing, Bacon posited (as he nearly always did once he had analyzed a situation into a conflict between mutually opposing extremes) a middle way, characteristically illustrating it with a horticultural image: "A good husbandman is ever proyning and stirring in his vineyard or field; not unseasonably (indeed) or unskilfully. But lightly he findeth ever somewhat to do."[40]

The most important schema which Bacon used to treat the problem of disorder was that of the vulgar and the select, an old commonplace which recurs repeatedly in his writings. The reason, in the long run, that religious disputes had gotten so out of hand, according to Bacon, was that the vulgar had been allowed to involve themselves in religious matters. The solution would come only when such issues were reserved for some select group. According to Bacon,

> *Another point of great inconvenience and peril is to entitle the people to hear controversies and all points of doctrine. They say no part of the counsel of God must be suppressed, nor the people defrauded: so as the difference which the Apostle maketh between* milk and strong meat *is confounded: and his precept* that the weak be not admitted unto questions and controversies *taketh no place.*[41]

Bacon regularly found in a small, enlightened group the cure for the failings of humanity at large—the "vulgar"—and here he recommended that a good part of the religious disorder could be ended if discussion of the disputed issues were confined to a small, select group. "The people," he wrote, "is no meet judge nor arbiter, but rather the quiet, moderate, and private assemblies and conferences of the learned."[42] Bacon's views on religion and particularly the moderation of the "Advertisement," are often cited as proof of a certain liberal, progressive animus in Bacon's thought. But this ignores the crucial fact that for Bacon not all men were capable of moderation. In the end, reasonableness in the discussion of religious affairs would be achieved only to the extent that discussion could be removed from the public sphere and contained in the councils of the elite. This solution to the problem of disorder is habitual with Bacon, and it connects his particular analyses of social disharmony with his views on social hierarchy and the maintenance of authority. Deliberation about public issues and decisions about change must be confined to small groups at the top of the social order.

What is most interesting about Bacon's insistent stereotyping of people and movements using schemata such as these is that he manages to deprive them of any specific meaning. They become instances of generic tendencies of humankind. No further understanding is necessary — only containment and repression. The stereotyping then becomes a kind of ideological analogue to the practical suppression of disorder and establishes an unconditioned need for the maintenance of authority as a key to social peace.

"SEDITIONS AND TROUBLES": THE EVER-PRESENT THREAT TO CIVIL PEACE

Though it is true that "seditions and troubles" in the political realm differ in important ways from the religious controversies that Bacon treated in his "Letter of Advice" and "Advertisement," it is likewise the case that Bacon tended to interpret political and religious disorder in much the same terms. Running through virtually all of his writings about political life is the belief that the political order was fragile and that the main threat came from the elemental, irrational tendency of the masses to short-sighted contentiousness and anarchy. Like religious controversy, political troubles took certain stereotyped forms and, as with religion, the solution to political turmoil was to deprive the vulgar of the chance for political initiative and to relegate them to a passive role in the political life of the commonwealth.

When Bacon discussed the change of regime which occurred in 1603 in the fragment, *The Beginning of the History of Great Britain,* he was keenly aware of the possibilities for disorder, and against the background of this awareness the very peacefulness of James's accession seemed a kind of wonder.

> *Nothing did more fill foreign nations with admiration and expectation of his succession, than the wonderful and (by them) unexpected consent of all estates and subjects of England for the receiving of the King without the least scruple, pause, or question.*[43]

In part the expectation that the succession would be attended by civil disturbance resulted from the scheming of disaffected English émigrés who sought to encourage foreign elements hostile to England.[44] But treachery and machination were not alone the cause of these expectations, and here appeared an idea near the heart of Bacon's political thinking.

> *[There were] within this realm divers persons both wise and well af-*
> *fected, who though they doubted not of the undoubted right, yet set-*
> *ting before themselves the waves of peoples' hearts (guided no less by*
> *sudden temporary winds than by the natural course and motion of the*
> *waters), were not without fear what mought be the event.*[45]

Even for those who were "wise and well affected," the precipitous deterioration of the political order into anarchy was always a possibility because the people, on whose obedience political order must ultimately
depend, were regarded as essentially irrational and unpredictable. The
belief that political order was unavoidably fragile and that right offered
no guarantee for its endurance shaped Bacon's thoughts on political life
generally and, indeed, on all the various collective enterprises of humankind.

In Bacon's political universe one of the principal meanings of the
Tudor regime was that it had brought to an end the Wars of the Roses.
Civil war and Tudor rule were not merely related in historical sequence;
rather, they formed logical alternatives with an either-or inevitability
that was as harsh as that later propounded by Hobbes. Either the government would retain enough repressive power to control the forces of
disorder that were always ready to well up, or the civil order would be
swept away. That the fear of civil war was omnipresent and intense does
not necessarily mean that it was realistic. The ideological function of this
perceived threat, however, was to allow all factional or popular opposition to be assigned to the general category of disorder, subjected to the
same stereotyping molds, and interpreted as an opening wedge to the
forces which might dissolve the civil order. What we must seek to understand his how the *idea* of political disorder formed a constant touchstone
of Bacon's political thinking, how it was rooted in his view of human
nature, and how it justified a particular view of government. The *Essays*
are a useful starting place, for in them Bacon's discussion of "seditions
and troubles" occurs in the context of a more general series of reflection
on the timeless verities of human nature. Here we may see quite clearly
that for Bacon political disorder is more than an exceptional and passing
affliction of the body politic. It is an ever-present threat and a condition
of political existence.

In the essay "Of Seditions and Troubles" Bacon surveyed the "signs"
and "predictions" of political disorders, their causes (material and efficient), and their remedies. One of the signs of impending disorder is that
"things grow to equality" in such a way that the hierarchical order of
society is threatened.[46] Accompanying the instability of equality is the
proliferation of what Bacon called "Fames" and we might call a danger-

ous instability in public opinion: "Libels and licentious discourses against the state, when they are frequent and open; and in like sort, false news, often running up and down, to the disadvantage of the state, and hastily embraced; are amongst the signs of troubles."[47] Another sign is when the Prince descends to participate in factional fighting. "For when the authority of princes is made but an accessary to a cause, and that there be other bands that ties faster than the band of sovereignty, kings begin to be put almost out of possession."[48] It is a sign of coming troubles, moreover, when men become open and "audacious" in their factional quarrels, as if they are no longer awed by the overarching power of the sovereign and "the reverence of government is lost."[49] Here, Bacon offered an image which gives some sense of his positive conception of political order:

> *The motions of the greatest persons in a government ought to be as the motions of the planets under* primum mobile, *according to the old opinion, which is, that every one of them is carried swiftly by the highest motions, and softly in their own motion. And therefore, when great ones in their own particular motion move violently . . . it is a sign the orbs are out of frame.*[50]

Bacon ended his discussion of "signs" and "predictions" by noting that if any of the "four pillars of government"—religion, justice, counsel, and treasure—are weakened "men had need to pray for fair weather."[51]

Bacon divides his account of the causes of political disorder in two: the "materials of sedition" and the "causes and motives of seditions," by which he means the deep causes and the occasions or the material causes and the efficient causes.

Bacon did not spend many words on the efficient causes, apparently believing that if a nation were ripe for rebellion virtually anything might precipitate it, and the "causes and motives" are summarized in one short paragraph framed in a way that emphasizes the catchall, contingent character of the list.

> *The causes and motives of seditions are: innovation in religion; taxes; alteration of laws and customs; breaking of privileges; general oppression; advancement of unworthy persons; strangers; dearths; disbanded soldiers; factions grown desperate; and whatsoever, in offending people, joineth and knitteth them in a common cause.*[52]

The one practical lesson that a government might draw from such a list is that every piece of policy must be fashioned cautiously.

It is to the material causes of sedition that Bacon devotes most of his attention in "Of Seditions and Troubles," and his account of these reveals ideas that are at the heart of his political outlook. The material causes of seditions are distinguished into two kinds, the distinction being crucial to Bacon's conception of the real problem of maintaining political order. The first kind of material cause Bacon designates as "poverty." Material hardship is particularly dangerous when it unites different orders of society in opposition to the Crown. "If this poverty and broken estate in the better sort be joined with a want and necessity in the mean people, the danger is imminent and great. For the rebellions of the belly are the worst."[53]

Although such rebellions may be "the worst," they are also the ones most avoidable by constructive policy. When Bacon took up the question of remedies, later in the essay, he argued that "the first remedy or prevention is to remove by all means possible that material cause of sedition whereof we spake; which is want and poverty in the estate."[54] It is instructive to note in this context some components of the kind of policy Bacon has in mind. He wants trade to be balanced, manufactures to be encouraged, idleness to be banished, waste and sumptuary display to be outlawed, husbandry to be promoted, prices to be regulated, taxes to be held within moderate bounds, population to be contained within limits dictated by the productivity of the nation, and the number of people not directly involved in production — nobles, clergy, and scholars — to be kept in due proportion to the total population. He envisioned the promotion of such policy taking place in the context of an international market situation in which "the increase of any estate must be upon the foreigner (for whatsoever is somewhere gotten is somewhere lost)."[55] All of this suggests that Bacon believed there to be a certain more or less rational and predictable relationship between poverty and policy and that "rebellions of the belly" could be prevented (within the limits set by natural disaster) by good government. This is not the case with the other material cause of sedition.

Alongside poverty Bacon places discontentment as a cause of sedition, and here the discussion leads to what was for Bacon the most problematic element of political life. "Discontentment" was the social face of what Bacon believed to be an irreducible irrationality in man and, because irreducible, one of the ultimate, stubborn facts of political life.

As for discontentments, they are in the politic body like to humours in the natural, which are apt to gather a preternatural heat and to inflame. And let no prince measure the danger of them by this, whether they be just or unjust; for that were to imagine people to be too reasonable, who do often spurn at their own good: nor yet by this, whether the griefs whereupon they rise be in fact great or small; for they are the most dangerous discontentments where the fear is greater than the feeling.[56]

Discontentment is not a function of the justice or benevolence of government policy; it is not rational or realistic; it is unpredictable. Unlike seditions which arise from poverty, those arising from discontentment cannot be avoided by providing material well-being and security to the population at large, for people do not do what is reasonable and frequently act against their own interests.

It is the irrational and perverse character of popular discontentment that renders it a greater challenge to government policy than poverty. Bacon even seems to suggest that it might not be possible to eliminate discontentments themselves but only to minimize the danger they pose. His first observation is that to be effective a revolt requires the simultaneous action of upper-class leaders and lower-class followers.

There is in every state (as we know) two portions of subjects, the noblesse and the commonalty. When one of these is discontent, the danger is not great; for common people are of slow motion, if they be not excited by the greater sort; and the greater sort are of small strength, except the multitude be apt and ready to move of themselves. Then is the danger, when the greater sort do but wait for the troubling of the waters amongst the meaner, that then they may declare themselves.[57]

We have already seen Bacon's characterization of leadership and followership in the making of religious factions; now he presents another variation on the same theme as he analyzes political tumult. Tumult comes when the discontented among the "noblesse" provide leaders and the discontented among the "commonalty" provide followers. One good piece of policy, then, is to prevent both social orders from becoming discontented at the same time or, if this is impossible, to prevent their union.

Bacon went on to suggest that sometimes discontent will dissipate itself if left alone.

To give moderate liberty for griefs and discontentments to evaporate (so it be without too great insolency or bravery) is a safe way. For he that turneth the humours back, and maketh the wound bleed inwards, endangereth malign ulcers and pernicious impostumations.[58]

Also, a government can counter the dangers of discontent by engendering "hopes" among the people such that they are carried "from hopes to hopes."[59] What Bacon had in mind here was the manipulation of appearances and of affections and opinions. A government should "hold men's hearts by hopes, when it cannot by satisfaction"; it should "handle things in such a manner, as no evil shall appear so peremptory but that it hath some outlet of hope."[60] A government should also try to prevent the rise of a person who might be fit to lead a rebellion.

> *I understand a fit head to be one that hath greatness and reputation;*
> *that hath confidence with the discontented party, and upon whom they*
> *turn their eyes; and that is thought discontented in his own particular;*
> *which kind of persons are either to be won and reconciled to the state,*
> *and that in a fast and true manner; or to be fronted with some other of*
> *the same party, that may oppose them, and so divide the reputation.*[61]

More generally, Bacon recommends a policy of playing factions off against one another—"dividing and breaking of all factions and combinations that are adverse to the state, and setting them at distance or at least distrust amongst themselves."[62] Bacon next cautioned Princes to make their public pronouncements with caution, particularly in times of troubles, "in tender matters and ticklish times, to beware what they say; especially in these short speeches, which fly abroad like darts, and are thought to be shot out of their secret intentions."[63]

As if to give final emphasis to the intractability of discontent and the need for prudence in addressing it, Bacon ends his essay on "Seditions and Troubles" by pointing out that the final defense against this kind of disorder will be military.

> *Let princes, against all events, not be without some great person, one*
> *or rather more, of military valour, near unto them, for the repressing of*
> *seditions in their beginnings. . . . But let such military persons be as-*
> *sured, and well reputed of, rather than factious and popular; holding*
> *also good correspondence with the other great men in the state; or else*
> *the remedy is worse than the disease.*[64]

The ultimate weapon of the state against the irrationality of its subjects is thus force.

The irrational core which Bacon attributed to discontent is central to his view of politics and is the basis of the deeply authoritarian role he assigned to government. Christopher Hill asserts that for Bacon almost all the causes of sedition were economic,[65] and on this ground has emphasized the progressive character of Bacon's pronouncements on policy and made him out to be something of a liberal. But as we have seen the kind of sedition that sprang from discontent was not, in Bacon's view, the result of poverty and would not be prevented by enlightened economic policy. Bacon's remarks on discontent are not casual or isolated. On the contrary, they represent a pervasive tendency to view the populace-at-large as fundamentally irrational and "humourous" and hence a perpetual threat to political order.

In his discussion of the irrational sources of political disorder, Bacon revealed a feature of his thought which is crucial to understanding all of his ideas about human community and cooperative enterprise. No matter how just, benevolent, or rational a social order might be, it is vulnerable to the irrational and elemental outbursts of its subjects. Prudent policy may limit the danger but will never eliminate it. The authority entrusted with the maintenance of that order must therefore be ever ready to coerce by military force. There is thus a sense in which people, however much they might be the beneficiaries of order, are at the same time its most dangerous enemies. The constructive aims of government, therefore, must always be pursued against a backdrop of political insecurity, and there can never be an absolutely secure peace between a government and its subjects.

Against the backdrop of human perversity and the fragility of the political order, Bacon fashioned his ideas about change. It is clear that good government was more for Bacon than a holding action against anarchy—that government had an obligation to undertake constructive policies as well as to maintain repressive ones. But even constructive changes ran the risk of destabilizing the political order. The aim, therefore, should be to see that change was controlled and not only change itself but also the appearance of change, since it was this that would register for good or ill in the public mind. In his essay "Of Innovations" Bacon suggested how complex the matter of reform must be in terms of the maintenance of political order.

Surely every medicine is an innovation; and he that will not apply new remedies must expect new evils; for time is the greatest innovator; and if time of course alter things to the worse, and wisdom and counsel shall not alter them to the better, what shall be the end? It is true, that what is settled by custom, though it be not good, yet at least it is fit; and those things which have long gone together, are as it were confederate within themselves; whereas new things piece not so well; but though they help by their utility, yet they trouble by their inconformity. Besides, they are like strangers; more admired and less favoured. All this

is true, if time stood still; which contrariwise moveth so round, that a
froward retention of custom is as turbulent a thing as an innovation;
and they that reverence too much old times, are but a scorn to the
new.[66]

Bacon was aware that he was living in an era of changes — deep
changes that had not been chosen but to which government must surely
respond. In answering these changes and fashioning adaptive innovations, government must attend to maintaining the customary order of
things and strive to make even its innovations bear the appearance of
stasis. Even reforms that are undertaken with the best of intentions and
in the most rational manner are liable to disrupt the continuity and
integration of the social order and customary life, tending to unleash the
very forces of irrationality and disorder they are intended to contain. In
principle, there is no solution to this dilemma. In practice the solution is
to disguise innovation as continuation:

It were good therefore that men in their innovations would follow the
example of time itself; which indeed innovateth greatly, but quietly, and
by degrees scarce to be perceived. For otherwise, whatsoever is new is
unlooked for; and ever it mends some, and pairs other; and he that is
holpen takes it for a fortune, and thanks the time; and he that is hurt,
for a wrong, and imputeth it to the author. It is also good not to try
experiments in states, except the necessity be urgent, or the utility evi-
dent; and well to beware that it be the reformation that draweth on the
change, and not the desire of change that pretendeth the reformation.
And lastly, that the novelty, though it be not rejected, yet be held for a
suspect; and, as the Scripture saith, that we make a stand upon the
ancient way, and then look about us, and discover what is the straight
and right way, and so to walk in it.[67]

At the end of his essay "Of Seditions and Troubles," it appeared that
the last resort of a government against the forces of irrationality was
military force. If that is true, it is equally true that the first resort must
be the maintenance of custom. In the management of society custom,
not reason, is the best first defense against anarchy. Some of the political
uses of custom are also suggested in the essay "Of Custom and Education."

Men's thoughts are much according to their inclination; their discourse
and speeches according to their learning and infused opinions; but their

deeds are after as they have been accustomed. And therefore as Machiavel well noteth (though in an evil-favoured instance,) there is not trusting to the force of nature nor to the bravery of words, except it be corroborate by custom.[68]

While custom thus does not reach to the depths of a person's nature to constrain or reshape the most basic impulses, it can serve to regulate actions. The political uses of custom are suggested in the following passage:

But if the force of custom simple and separate be great, the force of custom copulate and conjoined and collegiate is far greater. For there example teacheth, company comforteth, emulation quickeneth, glory raiseth: so as in such places the force of custom is in his exaltation. Certainly the great multiplication of virtues upon human nature resteth upon societies well ordained and disciplined.[69]

Custom, thus, is the bulwark of a society that is "well ordained and disciplined" against the perpetually threatening forces of dissolution.

These themes run through all of the essay and, indeed, are fundamental to Bacon's political outlook. That tumult is not solely the product of poverty, that it is rooted in human psychology and human nature, that it is a perpetual and not just a sometime danger, that a policy of reason and justice is no guarantee against it, and that ultimately a government must rely on custom and force to contain and control it—these are potent and pervasive ideas. As a consequence, in Bacon's view, there was a kind of perpetual war between human nature and political order—a war that was never to be won but which, on the other hand, could never be abandoned.

THE COSMIC DIMENSIONS OF POLITICAL DISORDER

In *On the Wisdom of the Ancients,* Bacon's account of political disorder took the form of an interpretation of a classical myth. The same themes appear again, only now in a genre that bestow upon them the quality of timeless and cosmic truth. In his interpretation of classical myths, Bacon ranges over a variety of political topics. We will concern ourselves here with the myths that touch on the questions of political disorder.

"Typhon; or the Rebel" concerns the phenomenon of civil uprising. Although the initial cause of the rebellion in this tale is the tyrannical behavior of the king, Bacon quickly suggested that the real problem is the inborn resistance of the people to authority.

> *The poets tell us that Juno being angry that Jupiter had brought forth Pallas by himself without her help, implored of all the gods and goddesses that she also might bring forth something without the help of Jupiter: to which when wearied with her violence and importunity they had assented, she smote the earth, which quaking and opening gave birth to Typhon, a huge and hideous monster. He was given to a serpent by way of foster-father to be nursed.*
>
> *As soon as he was grown up he made war upon Jupiter, whom in the conflict he took prisoner; and bearing him on his shoulders to a remote and obscure region, cut out the sinews of his hands and feet, and carrying them away, left him there helpless and mutilated. Then came Mercury, and having stolen the sinews from Typhon gave them back to Jupiter, who finding his strength restored attacked the monster again. And first he struck him with a thunderbolt, which made a wound the blood whereof engendered serpents; then, as he fell back and fled, threw upon him the mountain Aetna and crushed him beneath the weight.[70]*

This myth, wrote Bacon, concerns "the variable fortune of kings and the rebellions that occur from time to time in monarchies." In a properly functioning society the king and his kingdom should be like a married couple. In this tale, however, by bringing forth Pallas without the participation of his wife, Jupiter had sought to "[take] all into his own hands," just as the tyrant "administers the government by his own arbitrary and absolute authority." To this point the failure seems to belong to the king, but as Bacon proceeded to describe the anarchy that follows upon the attempted tyranny, he portrayed the "common people" in such terms that the initial misdeeds of the king fade in importance in comparison to the inherent unwillingness of the people to accept government. "The people aggrieved endeavour on their part to set up some head of their own. This generally begins with the secret solicitation of nobles and great persons, whose connivency being obtained, an attempt is then made to stir the people."[71]

Throughout Bacon's writings the alliance of "the great ones" and "the people" was consistently presented as the most dangerous of conditions. The picture of the anarchy which flows from this alliance is Hobbesian in its starkness.

Thence comes a kind of swelling in the State, which is signified by the infancy of Typhon. And this condition of affairs is fostered and nourished by the innate depravity and malignant disposition of the common people, which is to kings like a serpent full of malice and mischief; till the disaffection spreading and gathering strength breaks out at last into open rebellion; which because of the infinite calamities it inflicts both on kings and people is represented under the dreadful image of Typhon, with a hundred heads, denoting divided powers; flaming mouths, for devastations by fire; belts of snakes, for the pestilences which prevail, especially in sieges; iron hands, for slaughters; eagle's talons, for rapine; feathery body, for perpetual rumours, reports, trepidations, and the like.[72]

Order is restored when the king "by affability and wise edicts and gracious speeches . . . reconciles the minds of his subjects, and awakens in them an alacrity to grant him supplies, and so recovers the vigour of his authority."[73] Then he can turn on the rebels and destroy them.

If open rebellions are one sign of the inherent resistance of the people to government, the vicissitudes of public opinion, continually fed and fueled by rumor and "fame" are another. In "The Sister of the Giants," Bacon recounted the story of the creation of Fame.

The poets tell us that the Giants, being brought forth by Earth, made war upon Jupiter and the gods, and were routed and vanquished with thunderbolts, whereupon Earth, in rage at the wrath of the gods, to revenge her sons brought forth Fame, youngest sister of the giants.[74]

Bacon explained the passage as follows:

By Earth is meant the nature of the common people; always swelling with malice towards their rulers, and hatching revolutions. This upon occasion given brings forth rebels and seditious persons, who with wicked audacity endeavour the overthrow of princes. And when these are suppressed the same nature of the common people, still leaning to the worse party and impatient of tranquillity, gives birth to rumours and malignant whispers, and querulous fames, and defamatory libels, and the like, tending to bring envy upon the authorities of the land: so that seditious fames differ from acts of rebellion, not in race and parentage, but only in sex: the one being feminine and the other masculine.[75]

Taken together, "Typhon" and "The Sister of the Giants" present a gloomy assessment of human nature as it may be expected to bear on governmental and the social order. "The innate depravity and malignant disposition of the common people" and like notions suggest that a kind of blind anarchism is not an occasional and adventitious failing of the people but rather chronic and inborn—a fact of political life.

In "Orpheus," however, Bacon suggested that civil and moral philosophy can play a role in making men more suited to accept the yoke of government. Having lost Eurydice, Orpheus "betook himself to solitary places, a melancholy man and averse from the sight of women." So beautiful was his music that he brought peace to the wild beasts and "moved the woods and the very stones to shift themselves and take their stations decently and orderly about him." This state of happy tranquillity continued until the Thracian women, incited by Bacchus, destroyed the harmony that Orpheus had established with his music and furiously tore Bacchus himself to pieces.

Bacon explained the tale of Orpheus in the following way: "The meaning of the fable appears to be this. The singing of Orpheus is of two kinds; one to propitiate the infernal powers, the other to draw the wild beasts and the woods. The former may be best understood as referring to natural philosophy; the latter to philosophy moral and civil."[76] Because of the difficulties of the tasks it sets itself, natural philosophy generally fails to achieve its goals, commonly, Bacon added, "from no cause more than from curious and premature meddling and impatience."[77]

> *Then Philosophy finding that her great work is too much for her, in sorrowful mood, as well becomes her, turns to human affairs; and applying her powers of persuasion and eloquence to insinuate into men's minds the love of virtue and equity and peace, teaches the people to assemble and unite and take upon them the yoke of laws and submit to authority, and forget their ungoverned appetites, in listening and conforming to precepts and discipline; whereupon soon follows the building of houses, the founding of cities, the planting of fields and gardens with trees; insomuch that the stones and the woods are not unfitly said to leave their places and come about her.*[78]

Turning from the challenge of nature to the challenge of human nature, philosophy thus lays the foundation for civil order and paves the way for social and economic progress. "Ungoverned appetites" are made to submit to the "discipline" of authority. The human lot is improved through the renunciation of natural licentiousness. Humanity bends down to accept the "yoke" of social life. And yet, Bacon hastened to add, the solution was not a final one.

In the closing passage of "Orpheus," Bacon suggested a cyclical and pessimistic view of human history in which even the best-formed and most peace-loving of societies will fall victim to deterioration and decay, leaving men and women once again the victims of their own depravity.

> *Howsoever the works of wisdom are among human things the most excellent, yet they too have their periods and closes. For so it is that after kingdoms and commonwealths have flourished for a time, there arise perturbations and seditions and wars; amid the uproars of which, first the laws are put to silence, and then men return to the depraved conditions of their nature, and desolation is seen in the fields and cities. And if such troubles last, it is not long before letters also and philosophy are so torn in pieces that no traces of them can be found but a few fragments, scattered here and there like planks from a shipwreck; and then a season of barbarism sets in, the waters of Helicon being sunk in the ground, until, according to the appointed vicissitude of things, they break out and issue forth again, perhaps among other nations, and not in the places where they were before.*[79]

Bacon's interpretation of classical fables in *De Sapientia Veterum* discloses political ideas which are consistent with those we found in the *Essays* and *The History of the Reign of King Henry the Seventh:* the struggle between order and disorder as an essential feature of political life; the resistance to authority which is inborn in human nature; the limited prospects for ultimate solutions to the essential problems of political life.

De Sapientia presents itself as a collection of gleanings from ancient and apparently timeless wisdom. The interpretation of the Orpheus myth, for example, with its suggestion that the political problem will never find a permanent solution, would seem to speak not simply to the plight of England in early Tudor times but to all times — to the human condition. The resignation to this condition that is expressed in the myth, has a much more final quality than anything we found in the *History,* which, after all, recounted a clear — albeit provisional and ultimately transitory — political success.

In the final analysis, the fables of *De Sapientia* are didactic commentaries on human nature and the human predicament, and they show that for Bacon the problematic features of political life are ultimately reducible to ineradicable tendencies in the human constitution. Bad government can call forth and excite these tendencies; good government can only lessen the likelihood of their being unleashed. Even the best of governments have their "periods and closes," falling victim to destructive impulses and allowing the people to return once again to "the depraved conditions of their natures."

GOVERNMENT AS ARCANUM

G iven his view of "the people" as a political factor, it is clear that a great gulf separates Bacon's political outlook from modern ideologies of popular liberty and government. One may discern in his writing a mingling of fear and contempt for the mass of humanity. Yet all this does not necessarily mean that Bacon's frequent assertion that he was motivated by *philanthropia* was insincere. Bacon believed that it was the responsibility of princes and statesmen to act as benefactors of the people. This obligation did not depend on the merits of the people, nor on their active participation in government, but was enjoined by political and religious principle. In a curious way the irrationality, viciousness, and lawlessness of "the people," may even have strengthened the claims of *philanthropia,* since the people were not deemed capable of looking after their own well-being in any rational, realistic, and long-term sense. Thus *philanthropia* might go hand in hand with paternalistic authoritarianism.

Bacon did not expect the philanthropic actions of governors to be met with understanding or gratitude on the part of popular beneficiaries. The people were incapable of understanding actions that were in their own long-term interests and were much more likely to be moved by irrational impulse and the desire for immediate gratification. Not only were they unlikely to be good participants in the management of the commonweal but were quite often in opposition to policies directed toward the common good and the civil peace. Philanthropic social policies, therefore, would have to be implemented without the people's active participation and often against their active resistance. In any case, "the people" (and this term is variously construed in Bacon's writings) must be excluded so far as possible from an active role in political matters.

In one of his earliest writings on policy, Bacon recommended that religious turmoil could be largely contained if important religious matters were not opened to public discussion but rather adjudicated by "quiet, moderate, and private assemblies and conferences of the learned." He approved the precept that "the weak be not admitted unto questions and controversies" touching crucial points of doctrine or worship. The tendency to exclude "the vulgar" from the centers of deliberation and decision making is pervasive in Bacon's thought and one of his most important proposals for the maintenance of civil peace. It is central not merely to his treatment of religious controversy but, more generally, to his whole political outlook — and to his scientific outlook as well. Government, in his view, should be the business of a select elite, insulated from public participation, shielded from public scrutiny, and under no obligation to provide the public with knowledge of its doings. It is a political outlook which specifically denies a constructive political role to public enlightenment and discussion.

When Bacon came to the place in *The Advancement of Learning* where his plan dictated a discussion of political knowledge, he was largely silent, and in giving his reasons for this silence he set out one of the fundamental beliefs of his political outlook.

Concerning Government, it is a part of knowledge secret and retired, in both these respects in which things are deemed secret; for some things are secret because they are hard to know, and some because they are not fit to utter. We see all governments are obscure and invisible.

Totamque infusa per artus
Mens agitat molem, et magno se corpore miscet.
[In every pore diffused the great mind works,
Stirs all the mass, and thro' the huge frame lives.]

Such is the description of governments. We see the government of God over the world is hidden, insomuch as it seemeth to participate of much irregularity and confusion. The government of the Soul in moving the Body is inward and profound, and the passages thereof hardly to be reduced to demonstration. Again, the wisdom of antiquity (the shadows whereof are in the poets) in the description of torments and pains, next unto the crime of rebellion which was the Giants' offence, doth detest the offence of futility, as in Sisyphus and Tantalus. But this was meant of particulars: nevertheless even unto the general rules and discourse of policy and government there is due a reverent and reserved handling.

But contrariwise in the governors toward the governed all things ought, as far as the frailty of man permitteth, to be manifest and revealed. For so it is expressed in the Scriptures touching the government of God, that this globe, which seemeth to us a dark and shady body, is in the view of God as crystal: Et in conspectu sedis tanquam mare vitreum simile crystallo [*and before the throne there was a sea of glass, like crystal*]. *So unto princes and states, and specially towards wise senates and councils, the natures and dispositions of the people, their conditions and necessities, their factions and combinations, their animosities and discontents, ought to be, in regard of the variety of their intelligences, the wisdom of their observations, and the height of their station where they keep sentinel, in great part clear and transparent. Wherefore, considering that I write to a king that is a master of this science, and is so well assisted, I think it decent to pass over this part in silence, as willing to obtain the certificate which one of the ancient philosophers aspired unto; who being silent, when others contended to make demonstration of their abilities by speech, desired it might be certified for his part,* that there was one that knew how to hold his peace.[80]

Little or nothing of the arcana of government, in other words, should be revealed to the people, while the governors collectively should know everything there is to know about governing and about their subjects.

Bacon made frequent use of the idea of "the vulgar" as a critical and exclusionary concept. "The vulgar" and things "vulgar" were for him embodiments of the least rational and least virtuous tendencies of humankind. As suggested indirectly in the passage quoted, the idea of vulgarity is relative and mobile in Bacon's framework of thought. It can operate at virtually any level of the hierarchy to differentiate the select from the mass. Thus, it is not so much a matter of fixed characteristics inhering in human beings as of the inevitable relationship between governors and governed. Here it is important to note the manner in which Bacon's conception of hierarchy, however much it might draw upon and reinforce the traditional conception of society as a system of hereditary ranks and orders, is also moving toward a functional rationale. Though it is still very much a hierarchy of status, it is also increasingly a hierarchy of managerial skill and expertise. In the passage quoted, for example, political knowledge and the power to which it is requisite are conceived as being distributed on the basis of political function—the "station where they keep sentinel."

In Bacon's political world, power was most safely lodged in the smallest, highest circle of the political elite. Once he himself rose to political power, Bacon became a key member of James's conciliar government. It was to just such a position that all his efforts had been directed, and it was in the hands of men such as himself that Bacon most wanted to see power concentrated. Unlike the masses, the King and his small circle of advisers could (in Bacon's idealized scheme of things) represent the interests of the nation as a whole, rising above faction and interestedness. They could, moreover, acquire the expertise necessary to make decisions based on a sound, informed, and rational understanding of things rather than on the basis of generally held beliefs and sentiment. In a well-constructed polity the most delicate and potentially disturbing political matters would never make their way out of a group of responsible ministers and hence never become the plaything of popular perversity.

To the extent that the vulgar could simply be excluded from meddling in politics and government, the peace of society would be more likely. Bacon is very much an elitist in this sense, and efforts to democratize his thinking retrospectively do great damage to an understanding of his thought and to a proper appreciation of his attitude toward the movements of his time. In the third part of this book, we shall see that Bacon's contempt for the mass of humanity and his deep distrust of the "democratizing" tendencies of his age were not confined to his thoughts on the civil sphere but mark his scientific thinking as well. For Bacon, government was not to be a public affair, and to the extent that the populace mixed itself in the arcanum of government, disorder was likely to result. But Bacon was well aware that preventive prudence would not always succeed and that the crowds were always ready to gather like a sudden storm to bring sedition and tumult to the state. Therefore, the wise governor must be ever on guard and ever willing to use coercion and the threat of coercion, cannily mingled with manipulative enticements, to keep people in their places and to preserve the state from dissolution.

Though policy might have a forward and "progressive" aspect for Bacon, he certainly did not reject the common Tudor views on the perversity of men and the consequent necessity for coercion and fear as bulwarks of polity. Bacon's whole analysis testifies to his belief that though the dangers of civil disorder might be lessened they could not be eliminated by enlightened policy because the most incorrigible sources of disorder lay in the frailty of human nature. There is no sense in Bacon's writings that episodes of civil disorder laid bare an otherwise invisible but ultimately rational process of historical change or that tumults might reveal the difficult but necessary choices facing a society — no anticipation, in other words, of modern ideas on revolution. Instead, civil disorder is always treated as but another manifestation of generic human fallibility, irrationality, and error.

Bacon's views on civil disorder reflect in large part the ideas and prejudices which Bacon absorbed as a member of the upper class in Tudor England and partly, too, his choice of a political vocation. Bacon never viewed disorder as a detached observer but rather as one who aspired to make policy for the Crown. From the vantage point which he began to cultivate long before he actually achieved a policy-making posi-

tion, Bacon always viewed discontent as a representative of the governing establishment. A certain foreshortening of his social view followed
from this fact, and in this perspective he tended to see the disruptive
portions of the populace—whether Puritan dissidents, armed peasants,
or the vulgar in general—as acting in stereotyped ways which reenacted
timeless dramas of foolishness and sin.

The solutions which Bacon proposed to the problem of ever-threat-
ening disorder were not especially original. First and foremost, he
thought that the order of the polity would be safeguarded if the vulgar
were excluded not merely from political decision making but even from
the discussion of public issues. Given his convictions regarding the instability and irrationality of the popular mind, "rumors" and "fames" were
but a step removed from overt uprising. To the extent that custom could
be used to bolster the existing order, Bacon thought that it should be
maintained. To be more precise, what he warned against most emphatically was not so much the breaching of custom as the appearance of
deliberate innovation which might bring custom into popular contempt.
The "humourousness" of the popular mind might be as well checked by
the appearance of stasis as by stasis itself. If the stifling of public discourse and the maintenance of custom (or the appearance of customary
life) did not succeed in holding in check the popular tendency to irrational disorder, Bacon recognized the necessity for coercion. War against
the disorderly en masse and the prudent imposition of penalties against
tumultuous individuals—these were the ultimate weapons of government.

BACON'S CONSTITUTIONAL VIEWS

I n his schedule of political honors, Bacon awarded the highest place
to those who had succeeded in imposing order on chaos: the founders of states, the givers of laws, and the repairers of civil strife.
Order itself was the first political good, and measured against the need
to contain anarchy all other political needs were secondary. It is also
true, however, that Bacon envisaged the responsibilities of government
as widely encompassing, and it is to the uses of power once it has been
established—to "policy"—that we should now turn. Before taking up the
question of policy per se, it will be useful to begin with the constitutional
arrangements through which Bacon imagined constructive policies being
framed and executed.

Bacon did not give a great deal of explicit attention to the theoretical dimensions of constitutional issues. Quite probably his own constitutional convictions were not so much the result of philosophical reflection as of upbringing, experience, and practical aims. Having been reared in a political household and on the verge of the court and having decided on a political career early in life, Bacon seems to have committed himself to the Tudor constitution and administration by way of a vocational rather than a philosophical choice. From his youth he aspired to be a counselor to Elizabeth, and this overriding ambition meant for him that a whole range of constitutional questions would never be approached in the open-minded way that would have been required for radical philosophical reflection. He did not (like Machiavelli or Hobbes) have to come to terms with revolutionary situations which demanded a fundamental rethinking of political principles, and Bacon never seems to have questioned the Tudor monarchy as an adequate political framework for the achievement of his political goals. Moreover, though Bacon travelled in Europe as a youth and though, late in life, when he had been discouraged by his King and countrymen, he came to think of himself as writing for an international audience, Bacon's life as a whole was somewhat provincial. In his fundamental outlook he was English and his writings on politics — even his utopian *New Atlantis* — bear the unmistakable signs of his English point of view.

For these reasons, Bacon does not figure prominently in histories of political thought which are organized around grand constitutional themes. In his study of English political thought between 1603 and 1660, J. W. Allen wrote that Bacon "was a philosopher who gave no systematic thought to the State, and whose political opinions found only fragmentary and occasional expression."[81] Allen adds that Bacon's theory of government "does not seem to have been worked out in relation to anything but the England of his own day."[82] Despite the absence of explicit theorizing about constitutional issues, however, there is implicit in Bacon's writing a clear and thoroughgoing commitment to monarchy of the Tudor kind. He accepted a central role for Parliament because this was part of the political world into which he was born and bred, and in his role as the Crown's representative in Parliament and then as a member of the government itself he always sought to avoid the kinds of confrontations between King and Parliament which would clarify their constitutional relationship through conflict and struggle. Bacon still belonged to a world in which political wisdom dictated not only that the respective powers of Crown and Commons not be defined too precisely but more importantly that there be no real public discussion of fundamental political issues. As we have seen already, the true workings of government being deemed arcana not fit for public scrutiny or debate. Bacon's con-

stitutional outlook is thus not expressed by way of explicit theorizing.
(Bacon's *legal* activities sometimes involved him in questions of jurisdiction, and these often had constitutional implications, but by and large
his *political* writings and activities aimed at preventing the great constitutional issues from coming to the surface.)

When overt references to constitutional matters occur in Bacon's
writing, they are often casual in character, often figurative, and part of a
rhetorical apparatus for advocating some favored policy or giving some
advice. Thus in a letter to James immediately following his release from
prison after his fall from office, Bacon wrote "that doth well in church-
music when the greatest part of the hymn is sung by one voice, and then
the quire at times falls in sweetly and solemnly, and that the same harmony sorteth well in monarchy between the King and his Parliament."[83]
The role of Parliament in the government was clearly conceived to be
that of follower to the lead of the King. Bacon sometimes described
himself as a "peremptory royalist." The initiative of government — the
"melody" of policy — was to belong to the Crown alone.

Bacon made a fuller statement of his conception of the nature of
Parliament and its role in the English government in the advice which he
gave to Buckingham, then George Villiers, when the latter was raised to
the peerage.

> *I shall now put you in mind of some things touching the High Court of
> Parliament in England, which is superlative; and therefore it will be-
> hove me to speak the more warily of it.*
>
> *For the true constitution thereof consists of the two houses, of
> Lords and Commons, as the members; and the King's Majesty, as the
> head of that great body. By the King's authority alone, and by his writ,
> the members of both the houses are assembled, and by him alone are
> they prorogued and dissolved; but each house may adjourn itself.*
>
> *They being thus assembled, they are more properly a Council to
> the King, the great Council of the Kingdom, to advise his Majesty of
> those things of weight and difficulty which concern both the King and
> kingdom, than a court.*
>
> *No new laws can be made, or old ones abrogated and altered, but
> by common consent in Parliament, where bills are prepared and pre-
> sented to the two houses, and there seriously debated; but nothing is
> concluded but by the King's royal assent in person or by his commis-
> sioners delegated; they are but embryos, till he gives life unto them.*
>
> *Yet the House of Peers have power of judicature in some cases:
> properly to examine, then to affirm, or (if there be cause) to reverse the
> judgment which hath been given in the King's Bench, which is the court*

of the highest judicature in this kingdom for ordinary judicature; but in those cases it must be done by writ of error in Parliament: and then their proceeding is not absoluta potestas, *as in making new laws, in that conjuncture as before is said, but* potestas limitata, *according to the rule of the known laws of this land.*

But the House of Commons hath only power to censure the members of their own house, in point of election and misdemeanors in or towards that house; and have not, nor ever had the power so much as to administer an oath in any case whatsoever to prepare a judgment.

The true use of Parliaments in this kingdom is very excellent; and they would be often called, as the arduous affairs of the kingdom shall require; and continue as long as it is necessary and no longer: for then they are but burthens to the people, by reason of the privileges due to the members of the two houses and their attendants; which their privileges and rights are religiously to be observed and preserved: but if they should be unjustly enlarged beyond the true bounds, they might lessen the just power of the Crown, it borders so near upon popularity.[84]

Particularly interesting here is the cautious watchfulness which Bacon urges on royal servants toward Parliament: scrupulous observation of the "privileges and rights" which already belong to that body; but also an ever-watchful resolve to contain it within its present bounds lest it become a focus of popular sentiment and a challenger to the Crown itself.

Bacon was aware that the Crown would ever have to deal with conflicts between itself and Parliament on an ad hoc basis. Nowhere is the ad hoc character of this relationship more clear than in another piece of advice that Bacon gave to the future Buckingham on the role of favorites and ministers in the government and the use to which such men might be put. In answering the question why do kings create favorites, Bacon wrote:

They have done it sometimes out of their affection to the person of the man (for Kings have their affections as well as private men), sometimes in contemplation of their great abilities (and that's a happy choice), and sometimes for their own ends, to make them whom they so stile, and are contented should be so stiled, to be interposed between the Prince and the People.[85]

Bacon went on to warn the future Buckingham that the position of the favorite (and this applies to any minister of the Crown, as Bacon was himself to learn) exposed him to peculiar dangers.

Remember then what your true condition is. The King himself is above the reach of his people, but cannot be above their censures; and you are his shadow, if either he commit an error and is loath to avow it, but excuses it upon his Ministers, of which you are the first in the eye: or you commit the fault, or have willingly permitted it, and must suffer for it; so perhaps you may be offered as a sacrifice to appease the multitude.[86]

The King must maintain his position vis à vis Parliament and the populace in whatever way he can, even including the timely sacrifice of those around him.

Bacon's view of the political constitution bore a close relationship to his vision of society, and one of the other pieces of advice he gave to the future Buckingham in 1616 concerned the role of the nobility in public life.

It is now time that you should refer your actions chiefly to the good of your sovereign and your country. It is the life of an ox or beast always to eat, and never to exercise; but men are born (and specially christian men), not to cram in their fortunes, but to exercise their virtues; and yet the other hath been the humour of great persons in our times. Neither will your further fortune be the further off: for assure yourself that fortune is of a woman's nature, that will sooner follow you by slighting than by too much wooing. And in this dedication of yourself to the public, I recommend unto you principally that which I think was never done since I was born; and which not done hath bred almost a wilderness and solitude in the King's service; which is, that you countenance, and encourage, and advance able men and virtuous men and meriting men in all kinds, degrees, and professions. For in the time of the Cecils, the father and the son, able men were by design and of purpose suppressed; and though of late choice goeth better both in church and commonwealth, yet money, and turn-serving, and cunning canvasses, and importunity prevail too much.[87]

All social classes ("men in all kinds, degrees, and professions") but most particularly the nobility should wish to justify their place in society by royal service.

The rationale for the preeminent place of the monarch in government seems to lie in Bacon's conviction that the people and popular bodies (which Parliament was always in danger of becoming) were unsafe repositories for power. Only a wise and prudent king assisted by devoted and expert counsellors could hope to maintain the peace of society and, beyond that, safeguard and augment the well-being of the commonwealth.

Though not a constitutional theorist, Bacon thus took a clear stand on what was becoming in his lifetime the preeminent constitutional question: the respective powers of Crown and Parliament. He was a royalist, who accepted an important role for Parliament in government. That body was to be, as he told the future Buckingham in the passage already cited, a "Council to the King . . . to advise his Majesty of those things of weight and difficulty which concern both the King and kingdom." But though he accepted the role of Parliament thus defined in the government of the realm, he was ever wary that the body should become a mouthpiece for the populace and overstep its bounds. Its role, on the contrary, should be to serve the King when he desired it and to disband when he commanded.

In Bacon's view the monarchy was the agency most likely to stand above the play of faction and interest and therefore most able to frame and pursue rational policies, and for this reason it should possess constitutional primacy. Although the monarch might make timely and prudent concessions to pressures from below on an ad hoc basis, the principle of monarchy itself should never be compromised or derogated. Even explicit clarification of the respective roles of Crown and Parliament implied a certain danger in Bacon's view, for to clarify might mean to divide the powers of government and to limit the Crown, and this in turn might open the door to "popularity" and the "multitude."

THE ENCOMPASSING PURVIEW OF POLICY

Though not a searching constitutional thinker, Bacon was very much concerned with the uses of political power and the greatest part of his political thought throughout his life was concerned with policy-making. The term "policy" carried many meanings in the sixteenth century. It could mean government in general or the art of good government. Sometimes it was identified with political wisdom, but sometimes it carried the negative connotations of crafty amorality in politics. "Policy" for Bacon was everything that the government does — short of war — to attain its ends. Policy had two faces for Bacon: one (which we have already explored) defensive and "conservative"; the other, constructive and "progressive." Thus the first end of policy is to preserve the peace of society. Beyond the defense of order, however, policy must be directed to the enlarged provisioning of society, particularly in the pursuit of those goods whose future enjoyment is only to be secured by present planning and sacrifice.

Bacon's conception of policy shows most clearly the "progressive" animus of his political thought. We recall Hexter's apt characterization of Tudor government. "It was not the policy of the Tudors either to stand mulishly athwart the path of change, or to allow it free rein, but to guide it, to bring it as they said to some good rule conformable with good order."[88] Bacon's conception of policy fits Hexter's formulation precisely. For it was only *within* a stable and traditional constitutional framework that in Bacon's view the growing potential for material wealth and progress could be realized. Traditional authority must be maintained and made to work in the direction of economic and social change for the better provisioning of the Crown's subjects and the better ordering of the realm.

That the freeing of the new potentials for material growth probably required the destruction of a political order which, in retrospect at least, seems archaic and self-subverting is not the point. What is crucial here is the recognition that Bacon's whole outlook rested on the belief in a monarchy which was, if not absolute, at least so clearly preponderant in relation to all potentially competing social and political forces that royal policy could effectively shape the collective life of the nation. Only such an overarching authority, in Bacon's view, could manage change in such a way that the peace of the commonwealth was not undermined. Only such an authority could overcome the selfishness and shortsightedness of particular groups and interests and shape its policies with rationality, farsightedness, and wisdom. Only such an authority could maintain the customary order (or the appearance of customary order) in the face of momentous change. Against the troublesome background of human nature and human rationality, Crown policy became the single most important agent for organizing and rationalizing the nation's collective life.

The scope of policy was broad for Bacon and almost coextensive with the social order itself in that there was virtually no aspect of social life that was in principle immune to the attentions of the Crown. Thus social process in toto became the object of policy, and beyond this regulated realm lay only the individual lives of subjects and the renegade activities of rebellious groups.

That such a conception of the role of government policy might seem stifling to us now is partly a sign of our own ideological propensities, since modern ideologies of improvement have often been closely associated with ideas of liberation. For Bacon, improvement was associated with the opposite of liberation. His notion of policy, precisely in its comprehensively wide-ranging, rationalizing, managerial, and even coercive aspects, was the part of his political vision which harbored the utopianizing impulse of his political thought.

Two pieces of writing—one from early in his career, the other from late—will serve as good indicators both of the wide range of matters with which policy must concern itself and of the manner in which Crown policy was viewed as the principal agent of social improvement and progress. One is Bacon's *Certain Observations Made upon a Libel Published this Present Year, 1592;* the other, his already-mentioned letter of advice to George Villiers, the future Duke of Buckingham, upon his being raised to the peerage in 1616.

Certain Observations was Bacon's literary defense of Elizabeth and her government against attacks by Roman Catholic propagandists, and in the course of the piece Bacon had occasion to take up the topic "Of the present estate of this realm of England, whether it be truly avouched to be prosperous or afflicted."[89] As he dealt with this topic Bacon attempted an inventory of indices by which to judge the "felicity" of Elizabeth's reign.

> *If a man weigh well all the parts of state—religion, laws, administration of justice, policy of government, manners, civility, learning and liberal sciences, industry and manual arts, arms and provisions of wars for sea and land, treasure, traffic, improvement of the soil, population, honour and reputation—it will appear that, taking one part with another, the state of this nation was never more flourishing.*[90]

Though it is true that "policy of government" itself appears as an item on the list, the context of the inventory, i.e., proof of the wisdom and goodness of Elizabeth's reign, leaves no doubt that Bacon considered each item in the list to be in part at least the result of good policy. Taken as a whole the list forms a conspectus of the matters to which government policy must address itself.

However much it might be a result of the monarch's artfulness, Bacon is at pains to stress at the outset of his discussion, good policy may benefit from the works of fortune—those "parts of a government blessed of God."[91] Thus Elizabeth's reign has been a long one, the English people have been largely free from pestilential disease, there has been general peace, England has continued to be a wealthy nation, and population has increased. Bacon's measure of England's wealth—which Elizabeth did not create but did augment—is interesting as a would-be policymaker's vision of material well-being. He notes that there is an abundant supply of grain at reasonable prices, that England has become a food exporter, and that new land has been brought into tillage under

Elizabeth. Then he goes on to present signs of England's present wealth:

> *There was never the like number of fair and stately houses as have*
> *been built and set up from the ground since her Majesty's reign . . .*
> *There were never the like pleasures of goodly gardens and or-*
> *chards, walks, pools, and parks, as do adorn almost every mansion*
> *house.*
> *There was never the like number of beautiful and costly tombs and*
> *monuments, which are erected in sundry churches in honourable mem-*
> *ory of the dead.*
> *There was never the like quantity of plate, jewels, sumptuous mov-*
> *ables and stuff, as is now within the realm.*
> *There was never the like quantity of waste and unprofitable*
> *ground inned, reclaimed, and improved.*
> *There was never the like husbanding of all sorts of grounds by*
> *fencing, manuring, and all kinds of good husbandry.*
> *The towns were never better built nor peopled; nor the principal*
> *fairs and markets never better customed nor frequented.*
> *The commodities and eases of rivers cut by the hand and brought*
> *into a new channel, of piers that have been built, of waters that have*
> *been forced and brought against the ground, were never so many.*
> *There was never so many excellent artificers, nor so many new*
> *handicrafts used and exercised, nor new commodities made within the*
> *realm; as sugar, paper, glass, copper, divers silks, and the like.*
> *There was never such complete and honourable provision of horse,*
> *armour, weapon, ordinance of the war.*[92]

While a disproportionate number of these indices of national well-being concern the visible consumption of the nobility, it is also clear that Bacon is concerned with public works conducive to industrial and commercial development, with the development of industry itself, and with the improvement of agriculture – all signs (in part at least) of good government and successful policy.

Beyond these goods, which Elizabeth inherited as part of her national estate and merely preserved or augmented by her good policy, Bacon acknowledges another set of benefits which are largely to the Queen's own credit. Among these he cites her religious policy, which completed the change begun by her father, Henry VIII. Here, characteristically, Bacon looks to Tudor religious policy not just for its specifically religious effects but for a gamut of social goods.

> *Out of which purity of religion have since ensued, besides the principal*

effect of the true knowledge and worship of God, three points of great consequence unto the civil estate. One, the stay of a mighty treasure within the realm, which in foretimes was drawn forth to Rome. Another, the dispersing and distribution of those revenues (amounting to a third part of the land of the realm, and that of the goodliest and the richest sort) which heretofore were unprofitably spent in monasteries, into such hands as by whom the realm receiveth at this day service and strength, and many great houses have been set up and augmented. The third, the manumizing and enfranchising of the regal dignity from the recognition of a foreign superior. All which points, though begun by her father and continued by her brother, were yet nevertheless after an eclipse or intermission restored and re-established by her Majesty's self.[93]

Next, he cites her reform of the currency, which he compares with the religious reform. Elizabeth has restored the "fineness of money" by the "purging of the base money" just as she had purged "the dross of religion"[94] Finally, Bacon praised Elizabeth for the improvement of the navy and of maritime commerce and the fishing industry. By her policies "this island is become . . . the Lady of the Sea."[95]

Bacon is particularly concerned to answer two charges that are made against Elizabeth: The first that she has contributed to the "overthrow of the nobility," the second that her policies have led to the "oppression of the people." His answers to both charges are interesting for what they reveal about his conception of the social dimensions of policy.

Bacon clearly approved of royal policies which served to curb and domesticate the nobility. Indeed, against the background of the Wars of the Roses (one of Bacon's recurrent touchstones in his discussions of political history) this was one of the most significant accomplishments of the Tudor dynasty. Thus, while he might agree that under Elizabeth some great nobles had declined in their feudal status and powers ("commandment" in the following passage), Bacon saw this as a success rather than a failure of government policy.

Touching the commandment, which is not indeed so great as it hath been, I take it rather to be a commendation of the time than otherwise. For men were wont factiously to depend upon noblemen; whereof ensued many partialities and divisions, besides much interruption of justice, while the great ones did seek to bear out those that did depend upon them; so as the kings of this realm, finding long since that kind of commandment in noblemen unsafe unto their crown and inconvenient unto their people, thought meet to restrain the same by provision of

laws; whereupon grew the statute of retainers; so as men now depend
upon the prince and the laws and upon no other. . . . But otherwise it
may be truly affirmed that the rights and pre-eminencies of the nobility
were never more duly and exactly preserved unto them than they have
been in her Majesty's times.[96]

It was one of Bacon's lifelong beliefs that political disorder was most likely to result from an unholy joining of the ambitious few and the vulgar many, and in the interests of civil peace he always sought to attach both the "great ones" and "the people" directly to the Crown. This necessarily involved an attack on noble privileges that made possible factious resistance to the government and opened the way for "tumult." As his earlier list of signs of prosperity shows, Bacon was quite eager for the nobility to be wealthy and to display its wealth, but only within the stable peace provided by a strong monarchy.

Bacon likewise defends Elizabeth against the charge of oppressing the people, specifically refuting four points made by her critics: the suggestion that too many have died in wars, the idea that wars have disrupted trade, the argument that the court system was corrupt, and the claim that the people were overburdened with taxes. Bacon answers the first charge in a way that seems heartless to us and points up the difference between his ethos and our own. He admits that many have been lost in war but quickly adds that they are more than made up for by the natural increase of population and adds, to clinch his argument, that there are signs that England is becoming pressed with excess population anyway. The second charge he simply denies: warfare had not disrupted trade to any significant extent, and marginal commercial losses had been more than made up for by prizes taken at sea. In answer to the third charge, Bacon admits that there are some problems with the courts. "It is true," he writes, "that cunning and wealth have bred many suits and debates in law."[97] While admitting that the English legal system had its problems, however, Bacon nonetheless asserts that good legislation under Elizabeth had improved the situation and that the Star Chamber in particular has been active "in repressing forces and frauds." Specifically Bacon emphasizes the role of royal justice in protecting the interests of the poorer classes against the rapacity of the wealthy, citing "the great favours that have been used towards copyholders and customary tenants, which were in ancient times merely at the discretion and mercy of the lord, and are now continually relieved from hard dealing in chancery and other courts of equity."[98] Lastly, Bacon disputes the suggestion that Elizabeth has overburdened her subjects with taxes. Some taxes have been increased, he admits, but generally these have been on luxury items.

The subsidies that have been granted the Crown are necessary, well used, and cheerfully given.

> *Touching the number of subsidies, it is true that her Majesty, in respect of the great charges of her wars both by sea and land against such a lord of treasure as is the King of Spain; having for her part no Indies nor mines, and the revenues of the crown of England being such as they less grate upon the people than the revenues of any crown or state in Europe; hath by the assent of Parliament according to the ancient customs of the realm received divers subsidies of her people; which as they have been employed upon the defence and preservation of her subjects, not upon excessive buildings nor upon immoderate donatives nor upon triumphs and pleasures or any the like veins of dissipation of treasure, which have been familiar to many kings, so have they been yielded with great good-will and cheerfulness; as may appears by other kinds of benevolence, presented to her likewise in Parliament, which her Majesty nevertheless hath not put in use. They have been taxed also and assessed with a very light and gentle hand; and they have been spared as much as may be, as may appear in that her Majesty now twice, to spare the subject, hath sold of her own lands.*[99]

The survey "of the present estate of this real of England" is only one part of Bacon's *Certain Observations,* but it is a good indication of the criteria by which, as a young man, he sought to judge the success of Elizabeth's policy. Indirectly it provides an indication both of the domain over which policy itself was conceived to operate and of the ends toward which it was directed. Policy must thus concern itself with the peace and prosperity of the realm, with the myriad factors affecting agriculture, commerce, and industry, with religion and the realm of social opinion, with justice, with taxation, and, significantly, with the effects of government action in all these areas on the social equilibrium of the whole.

Late in his life Bacon provided another conspectus of policy issues in his letter of advice to the future Buckingham. Two versions of the "Letter" survive, one longer and one shorter, but since I am here concerned with the works not as literary productions or biographical evidence but rather as illustrating some of Bacon's views on the domain and direction of policy, I will move between the two versions, drawing freely on each.

What Bacon seems to have wanted to provide with this advice is a sort of primer on policy. "All matters of difficulty which will be presented to you," Bacon wrote, "will be one of these eight sorts," and he listed the following:

1. *Religion and Church-men, or Church-matters.*
2. *The Laws and the Professors thereof.*
3. *The Council Board, and matters of State.*
4. *Negotiation with foreign Princes or States.*
5. *War by Sea or Land.*
6. *Foreign Plantations and Colonies.*
7. *Matter of Trade.*
8. *The Court or Curialities.*[100]

That Bacon conceived of policy in this wide-ranging and comprehensive way is, again, interesting in itself, but as we turn to an examination of his remarks under several of these rubrics it is interesting further to see the extent to which Bacon thought of policy as the principal rationalizing and progressive force in the life of the nation over and against the spontaneous activities of individuals and groups.

In his advice on religion, Bacon reiterated the middle Anglican position that marked his entire career. "If any question be moved concerning the doctrine of the Church of England expressed in the 39 Articles, give not the least ear to the movers thereof. This is so soundly and so orthodoxally settled as cannot be questioned without extreme danger to the honour and stability of our Religion." Religious peace must be protected against "enemies and underminers" on two flanks: from "the Romish Catholiques (so stiling themselves) on the one hand, whose tenents are inconsistent with the truth of Religion. . . . and the Anabaptists and Separatists, and Sectaries on the other hand, whose tenents are full of schism, and inconsistent with monarchy."[101] Bacon did not believe that the government's defense of religious peace required extraordinary measures but only the consistent application of the existing laws.

When Bacon turns to "the Council Board, and matters of State," he is characteristically guarded. We have already seen that Bacon regarded secrecy as one of the principal requisites for stable government, and we have seen why he did so. To the future Buckingham he wrote: "For the matter of state and affairs proper for Council board, I dare not take upon me to say much; they are *secreta & arcana,* and are not fit to descend to too low, to too petty matters, or private interests."[102] Initiation into such *secreta & arcana* would presumably wait until his pupil was actually taken into the highest circles of power.

If in his remarks on religion and secrets of state we may recognize the "conservative" and "defensive" Bacon that we explored in the preceding chapter, in the remarks on colonies we begin to glimpse Bacon's conception of the constructive uses of policy and of the way in which he viewed the social order (the order of both the mother country and the colony) as a system requiring deliberate management and cultivation. Here Bacon presented colonies first as a means for dealing with excess population in the mother country — as a way "both honourable and profitable to disburthen the land of such inhabitants as may well be spared, and to employ their labours in the conquest of some foreign parts without injury to the natives."[103] (In his essay "Of Plantations," Bacon presented the problem of colonies in broad terms that made it seem paradigmatic of the predicament of government in general; here he confined himself to a series of practical admonitions.) Bacon did not want people to be sent to plantations under compulsion, "for that were a banishment, not a service fit for a freeman." He was wary of sending "known schismaticks, outlaws, or criminal persons," but if such were allowed to go advised that they be kept under strict surveillance.[104] He saw dangers in attempting to establish colonies in lands that were already inhabited and advised against making any "extirpation of the natives under pretence of planting Religion: God surely will no way be pleased with such sacrifices." He proposed that colonies be "governed according to the laws of this realm" and that colonists be considered English subjects. He thought that the Anglican Church must be established and the same care taken in the colonies to preserve the "same purity of Religion" as was guarded at home and "the same discipline for Church-Government without any mixture of Popery or Anabaptisme; lest they should be drawn into factions and schisms." He advised that the economic life of the colony be planned, that the people be engaged in "profitable trades and manufactures, such as the clime will best fit, and such as may be useful to this Kingdom," and that each colony trade the things it could produce for the things it needed from England. He thought that colonies must be prepared to defend themselves from foreign encroachment and saw that England's struggles with other powers would be carried into the colonial sphere. He warned against allowing the colonies to fall prey to unscrupulous and profit-mongering merchants who "under colour of furnishing the colony with necessaries, [might] grind them, so as shall always keep them in poverty." He advised that care be taken in settling government on the colony, that qualified governor be appointed, and that government be so conducted as to "lay the foundation of a new kingdom." Finally, foreseeing that England might accumulate a community of colonies (as had Spain) he recommended the formation of a body to manage colonial affairs generally: "That the King will appoint Commissioners in the nature of a Council, who may superintend the works of this nature, and regulate what concerns the colonies, and give an accompt thereof to the King or to his Council of State."[105]

It is clear from these remarks that colonies presented a dual set of problems. On the one hand, they must be considered extensions of the national economy and made to benefit the mother country economically. On the other hand, they must be seen as microcosmic societies in their own right and therefore be planned in such a way as their future peace and internal productivity might be assured. It was to this second problem that Bacon returned in his essay, "Of Plantations."

That Bacon thought of policy in terms that fit the narrower definitions of mercantilism is amply demonstrated by his remarks on trade. Here Bacon begins by confessing that these matters are "out of my profession," but this does not keep him from enunciating several principles which he thinks might be useful to guide the young favorite. The first piece of advice is a classic statement of what might be taken as the cardinal principle of mercantilism:

> *Let the foundation of a profitable Trade be thus laid, that the exportation of home commodities be more in value than the importation of foreign, so we shall be sure that the stocks of the kingdom shall yearly increase, for then the balance of trade must be returned in money or bullion.*[106]

To secure such a favorable balance of trade, he goes on to advise against allowing foreign credits to be squandered on luxury items. "Let not the merchant return toys and vanities (as sometimes it was elsewhere Apes and Peacocks) but solid merchandize, first for necessity, next for pleasure, but not for luxury." Specifically, Bacon here mentions the need to curtail the consumption of fashionable clothes and costly food and drink. Interestingly Bacon identifies the contaminating influence of foreign fashions as a potential source of economic danger. "Let the vanity of the times be restrained," he urges, "which the neighborhood of other nations have induced."[107] Such frivolities might be permitted on the stage, but not to "sober men and matrons." Wise men will naturally shun the consumption of exotic imported wines, but for those many who are not wise, Bacon proposes that a law be passed to prevent it.

In addition to controlling domestic consumption of foreign luxury items, Bacon would have England promote the domestic manufacture of certain goods.

> *If we must be vain and superfluous in laces and embroideries which are more costly than either warm or comely, let the curiosity be the manufacture of the natives: then it should not be verified of us* Materiam superabat opus.

> *. . . in stead of crying up all things which are either brought from beyond sea or wrought here by the hands of strangers, let us advance the native commodities of our own kingdom, and employ our countrymen before strangers: let us turn the wool of the land into cloaths and stuffs of our own growth, and the hemp and flax growing here into linen cloth and cordage; it would set many thousand hands on work, and thereby one shilling worth of the materials would by industry be multiplied to five, ten, and many times to twenty times more in the value being wrought.*[108]

Above all, Bacon hoped that the government would attend to the well-being of English agriculture, the industry on which all others depended, and urged a concerted policy of "improving lands for tillage." The land was a limited resource and must be used efficiently for "the King cannot enlarge the bounds of these Islands, which make up his Empire, the Ocean being the unremovable wall which encloseth them."[109]

To encourage the productive growth of the domestic economy, Bacon recommended that the government undertake public works — specifically the maintenance of navigable rivers — and urged that these "indrafts to attain wealth" not be left to "private profit."[110]

Bacon believed that the English should emulate the Dutch in exploiting the food resources of the oceans by improving its fishing.

> *I beseech you take into your serious consideration that Indian wealth, which this island and the seas thereof excel in, the hidden and rich treasure of Fishing: do we want an example to follow? I may truly say to the English go to the pismire thou sluggard. I need not expound the text; half a day's sail with a good wind will shew the mineral, and the miners.*[111]

As in the case of colonies, Bacon believed that trade should be kept under secure control by the Crown through the creation of a government body whose specific function it was to order trade and "give an accompt thereof to the State."

The longer version of Bacon's advice to the future Buckingham goes much further in specifying the way in which the domestic economy should be managed and encouraged, and here Bacon the Crown minister sounds awfully much like Bacon the reformer of learning. He is quite detailed in the recommendations for domestic production, to the point even of recommending government encouragement of particular crops. Also of interest is his perception of the systemic relations of agriculture to industry, which must be developed together. A sample of his suggestions will suffice:

1. For the home trade, I first commend unto your consideration the encouragement of Tillage, which well furnisheth the kingdom with corn for the natives, and to spare for exportation: and I myself have known more than once when, in times of scarcity and dearth, in the days of Queen Elizabeth, it was a means to drain much coin out of the kingdom, to furnish us from foreign parts.

2. Good husbands will find the means, by good husbandry, to improve their lands, by lime, chalk, marle, and sea-sand, where it can be had: but it will not be amiss, they be put in mind thereof, and encouraged in their industry.

3. Planting of orchards, in a soil and air fit for them is very profitable, as well as pleasant; perry and cider are both notable beverages in long sea voyages.

4. Gardens are also very profitable, if well planted with artichokes, all sorts of roots, as parsnip, turnip, carrot, and such things as are fit for food; whence they are not unfitly called kitchen-gardens, but very properly so named.

5. The planting of hop-yards, sowing of woad, rape seed, and coleseed are very profitable to the planter, in places apt for them, and consequently profitable to the kingdom, which for divers years was furnished with them from Holland and other parts beyond the seas.

6. The planting and preserving of wood, especially for timber, is not only profitable, but commendable, therewith to furnish posterity, both for shipping and building.

7. The kingdom would be much improved by draining drowned lands, and gaining them from the overflowing of the sea and the salt waters, and from fresh water also.

8. And many of these grounds so drained would be exceeding fit for dairies, which, being well housewived, are very profitable and commodious.

9. Much good land might be gained from forests and chases, more remote from the King's access, and from other commonable places, so as there be always a due care taken of the poor commoners, that they have no injury by such improvement. . . .

11. The planting of hemp and flax would be an unknown advance to the Kingdom, many places therein being as apt for it as any foreign parts.

12. But let these commodities be converted to cordage or linens, and the benefit by those manufactures will be multiplied.

13. The wool which in England in plentiful and good, and leather, are very profitable, if they also be converted into industrious manufactures.

14. English dames are much given to the wearing of very fine and costly laces; if they be brought from Italy, or France, or Flanders, they are with them in great esteem; whereas, if the like laces were made by the English, so much thread as would make a yard of lace, put into manufacture, would be of five times, nay, perhaps, of ten or twenty times the value.

15. The breeding cattle is of much profit, especially the breeding of horses, in many places, not only for travel, but for the great saddle; the English horse, for strength, and courage, and swiftness together, not being inferior to the horse of any other country.

16. The minerals of the kingdom, as lead, copper, iron, and tin, are of great value, and set very many able-bodied subjects on work; it were to be wished that care be taken that they be industriously followed. . . .

20. But especially care must be taken, that monopolies, (which are the canker of all trades,) be by [no] means admitted under the pretence or the specious colour of the public good.[112]

As in the shorter version, Bacon concluded this list of economic counsels with the suggestion that the entire economy be put under the supervision of an overseeing board.

Bacon's remarks on policy—those given early in his life in his defense of Elizabeth and those given later in his advice to the future Buckingham—are interesting not because all of the ideas are original but rather for what they show about his conception of the constructive uses of political power, about his comprehensive vision of the purview of policymakers, and, finally, of the extent to which he conceived of society as a more or less closed system, with its own internal order and dynamics, which must be rationally managed in order to thrive. The range of policy was for Bacon virtually coextensive with the social order, and there is no sign that he recognized limits in principal to the domain of policy. In his remarks on colonies, foreign trade, and the ordering of the domestic economy, Bacon shows the extent to which he regarded a wide range of economic and social goods to be dependent on the rationalizing, future-oriented policies of the state. These remarks also show the degree to which he recognized the social order to be complex and conceived of good policies themselves as necessarily circumspect and designed with an eye to the wide range of consequences that must follow any particular policy decision.

THE PLANTATION AS A MICROCOSMIC COMMONWEALTH

B acon included the matter of colonies in his advice to the future Buckingham a principal department of policy. For Bacon a colony or "plantation" was not only an extension of the mother country, designed to augment national wealth and security, but was also a microcosmic society, requiring the same careful planning and administration as the larger society. At the same time it offered a clearer field for rational policy since it was not encumbered by the inevitable accumulations of history. Because colonies were made by a deliberate act of government they offered special opportunities for the rational policymaker and required systematic and comprehensive planning. Colonies thus present themselves as both problematic and interesting in two senses: first, as microcosms of social order itself; second, as new beginnings which bring both opportunities and challenges.

In his essay "Of Plantations" Bacon reflected generally on the "planting" of colonies. Though his remarks do not differ in marked respects from the ideas we have already encountered in his advice to Buckingham, they fill out his conception of colonization in a way that highlights the challenge that colonies pose for the social planner and policymaker.

Bacon's statement at the very outset that "plantations are amongst ancient, primitive, and heroical works," echoing the language he had used to praise the founders and rescuers of the great states themselves, immediately raised the topic of colonies to a plane of premier political importance. To plant a colony was to create a new society, "for I may justly account new plantations to be the children of former kingdoms." Ideally each new colony would be an absolutely new beginning, unburdened by the weight of history—a kind of social tabula rasa: "I like a plantation in a pure soil; that is, where people are not displanted to the end to plant in others. For else it is rather an extirpation than a plantation."[113] In the ideal case, therefore, where a colony is laid down in a virgin land, the task of colonial planning borders on a kind of practical utopianizing.

The portrait that Bacon goes on to paint (by way of a series of counsels) is that of a rationally-ordered community in which each major social function—government, economy, population, social groupings, ideology—is planned. In terms of its domestic government, Bacon would "let it be in the hands of one, assisted with some counsel; and let them have a commission to exercise martial law, with some limitation."[114] He was keenly aware of the hazardousness of life in a newly planted society, and this no doubt partially explains his resort to martial law, but, as we have already seen, Bacon believed social life in general to be somewhat precarious and his authoritarian proposals for colonial government may be related to this more general disposition as well.

For the economy of the new society, Bacon recommended a full range of productive activities. At the beginning the colony should be particularly concerned to feed itself. A site should be chosen which offered natural foods: "chestnuts, walnuts, pine-apples, olives, dates, plums, cherries, wild honey, and the like." Initially colonists should be directed to grow things that were easy and sure: "parsnips, carrots, turnips, onions, radish, artichokes of Hierusalem, maize, and the like"; peas and beans rather than cereal crops; swine, goats, and fowl rather than larger and more delicate animals.[115]

Productive activities would govern immigration policies, social groupings, and the general social ethos within the new colony. First, unproductive men would not be permitted to immigrate:

> It is a shameful and unblessed thing to take the scum of people, and wicked condemned men, to be the people with whom you plant: and not only so, but it spoileth the plantation; for they will ever live like rogues, and not fall to work, but be lazy, and do mischief, and spend victuals, and be quickly weary, and then certify over to their country to the discredit of the plantation.[116]

Immigrants should be chosen for their productive contribution to the colony, and the nearest thing which Bacon provides to a social structure for his colony is the listing of occupational groupings: "The people wherewith you plant ought to be gardeners, ploughmen, labourers, smiths, carpenters, joiners, fishermen, fowlers, with some few apothecaries, surgeons, cooks, and bakers."[117] This list of sought-for immigrants also suggests that Bacon would have the colony be economically diversified and as fully self-sufficient as possible. At the beginning (at least), Bacon would have the production and consumption of goods be rigidly controlled: "The victual in plantations ought to be expended almost as in a besieged town; that is, with certain allowance. And let the main part of the ground employed to gardens or corn be to a common stock; and to be laid in, and stored up, and then delivered out in proportion."[118] While the mercantilist aims of the colonial effort should take second place to the requirements of survival, Bacon foresaw a time when the society might become an exporter, and he mentions specifically tobacco, timber, iron (where waterpower and fuel wood along with iron ore were plentiful), salt, silk, pitch and tar, drugs and sweet woods, and soap ashes. Repeatedly, Bacon warned against the desire for easy wealth and premature profits, and it was in this connection that he cautioned against the hope for mineral wealth, first because it was so uncertain, and second because it would destroy the work ethic in the colonists. It was this ethic of productivity along with godliness that would provide the new society with its overriding values: "Above all, let men make that profit of being in the wilderness, as they have God always, and His service, before their eyes."[119]

Once political order and economic productivity were assured, Bacon (echoing Livy's account of the early history of Rome) would provide for the perpetuation of the colonial population by permitting the immigration of women: "When the plantation grows to strength, then it is time to plant with women as well as with men; that the plantation may spread into generations, and not be ever pieced from without."[120]

It is clear from all this that Bacon envisaged the colony first as a small, rationally constructed society and, comparing his remarks here to what we have already seen of the policy he recommended for England itself, that he saw colonial policy as general state policy writ small. Each colony should become, like England itself, a small workshop, with all its arrangements geared to the stable production of wealth.

Bacon was well aware that the motives which urged the establishment of such new, productive communities might just as well undermine them. (His caution in this regard extends, as we shall see, to science.) Bacon's "bourgeois" desire for productivity and growth was regularly qualified by an equally bourgeois distrust of premature profit taking and by a political realism which saw the dangers of narrow, short-term interests prevailing over long-term goods. This caution is connected to his already-mentioned advocacy of a strict internal regimen ("as in a besieged town") to prevent the colonists themselves from undoing their enterprise by unrestrained consumption. He also worried lest those who sponsored and controlled the enterprise from the mother country undermine their project through short-sightedness and greed:

> Planting of countries is like planting of woods; for you must make account to leese almost twenty years' profit, and expect your recompense in the end. For the principal thing that hath been the destruction of most plantations, hath been the base and hasty drawing of profits in the first years. It is true, speedy profit is not to be neglected, as far as may stand with the good of the plantation, but no further.[121]

It was for this reason that Bacon did not want merchants at home controlling colonial enterprises. As he addressed the question of England's administration of her colonies, he warned that the counsellors who oversaw colonial affairs should "be rather noblemen and gentlemen, than merchants; for they look ever to the present gain."[122]

Thus for all its emphasis on the growth of wealth, what is perhaps most striking in Bacon's portrait of colonial enterprise is a belief that we have now encountered regularly in his thought and should come to see as one of its hallmarks: Social productivity is the fruit of rational planning from above and control by a rationalizing authority which prevents people from undoing their enterprises through irrational short-sightedness. We may doubt that "noblemen and gentlemen" in Bacon's age were more self-restraining than merchants when faced with the prospect of quick riches. Certainly Bacon himself was not a model of such restraint. But the idea is clear that social productivity will be achieved only to the extent that the spontaneous workings of human nature are restrained by an overarching system of authority.

THE COMMONWEALTH AND THE COMMONWEALTH OF LEARNING

For Bacon the future represented a crucial and highly problematic dimension of policy-making. People were all too prone to sacrifice future goods, however great, for present pleasure, however trivial. This cardinal fact of human nature jeopardized all efforts at rational planning and was one of the key reasons that government must necessarily be coercive if it were to achieve important collective ends. Nowhere does Bacon state this problem of the future more clearly than in his reflections on the government's role in providing for the educational needs of society. The *Advancement of Learning,* begun in 1603 and published in 1605, has so frequently been studied as a survey of human knowledge (which it is) that its character as a practical proposal is sometimes neglected. But it is quite clear from his remarks at the beginning of Book Two that in writing the piece Bacon was making a policy proposal to James I.

Bacon situated the matter of education and learning squarely in the domain of policy and at the same time presented it as a problem of future versus present rewards:

> *It might seem to have more convenience, though it come often otherwise to pass, excellent King, that those, which are fruitful in their generations, and have in themselves the foresight of immortality in their descendants, should likewise be more careful of the good estate of future times, unto which they know they must transmit and commend*

over their dearest pledges. Queen Elizabeth was a sojourner in the world in respect of her unmarried life, and was a blessing to her own times; and yet so as the impression of her good government, besides her happy memory, is not without some effect which doth survive her. But to your Majesty, whom God hath already blessed with so much royal issue, worthy to continue and represent you for ever, and whose youthful and fruitful bed doth yet promise many of the like renovations; it is proper and agreeable to be conversant not only in the transitory parts of good government, but in those acts also which are in their nature permanent and perpetual: amongst the which, if affection do not transport me, there is not any more worthy than the further endowment of the world with sound and fruitful knowledge. For why should a few received authors stand up like Hercules' columns, beyond which there should be no sailing or discovering, since we have so bright and benign a star as your Majesty to conduct and prosper us? To return therefore where we left, it remaineth to consider of what kind those acts are which have been undertaken and performed by kings and others for the increase and advancement of learning: wherein I purpose to speak actively without digressing or dilating.[123]

The "advancement of learning," then, is assuredly for Bacon one of the "parts of good government," and it is a part, moreover, that is in danger of being neglected because it yields rewards which are long-range rather than immediate, but at the same time "permanent and perpetual" rather than "transitory." In the discussion that follows his introduction, Bacon proposes six concrete acts by which James might inaugurate a policy of intellectual advancement.

Bacon establishes the major direction of his proposals by noting that in the past government policy toward education, however well-intentioned, has been conservative and backward-looking rather than future-oriented. The "works and acts" of past princes have been "rather matters of magnificence and memory, than of progression and proficience; and tend rather to augment the mass of learning in the multitude of learned men, than to rectify or raise the sciences themselves." First, princes have endowed "seats and places of learning . . . foundations and buildings, endowments with revenues, endowments with franchises and privileges, institutions and ordinances for government," all of which have served more as places of refuge for men of learning than as workshops for the creation of new knowledge. Second, they have provided support for "the books of learning," both libraries ("which are as the shrines where all the relics of the ancient saints . . . are preserved and reposed") and new editions of already hallowed authors. Third, they have supported the "persons of the learned" by rewarding men who are already eminent in their fields.[124]

Without denigrating any of these supports for learning, Bacon urges James to follow a more forward-looking policy. As will be clear, Bacon's proposals are aimed principally at revivifying the existing university system rather than inaugurating a new institutional order for learning. Therefore they have a reformist and civic character which make them seem in some ways more an extension of sixteenth-century humanism than an inauguration of seventeenth-century scientism.

In the first place, Bacon wished to see a greater place made for what we might call "liberal" education in the universities. "I find it strange," he writes, "that [the great colleges in Europe] are all dedicated to professions, and none left free to arts and sciences at large."[125] The unbalanced emphasis on professional training in medicine, law, and theology at the expense of what Bacon calls "fundamental knowledges" has had a stultifying effect on the production of new knowledge. Far from being mere ornamentation, the study of "philosophy and universality" nourishes the advancement of all more special and practical particular knowledges. It would be a mistake, however, to imagine that a liberal education was not, in Bacon's eyes, also an education for use. The undue emphasis on professional education had robbed the state of much-needed civil servants:

For hence it proceedeth that princes find a solitude in regard of able men to serve them in causes of state, because there is no education collegiate which is free; where such as were so disposed might give themselves to histories, modern languages, books of policy and civil discourse, and other the like enablements unto service of estate.[126]

The business of government, in other words, required generalists who were liberally educated, and the state should support an educational establishment which provided for these a liberal education.

Bacon's second proposal concerned the salaries of learners and teachers, which he considered to be altogether inadequate. The result of low pay scales was that "public lectures" became a mere stepping-stone for able men, who as soon as they were able were often tempted to abandon intellectual pursuits for more lucrative occupations, leaving both teaching and the enlargement of knowledge in the hands of mediocrities.

It is necessary to the progression of sciences that readers be of the most able and sufficient men; as those which are ordained for generating and

propagating of sciences, and not for transitory use. This cannot be,
except their condition and endowment be such as may content the
ablest man to appropriate the whole labour and continue his whole age
in that function and attendance; and therefore must have a proportion
answerable to that mediocrity or competency of advancement, which
may be expected from a profession or the practice of a profession.[127]

Those who are "the guardians of the stores and provisions of sciences"
must, in other words, be paid as well as those men of practical affairs
whose practice depends upon their learning.

Third, Bacon notes that the dawning sciences of nature require a
kind of initial investment which might most appropriately be made by
the state. Citing the alchemists ("who call upon men to sell their books,
and to build furnaces") as an example of the new approach to scientific
research, Bacon suggests that experimental science will require a much
larger supply of what we would now call "fixed capital" and much higher
"operating expenses" than did the speculative science of the past:

Certain it is, that unto the deep, fruitful, and operative study of many
sciences, especially natural philosophy and physic, books be not the
only instrumentals; wherein also the beneficence of men hath not been
altogether wanting: for we see spheres, globes, astrolabes, maps, and
the like, have been provided as appurtenances to astronomy and cos-
mography, as well as books: we see likewise that some places instituted
for physic have annexed the commodity of gardens for simples of all
sorts, and do likewise command the use of dead bodies for anatomies.
But these do respect but a few things. In general, there will hardly be
any main proficience in the disclosing of nature, except there be some
allowance for expenses about experiments; whether they be experi-
ments appertaining to Vulcanus or Daedalus, furnace or engine, or any
other kind: and therefore as secretaries and spials of princes and states
bring in bills for intelligence, so you must allow the spials and intelli-
gencers of nature to bring in their bills; or else you shall be ill adver-
tised.[128]

The last comparison of international "intelligence" to natural "intelligence" places the whole question of the new science in a very traditional
political context so that the problem of initiating a new study of nature is
subsumed by policy more broadly construed.

Fourth, Bacon recommends that the state take a much more active
role in regulating the "customs" and the curriculum of the universities.
Bacon clearly believed that the universities (like all other social institu-

tions) were answerable to the government as representative of the commonweal. In this respect, their corporate charters would be not so much bulwarks of their autonomy as tokens of their social obligation. Bacon noted as a defect, in any case, the "intermission or neglect in those which are governors in universities, of consultation; and in princes or superior persons, of visitation: to enter into account and consideration, whether the readings, exercises, and other customs appertaining unto learning, anciently begun, and since continued, be well instituted or no.[129]" Mere precedent or tradition was not enough to warrant a given practice. Practices, on the contrary, must be continually reevaluated as to their current soundness. Here Bacon cited one of James's "own most wise and princely maxims":

> *That in all usages and precedents, the times be considered wherein they first began; which, if they were weak or ignorant, it derogateth from the authority of the usage, and leaveth it for suspect.*[130]

The learned community must not, in any case, be allowed to go its own way, independent of state scrutiny, and Bacon's desire to free the educational community from the burden of outmoded tradition must in no way be interpreted as a desire to establish some general and untrammelled intellectual liberty. The state, on the contrary, must take a much more active role than it had in the past in reviewing the usages of the universities and in initiating "as amendment or reformation in that which shall be found inconvenient."[131] Interestingly, the specific "inconveniences" which Bacon cites in this passage do not (as one might expect) concern natural philosophy, but rather logic and rhetoric, whose teaching Bacon believes to be misplaced in the curriculum and ill-taught for use in the world.

Bacon's fifth proposal is for more international communication among institutions of learning. While learning might be immeasurably improved by the reordering of its institutions and practices within national boundaries, "so it would be yet more advanced, if there were more intelligence mutual between the Universities of Europe than now there is."[132] Indeed, given the analogies he invokes, Bacon seems to envision here some more or less formal association of learned men on an international scale:

> *Surely, as nature createth brotherhood in families, and arts mechanical contract brotherhoods in commonalities, and the anointment of God superinduceth a brotherhood in kings and bishops; so in like manner there cannot but be a fraternity in learning and illumination, relating to*

that paternity which is attributed to God, who is called the Father of illuminations or lights.[133]

However much such an association might be warranted by this common "paternity," Bacon's inclusion of this proposal in this particular list leaves no doubt that the actual promotion of international communication and exchange among scholars and institutions of learning would require the active assistance of governments.

Bacon's sixth proposal is for the "public designation of writers or inquirers concerning such parts of knowledge as may appear not to have been already sufficiently laboured or undertaken." Bacon believed that "the opinion of plenty is among the causes of want"; that is, that as long as people believed themselves to be well supplied with knowledge they would lack the incentive to go out and enlarge what was, in Bacon's opinion, a rather paltry store.[134] The point to be noted here—where we are concerned with learning as an object of state policy—is that Bacon would have the direction of new learning indirectly under the control of the state by way of state-appointed officers. The idea is similar to that of increased supervision of the universities and of university curriculum, only now applied to research rather than teaching. Bacon did not trust the existing community of learning to undertake its own renewal and redirection spontaneously and wished the government to take an active role in this as in so many other aspects of the advancement of learning.

These six proposals Bacon called *opera basilica,* "royal works," in the sense that they must be the object of public policy, and it is in the context of these that the rationale for the *Advancement* as a whole, whose purpose was the well-known "perambulation of learning," must be understood. Scholars and commentators have rightly interested themselves in the intellectual and philosophical import of Bacon's survey of the arts and sciences which is contained in the *Advancement,* without always keeping in view the fact that this survey was only a preliminary and private initiative in a much larger program to be organized and overseen by the state. In initiating the sixth of the proposals, Bacon believed, "the endeavours of a private man" might lay a foundation for state action, by serving as "an image in a crossway." They might, that is, provide a first approximation of the work which was to be done by that official and publicly designated group of "writers or inquirers."[135]

Since we shall return to Bacon's reflections on learning, it is enough to note here that, like religious life and the economy (and indeed like all the productive functions of society) intellectual pursuits were considered to be in need of organization and direction by public authority and were therefore fit subjects for policy deliberation. Bacon had as little tolerance for anarchy in the intellectual sphere as he did in any other sphere of social life and saw the only hope for productive efficiency to lie in the rationalizing power of authority. The six proposals discussed here are enough to show that Bacon wished for the state to introduce a much more secure order into intellectual life—an order which would provide both peace and direction.

THE DOUBLE FACE OF POLICY AND ITS RELEVANCE FOR BACON'S CONCEPTION OF ORGANIZED SCIENCE

Conservative" and "progressive" elements interpenetrate and balance one another in Bacon's political thought. Bacon's disparaging views on human nature and his consequent belief in the fragility of the social order made him a conservative on issues that might broadly be called constitutional. The interests of both peace and progress demanded that power be entrusted to a small circle at the top of society. Bacon's abstract account of the requirements of social peace corresponds closely to an idealized image of the Tudor monarchy in which real power resided in the Crown and the Crown's ministers. The consultative role of Parliament was legitimized precisely to the extent that the body did not become an organ for the expression of popular sentiment but remained the preserve of a responsible and properly submissive elite. It was within a stable and conservative social and political constitution of this sort, in Bacon's view, that constructive policy could be undertaken by a governmental authority that was firmly in control.

Policy was the dynamic element in Bacon's vision of social and political process. In his idealized account, policy must be comprehensive, rational, and future-oriented. There were, in principle, no discernible limits to Crown policy beyond the limits of God and nature—and certainly no constitutional limits—so that in theory every aspect of collective life might be conceived as a legitimate object of the government's attention and regulatory authority. Policy must address itself to public opinion and sentiment quite as much as to public works and foreign trade. Policy must stand against both the timeless perversity of human nature and the self-interestedness of particular, historical social groupings as a bulwark of reason in the state. Most particularly, since human selfishness always tended toward short-range gratification, policy must look to the future as did the estate management of a good steward.

Beyond this conception of policy lies a vision of the social future with ample room for change, growth, and improvement. Bacon was quite well aware that his was an age of rapidly expanding opportunity and that there were powerful new forces at work in society, which carried with them the potential for a vastly increased human productivity in all departments of life. It is inaccurate, however, to portray Bacon's intention toward these forces as one of *liberation,* even if the rhetoric of liberation were occasionally invoked against archaic forms of constraint. In his writings on policy Bacon made abundantly clear that what he wished was not so much to liberate the forces of change as to harness and manage them.

Controlled change, managed progress—these are the keys to understanding Bacon's ideas on the constructive uses of policy. Just as the spontaneous workings of human nature threatened the social order itself, so did spontaneity—a free rein for people's individual and collective impulses—threaten the effective mobilization of that order for the attainment of constructive ends.

Bacon's conservative intent—the maintenance of a rigidly hierarchical and authoritarian social and political order—must not therefore be understood as standing in opposition to or even merely coexisting with his progressive intent. It is only retrospectively and from the vantage point of modern ideologies, which closely identify liberty with progress, that Bacon's political outlook can be portrayed as harboring competing or even conflicting components. To this extent it is a historical distortion to organize his political thought into "forward-looking" and "historically bound" parts. When viewed from within, on the contrary, Bacon's ideas about politics and social organization are seen to display a coherence which is both historical and logical and in which tradition and innovation, stasis and change, hierarchy and social mobilization, central control and collective productivity are all faces of a single paradigm.

To anyone familiar with the Great Instauration it is obvious that Bacon's vision of science bears a close relation to his political thought. Most immediately, a redirected science would carry with it the possibility of previously unimaginable material increase. In this respect, science becomes one of those social functions in which government policymakers must have a special interest and to which they must provide special support. From the standpoint of the government, science is one among many means toward social progress.

What is perhaps less obvious is that Bacon's vision of science also mimics his vision of the political world. Bacon made an important contribution to the history of philosophy and scientific thought when he sought to conceptualize scientific activity as the business of individuals and groups working in concert—or conflict—with other individuals and groups. It is historically premature and misleading to speak of Bacon's insights into the social dimensions of learning as a "sociology of knowledge,"[136] for this suggests that he was working to develop methods and principles appropriate to a new and distinct discipline with its own proper subject matter. Bacon's reflections on the social dimensions of knowledge reflect a managerial interest rather than strictly scientific one, for he was above all interested in discovering the social changes necessary to launch a new natural science. It would be equally misleading to treat his remarks on the social conditions of science as merely rhetorical trappings for an essentially philosophical enterprise. Bacon was keenly attuned to the social aspects of scientific activity, and one of his most consequential offerings to seventeenth-century science was the argument that inquiry into the natural order must become the work of an organized community working according to a single method and under a single regimen. Explicitly rejecting both genius and chance as reliable keys to scientific discovery, Bacon redefined inquiry as a kind of collective labor and sought to find a place for such inquiry in the social order at large. Having once posited that science must be collective, that the activity and the people who performed it be organized and directed, and that there be some directing authority, Bacon had, in effect, defined the predicament of science in terms that we are already familiar with from the political realm. The task of reforming science became that of founding a community, reducing it to obedience and good order, and managing it for the performance of productive tasks.

Like Bacon's political conceptions generally, his approach to organizing science along collective lines displayed elements that were both conservative and progressive. The conception of human nature which lies near the foundations of Bacon's political thought — the view of humans as fallible, even perverse, short-sighted, impatient of order, irrational — also informs his vision of organized science. The scientific worker, therefore, no less than the political subject, must be made to submit to an outside authority, to a rationalizing agency. Scientific inquiry, no less that social life in general, must be governed if it is to achieve the order and organization necessary for the accomplishment of its ends.

The conception of authority and order that Bacon brought to the task of organizing science was of a piece with his views of politics and government. In the intellectual realm, no less than in the economic and social realms, Bacon was aware that new forces had arisen and further that these forces could be either disruptive or productive depending on whether they were properly controlled and channeled. In the proper channeling of the new intellectual currents — in their proper government — lay the hope of intellectual progress and, because he conceived a properly directed science as serving socially useful ends, the hope of general human improvement as well. But the hoped-for improvement of our estate through science depended, for Bacon, on the willingness of scientists themselves to accept a discipline which was stringent and which left little to the free workings of the human intellect.

Bacon's attention to scientific organization is central to his conception of science in a way that has been insufficiently appreciated. It offers, moreover, a point from which one may begin to understand the relation between Bacon's two careers — that of statesman and that of philosopher or scientific reformer — the elucidation of which has been a great long-standing gap in Bacon studies. It gives us, finally, a starting point for exploring the little-understood process of mutation which went on within the seventeenth-century tradition known as "Baconianism," for it shows how certain standard Baconian ideas and slogans could take on different coloration and meaning when they were fitted into different organizational, political, and ideological frameworks.

Much of the existing body of Bacon literature — and none more than that which makes Bacon a prophet of one or another aspects of what we call "modernity" — leaves us with the perplexing sense that Bacon-the-scientific-reformer could hardly have been a man of his age. Our perplexity is heightened when we turn from the abstracting (and often distorting) commentary to the unabstracted texts of Bacon himself, for in his writings Bacon speaks a language that is patently different from our own, different from that of the Enlightenment, different even from that of the Royal Society, which was founded in his name. It is not only a matter of language and style but also of substance. Bacon's prescription for the organization of science forms a point of nexus between a range of scientific conceptions and aspirations which have survived and a political outlook — including a general view of humankind and human enterprise — which has passed. It is thus one of those topics especially helpful in allowing us to restore to Bacon his historical specificity and to see him as a man who thought and acted within the context of his times.

Fr. Baconi
DE VERULAMIO
SERMONES FIDELES,
ETHICI,
POLITICI,
ŒCONOMICI:
Sive
INTERIORA RERUM.
Accedunt
FABER FORTUNÆ
COLORES BONI ET MALI, &c.

AMSTELODAMI,
Ex officina Elzeviriana. 1662.

I I I

The Commonwealth of Science

4

Collaboration, Organization, and Government

SCIENTIFIC ORGANIZATION

B acon's intellectual concerns and literary productions are so richly varied that there is considerable disagreement among scholars about how to categorize him as a thinker. He figures in histories of the arts tradition, of Renaissance encyclopedism, of philosophy, of law, of historiography, of political thought, and, of course, of science. But even among those whose interest is the history of science, there is disagreement as to Bacon's contribution to the scientific tradition. In the nineteenth century Spedding and Ellis might argue over whether induction or natural history was the heart of Bacon's method, but in the twentieth, when the very existence of "a scientific method" has come to be doubted, Bacon's elaborate scheme for methodizing the Great Instauration can seem quite irrelevant to the decisive scientific shifts — the "Scientific Revolution" — which took place in Bacon's age. Then, Bacon made no important discoveries and formulated no consequential theories. In this respect, there is little justification for classing him with such men as Copernicus, Brahe, Kepler, Galileo, Descartes, Boyle, and Newton. Some recent scholars like Graham Rees have placed him in an alchemical tradition of natural philosophy, but this very tradition had gone underground by the late seventeenth century and its relation to the mainstream of scientific development continues to be a matter of debate. Indeed, as positivistic nineteenth-century convictions about what science is recede into the historical distance, claims for Bacon's importance in the early history of science have become increasingly soft. Most recent scholarship has tended to see his importance and contribution as more diffuse and subtle than did the nineteenth-century enthusiasts. They have supported their claims for his importance by arguing that what he did was to establish certain psychological, ethical, rhetorical, and ideological preconditions for the "rise of science." Bacon is thus taken to have encouraged in a general way such habits as observation, experimentation, and natural history, to have inspired people with a vision in which scientific progress was closely linked with social improvement, and to have provided the seventeenth-century British with a language and ideology conducive to scientific research.

In attempting to explore the internal unity of Bacon's thought rather than to assess his importance for the history of science, I believe that his conception of organized science must occupy a central role. It provides, moreover, a new way of understanding the connections between Bacon's life as a political man and his life as a man of learning and a new way of looking at the Great Instauration.

There has been a tendency among Bacon's more philosophic-minded commentators to dismiss Bacon's ideas about scientific organization as merely ancillary and instrumental to his real aim, which, they argue, is a shift in the way people think. From this perspective, Jeffrey Barnouw has criticized what he believes to be an "undue and distorting emphasis on the external aspects of [Bacon's] efforts to further science as an endeavor and institution."[1] I believe that this view hits wide of the mark and that the matter of organization — broadly conceived — is central to Bacon's whole effort on behalf of natural learning.

While Bacon certainly wished to redirect the way people think, it was at least as important to him to reshape the way they behave. Thoughts, for Bacon, are shaped by ways of living. To change the way scientific inquirers think about nature, the reformer must change the way they go about doing science. But the transformation which Bacon sought to accomplish was even more radical than this, and in a very real sense his vision was deeply antiphilosophic in that he was deeply distrustful of thinking per se. Thinking is above all an activity of the individual mind. It is intrasubjective and personal. Its great modern exemplar is Descartes, who, away from his native land in 1619, with all of Europe descending into a long war, holed up in a stove-heated room, and with no one to talk to but himself, thought the thoughts that led to the great *Discours*. For Descartes it was solitude which allowed thinking and thinking in turn — even prior to the observation of nature — which laid the foundations for science.

Bacon's effort was entirely different, so that it is not too much to say that he wished to remove natural inquiry from the domain of individual thinking altogether and to assign it instead to the domain of collective labor. This entailed an externalizing and routinizing of what had previously been intrapsychic processes, so that what had formerly belonged to the domain of the thinking individual was now made part of the regimented routine of the organized community. Phases of inquiry were no longer conceived as successive subjective activities of a single thinking individual but as the successive objectified labors of specialized groups of workers. And the rule which governed the process as a whole was not a philosophic, Cartesian self-discipline but rather a social discipline whose paradigms were drawn from the realm of government and law. Put this way — admittedly a radical and provocative formulation — Bacon's schemes for organizing science cannot be seen as merely ancillary to an essentially philosophic program. On the contrary, they constitute what is perhaps most startlingly new in his attempted reformation of the commonwealth of learning.

Bacon's scheme to organize scientific inquiry on a collective basis has not, of course, gone unnoticed by scholars, and indeed, it has become a commonplace to find in Bacon's writings, and particularly in the description of Salomon's House which occurs in the *New Atlantis,* an inspiration for the Royal Society founded shortly after the Restoration. The tendency to see the Royal Society as an embodiment of Bacon's ideas has become so habitual that few scholars have read what Bacon has to say about scientific organization with sufficient care to recognize the tremendous differences between Bacon's conception and the self-styled "Baconian" society of the 1660s.

Among the scholars who make more than a passing mention of his organizational ideas, most assimilate these conceptions too quickly to an overall assessment of Bacon as an intellectual progressive without pausing sufficiently to grasp the specific character of these ideas or to interpret them in the light the whole body of his thought about human affairs. Thus Paolo Rossi has written of the "public, democratic, and collaborative character" of Bacon's vision of organized science; Benjamin Farrington, of Baconian science as "publicly organised collaboration" which is "democratic." Christopher Hill has suggested that Bacon's ideas about collaborative science amount to a "democratization" of intellectual life.[2]

Indeed, retrospectively, it might seem natural that a man so committed to progress through collaboration should likewise share the modern predilection for democracy, equality, and freedom. Such an idea is obviously congenial to Rossi, Farrington, and Hill, all of whom are intent on making Bacon a prophet of modernity in a wide range of senses including his views on human beings and human organization. Such a construction of Bacon's organizational ideas, however, flies so wide of the mark as to create serious misconceptions.

When we turn to Bacon's ideas about the organization of science we will find that he urges a tightly controlled, rigidly regimented, and deeply authoritarian organization for science and that the whole conception is very nearly the complete opposite of those accounts which seek to impute to it democratic, egalitarian, and libertarian impulses. Indeed Bacon's ideas about scientific organization closely parallel his thoughts about organizing human enterprise in general and appear to draw heavily on his ideas about civil life and civil government at large.

As he set out to conceptualize an organized science, Bacon first sought to establish a select and exclusive membership, a community of scientists which was set apart from the mass of vulgar humanity in order to rise above them and accomplish the special tasks of scientific inquiry. This select and exclusive community, moreover, was itself subject to an internal regimen in which the labors of scientific inquirers were not merely joined (as in a team), but also rigidly regulated — a regimen which narrowly directed the members of the community, which constrained them, and which prescribed what they might and might not legitimately do. The organization which Bacon envisioned aspired to be comprehensive in the sense that virtually all the human factors which might bear on the success of scientific inquiry were to be brought under the jurisdiction of the regimen with little left to chance or to the free play of human faculties. Finally, like his conception of society at large Bacon's conception of scientific organization was essentially hierarchical and authoritarian, with clear lines of control running from the top downward so as to rationalize and direct the entire enterprise.

The plan to organize science is often conceived principally as an attempt merely to multiply the human collective power to dominate nature by coordinating the efforts of individuals and assuring the continuity of these efforts across generations. Although this interpretation is accurate as far as it goes, it is too limited since it neglects Bacon's conviction that an increase in collective power requires a curtailment of individual freedom. In Bacon's view the program for the discovery of true and useful knowledge required that human energies and efforts be harnessed, rationalized, directed, and controlled in a new way.

Thus Bacon's program for a new natural science, so often conceived as signaling the advent of a new relationship between man and nature, also reflects a new attitude toward humanity. People are now seen as factors in the production of knowledge. They must be understood as such and deployed as crucial elements in a rational system for the discovery and refinement of natural knowledge. They become, in other words, a kind of matériel to be used and, from the standpoint of the scientific planner or director, objects to be arranged, manipulated, and deployed, rather than fellow subjects to be counselled and advised.

All of this brings into focus one of the central intentions of Bacon's organizational efforts: control. Bacon was not content merely to exhort people to scientific inquiry nor, in turn, to furnish them an edifying example. His conception of human nature gave him little confidence that exhortation or example would establish the conditions for good science. The control he sought would operate at nearly every level of the scientific enterprise, and amounted to a kind of government.

There are many unmistakable similarities between his conception of science and his larger political outlook, but there is one point, at least, where the task of organizing science presented a peculiar set of problems. Whereas Bacon could enter the already established government of Elizabeth or James and shape the policies of an authority that was already constituted, the commonwealth of learning must be founded. Thus Bacon's ideas about organizing science necessarily addressed some of the problems of founding in general and called for a special kind of wisdom and cunning. Bacon regarded the existing community of scholars to be an anarchy — without legitimate authority and without law. From this perspective, much of Bacon's rhetorical effort will be seen not so much as a general call for men to do science as an attempt to persuade them to acquiesce in the establishment of a new quasi-governmental authority in the realm of learning and to submit to a regimen which, though directly at odds with the spontaneous impulses of human nature, was nonetheless necessary to scientific progress.

The predicament of the founder, however, only partly indicates Bacon's problem, for the organization or community which he hoped to inaugurate was not, of course, an autonomous and self-contained society made from the unsocialized but a new community with a special mission formed within an already existing state. This meant that he might be able to count on assistance of the existing political authorities to aid in the founding and support of the new community and shelter the scientific enterprise within the existing social order. From this perspective, the establishment of an organized science resembles not so much the founding of an absolutely new state as, say, the planting of a colony. We have already seen that in his remarks on plantations Bacon was concerned to see that the right men were selected to begin the enterprise, that some were chosen for certain virtues while others were excluded on account of their vices, that the relationship between the colony and the impatient sponsors of the colony in the mother country be carefully regulated to prevent the subversion of the enterprise by premature profit taking, that a suitable political regimen be instituted, and so forth. But, the fact that the scientific enterprise must be launched within an existing social order also meant that Bacon had to concern himself with certain potentially disturbing effects that a dynamic intellectual community dedicated to innovation might have upon the larger civil order which rested on apparently changeless custom.

Thus as a founder, Bacon had to balance his concern with the internal dynamics of the new community of science against his solicitude for the problematic relations between this body of scientists and the larger body politic. In his attempts to address both sets of issues, Bacon's conservative instincts never failed him.

ORGANIZATION, NATURE, AND METHOD

Bacon's conception of organized science is closely related to his belief that the discovery of nature's fundamental laws was an essentially finite task. Put simply, Bacon believed that the profusion of natural effects resulted from a relatively simple set of causes and cloaked a simplicity of structure. The fundamental constituents of nature were a finite set of "forms," the discovery of whose operation was the task of science and the key to whose laws was the inductive method.

While there has been considerable disagreement about Bacon's view of nature — whether it is, for example, mechanistic or alchemical — there are certain features which it must possess if Bacon's conception of method is to make sense. Mary Hesse has identified some of the assumptions about nature which lie at the heart of Bacon's entire project. Essentially, Hesse points out, Bacon holds to a closed or "finite" view of nature: "Bacon remarks that whereas the number of particulars in the universe is very large and perhaps infinite, the number of species or abstract natures or forms of things is few."[3] Bacon's method further assumes that the "simple natures" (i.e., the visible footprints of forms by which forms come to be known) are likewise finite and can be exhaustively enumerated at the outset. Thus, not only are the ultimate constituents of nature finite in number, but also finite are the sensible units which are to be sifted by the process of induction. Without this assumption it would not be possible to draw "conclusive inductions" by the method of exclusions by negative instances. The method assumes that the scientist can always contrive experiments to eliminate all natures which are secondary and accidental to the fundamental forms whose workings are sought. Finally, Bacon assumes "a one-to-one correspondence between the form and the nature under investigation," or, one might say, between the elemental units of phenomenal nature and the hidden elements of working nature. Given these assumptions about the constitution of nature, Hesse notes in a striking conclusion to the section, Bacon's famed *induction* is actually a kind of deduction "based on experimental rejection of the consequents of all but one of a limited number of possibilities."[4]

Bacon himself sometimes called nature "labyrinthine," to communicate its complexity and the difficulties facing the scientist. But a labyrinth is really quite a simple structure, capable of systematic and exhaustive exploration, if only one can be sure at the outset that it is finite. Paths may be systematically explored and dead ends systematically eliminated until the correct passage is discovered. Bacon's image thus betrays (unconsciously perhaps) a set of simplifying assumptions which give an important clue to the outlook by which both his method and his conception of organization seemed warranted. Bacon's method presupposes that it is possible to move systematically from the appearances of the phenomenal world to the ultimate constituent parts of nature—the forms—and, in the application of scientific knowledge to the manipulation of nature, and back again. The method is a kind of systematic sifting which makes use of both observation and experiment. Inquiry by this method is seen as having an end—a conclusion in which the fundamental parts and the fundamental laws of nature come to be known finally and fully.

Bacon's whole approach to the problem of scientific inquiry, which is only partially and imperfectly conveyed when the focus is on observation and experimentation, relies on the closed character of the natural order which is under investigation. It is this view of nature that makes systematic induction imaginable. It is this view that makes the study of nature, in turn, a work to be done—in the sense of completed—rather than an ongoing and open-ended inquiry. It is the completable character of the inquiry, finally, which gives rise to the grandiose rhetoric of the project—the "Great Instauration," the restoration of Adam's dominion over the creatures—and promises the grand fruits that would so dramatically improve the human estate.

If this view of nature stands logically behind Bacon's view of method, it likewise furnishes the psychological and moral justification for the severe conception of organization in which liberty is to be sacrificed in the interest of productive discipline. Bacon is well aware that the demands which science makes are great and further that they run sharply against the grain of human nature. People are impatient of the constraints that the regimen of science will impose on them and find it difficult to defer the dangerous satisfactions of hastily drawn conclusions and premature attempts at useful application. It is precisely because the unravelling of nature can be completed in a way that is both exhaustive and certain that Bacon thinks some at least may find the will to submit themselves to the regimen and delay the gratification of premature axiomizing and application. The vision of a closed natural system which is susceptible to systematic and exhaustive inquiry and which can thus be made to yield certain and useful knowledge, therefore, makes possible a promise of completion which will function psychologically and morally as a kind of landfall that makes possible the hardships of the voyage.

To Bacon the cosmos itself seemed to mirror in its simplicity, intelligibility, and ultimate manageability the civil order of England. It had its ranks and orders, its hierarchy, and its principles of functional integration. Knowledge of these would allow its manipulation by means of rationally applied policy. Though there is still much to be known about Bacon's philosophy of nature, these things may be said with some confidence, and they provide an important key to understanding the conviction that lay behind his efforts at organizing scientific inquiry along new lines.

THE PARABLE OF THE OBELISK AND THREE CORE CONCEPTS

I n his preface to the *Novum Organum* Bacon used a provocative parable to convey the predicament of science and to indicate the course that it must follow.

Let us suppose that some vast obelisk were (for the decoration of a triumph or some such magnificence) to be removed from its place, and that men should set to work upon it with their naked hands, would not any sober spectator think them mad? And if they should then send for more people, thinking that in that way they might manage it, would he not think them all the madder? And if they then proceeded to make a selection, putting away the weaker hands, and using only the strong and vigorous, would he not think them madder than ever? And if lastly, not content with this, they resolved to call in aid the art of athletics, and required all their men to come with hands, arms, and sinews well anointed and medicated according to the rules of the art, would he not cry out that they were only taking pains to show a kind of method and discretion in their madness? Yet just so it is that men proceed in matters intellectual — with just the same kind of mad effort and useless combination of forces — when they hope great things either from the number and cooperation or from the excellency and acuteness of individual

*wits; yea, and when they endeavor by logic (which may be considered
as a kind of athletic art) to strengthen the sinews of the understanding,
and yet with all this study and endeavor it is apparent to any true
judgment that they are but applying the naked intellect all the time;
whereas in every great work to be done by the hand of man it is mani-
festly impossible, without instruments and machinery,* [sine instrumen-
tis et machinis] *either for the strength of each to be exerted or the
strength of all to be united.*[5]

Neither the individual mind, no matter how brilliant or well-directed by
method, nor the collective efforts of many, no matter how well-intentioned and hard-working, would allow men to raise the obelisk. The
work of each must be properly directed while the exertions of all were
united and coordinated for the feat to be done. For this, men needed
"instruments" and "machines."

There has been so much written on the growing role of scientific
instruments in the progress of natural inquiry during the seventeenth
century that it is tempting to imagine that such devices are what Bacon
had in mind when he wrote of "instruments and machines," and yet the
context clearly refutes this construction. The instruments and machines
which Bacon describes here are not the mechanical, chemical, or optical
devices used to conduct inquiries but rather devices that allow the labor-
ers themselves to be deployed and directed. They are the means by which
the entire enterprise of science was to be organized.

The parable illustrates the way in which Bacon's plan for the reform
of science demands more than the redirection of mental operations at the
level of the individual psyche and more than the enlisting of many in a
common task. Bacon conceived the inquiry into nature as a single grand
work, toward the accomplishment of which people must be organized
and directed in a radically new way. It is people themselves upon which
Bacon's imagination has set to work here. It is people who pose the most
problematic challenge to the would-be reformer of science. It is people—
even more than nature—who form the proper object of Bacon's attention, and it is to the reorganization of the social aspects of science that
Bacon devoted his most concerted and interesting efforts. The problem
of organization was hardly ancillary in Bacon's view, hardly a secondary
matter of implementing an essentially philosophical shift. Rather, it was
the core issue of the intellectual reformation to which this deeply political man devoted himself.

It is to the various "instruments and machines" which Bacon created
to deploy and direct the energies of human beings—to his ideas about

the organization of science—that the remainder of this book is devoted. In the parable of the obelisk, Bacon used the images and language of work to depict the problematic character of organization. In other places, as we shall see, he would use political or military imagery. At times he seemed to discuss the new enterprise almost as if it were to be a new religion, though more often his approach is purely secular. We have already seen that Bacon's conception of public policy was broad enough to embrace work, war, and religion. His shifts in imagery when discussing science must not be allowed to obscure the fact that here, too, Bacon saw himself as a policymaker arranging and directing activities for the accomplishment of socially desirable ends.

Three ideas and three texts will serve to suggest the major axes of Bacon's scheme for organizing science. The first is the idea of collaboration, and the text is *Valerius Terminus,* probably written around 1603. The idea of scientific collaboration seems so natural to us that a discussion might appear unnecessary. For Bacon, however, the need for collaboration was something that had to be established, and it is closely and substantively tied to many of his other ideas about what science should be and what it should accomplish. Second is the idea that the activity of science must not merely be carried on by a group of collaborators but must also be organized, and here the crucial text is the *Great Instauration* of 1620. The very idea that the activity of inquiry can be broken down into a prescribed sequence of discrete steps and that the labors of people must be subjected to a prescribed regimen is an interesting notion. It presupposes a certain view of nature and a distinctive attitude toward humans and to the human intellect. Finally, there is Bacon's explicit suggestion in the *De Augmentis* of 1623 that the commonwealth of learning, like the greater commonwealth, might be ordered by a kind of intellectual government. Here Bacon formulated the problem of organized learning in a way that is explicitly political and gave reasons why he believed a political treatment of science was warranted.

THE NEED FOR COLLABORATION

T he *Valerius Terminus on the Interpretation of Nature* is one of Bacon's earliest writings to explore in nascent form many of the ideas and themes which would come to define Bacon's project for a new natural science. At the very outset, Bacon is eager to make clear the "limits and ends" of natural knowledge, and it is here that he most clearly subordinates (though in a perfunctory way) natural science to religion. Knowledge of nature must not be confused with religious or moral knowledge and must forever be subordinate to these. If this is accepted, however, there can be no danger attaching to the inquiry into nature; indeed natural science would seem to be religiously sanctioned. Adam was the first scientist, possessing the "pure light of natural knowledge" whereby he was able "to give every living creature a name according to his propriety." It was not this knowledge of nature that caused his fall, but rather "an aspiring desire to attain to that part of moral knowledge which defineth of good and evil, whereby to dispute God's commandments and not to depend upon the revelation of his will."[6] God has made man to know and to want to know nature, and he "hath set the world in man's heart."[7] Moreover, Bacon interprets the prophecy of Daniel — "Many shall pass to and fro, and science shall be increased" — to indicate the special blessing of his own age, "as if the opening of the world by navigation and commerce and the further discovery of knowledge should meet in one time or age."[8] Finally, Bacon finds in science a means of fulfilling the Christian injunction to charitable works, "the benefit and relief of the state and society of man."[9]

Having thus suggested the Christian and transcendent boundaries of science and having invoked the image of Adam naming the creatures with the "pure light of natural knowledge," Bacon goes on to make an important and often-ignored qualification which — the allusion to Daniel's prophecy notwithstanding — decisively establishes science as a post-lapsarian, secular enterprise demanding worldly wisdom for its fulfillment. This cautions strongly against an eschatological interpretation of Bacon's practical program. In some points, he says, the curse of Adam is "peremptory and not to be removed."[10] Bacon argues therefore "that vanity must be the end in all human effects, eternity being resumed, though the revolutions and periods may be delayed." He also asserts "that the consent of the creature being now turned into reluctation, this power [over nature] cannot otherwise be exercised and administered but with labour, as well in inventing as in executing."[11]

This definition of scientific inquiry as labor is important not only to the remaining arguments of the *Valerius Terminus* but to the character of Bacon's entire enterprise, since it clearly assimilates the predicament of science to a familiar category of human activity and suggests that new attention must be paid to the organization of human effort. Throughout his life Bacon would return to religious rhetoric when discussing the ends of science and its lofty moral character, yet the program which he devised and refined in his subsequent writings is overwhelmingly secular in character. In nominally subordinating science to religion, Bacon had also drawn a line of demarcation, such that natural science would be guaranteed almost complete autonomy within its own sphere, so long as it did not cross the line.

The secular character of Bacon's approach becomes clear in the remainder of the *Valerius Terminus* where Bacon turns to analyzing the failure of natural science in the past and to prescribing some of the ways by which it might be successful in the future. Here Bacon enunciates many of the ideas which were to become hallmarks of his thought.

Among the "impediments" which Bacon discusses in the remainder of the *Valerius,* one of the most important is that there was little or no collaboration or continuity of scientific labor in the past. His first point in this regard concerns the overwhelmingly local character of life in distant times:

> At that time the world was altogether home-bred, every nation looked little beyond their own confines or territories, and the world had no through lights then as it hath had since by commerce and navigation, whereby there could neither be that contribution of wits one to help another, nor that variety of particulars for the correcting of customary conceits. [12]

Just as there was no larger community of scientists, whose labors might supplement and correct one another's, so there was no cumulative development of science over time:

> As there could be no great collection of wits of several parts or nation, so neither could there be any succession of wits of several times, whereby one might refine the other, in regard they had not history to any purpose. And the manner of their traditions was utterly unfit and unproper for amplification of knowledge. [13]

To the extent that people in this distant time were moved at all by a spirit of collective or collaborative enterprise, their energies were absorbed, according to Bacon, by the immediate need to stabilize and build civil society.

> The studies of those times, you shall find, besides wars, incursions, and rapines, which were then almost everywhere betwixt states adjoining (the use of leagues and confederacies being not then known), were to populate by multitude of wives and generation, a thing at this day in the waster part of the West-Indies principally affected; and to build sometimes for habitation towns and cities, sometimes for fame and

memory monuments, pyramids, colosses, and the like. And if there
happened to rise up any more civil wits; then would he found and erect
some new laws, customs, and usages, such as now of late years, when
the world was revolute almost to the like rudeness and obscurity, we see
both in our own nation and abroad many examples of, as well in a
number of tenures reserved upon men's lands, as in divers customs of
towns and manors, being the devices that such wits wrought upon in
such times of deep ignorance.[14]

"Civil" talents, in other words, were otherwise occupied than with science.

In such a condition "the length of one man's life hath been the greatest measure of knowledge,"[15] and there commenced the long tradition in which philosophizing was only an activity of the individual. To clarify his point by way of contrast, Bacon adduces the example of the mechanical arts. In the perfecting of mechanical devices, one person may invent but many come along to refine, improve, and perfect. In the realm of science, however, there are only dominating individuals who philosophize egocentrically and crowds of followers who "compound and abridge." There is no true collaboration and no true improvement.

It is true that the past has produced a kind of pseudocollaboration — a "pretended succession of wits" — insofar as each of the great individual thinkers has attracted a crowd of followers. But the schools or sects which arose upon the thought of some great philosopher did not build on whatever kernels of truth or promising beginnings they had inherited. On the contrary, because there was no order or system to any of these pseudocollaborations, valuable ideas tended to be lost. Cicero is supposed to have said that "time weeds out the fiction of 'Opinion' and eliminates 'ungrounded persuasion.' "[16] Bacon's view is precisely the opposite:

Time is like a river which carrieth down things which are light and
blown up, and sinketh and drowneth that which is sad and weighty. For
howsoever governments have several forms, sometimes one governing,
sometimes few, sometimes the multitude; yet the state of knowledge is
ever a Democratie, *and that prevaileth which is most agreeable to the*
senses and conceits of people.[17]

The "Democratie" of public opinion, therefore, does not constitute true collaboration when truth is sought.

True collaboration, according to Bacon, will require organization, and when he offers a political image to indicate what organization might mean it is far from that of Democratie. As he prepares to leave the question of collaboration, the image he invokes is an imperial one.

> So then we see that this note leadeth us to an administration of knowledge in some such order and policy as the king of Spain in regard of his great dominions useth in state; who though he hath particular councils for several countries and affairs, yet hath one council of State of last resort, that receiveth the advertisements and certificates from all the rest.[18]

True collaboration can occur, in other words, only where there is an organizing authority to divide the work to be done into parts and to oversee the completion and integration of those parts.

The *Valerius Terminus* offers a clear, if brief and undeveloped, statement of the need for scientific collaboration, of the inadequacy of past pseudocollaboration, and of the organizational preconditions for collaboration in the future. By establishing that natural science must be considered an attempt at postlapsarian improvement — that it is a variety of labor and that, however much it must obey the laws of charity and religion as to its boundaries and ends, it is in its accomplishment a secular task — Bacon lays the groundwork for addressing the predicament of science in secular terms. In his analysis of the causes for the failure of science in the past, Bacon places the question of collaboration in an essentially civil framework. In the future, the search for natural truth must be organized more tightly and as a kind of imperial enterprise in which oversight and the power to regulate are invested in a single supreme authority.

Already in this early work, we see a clear indication of some of the ways that collaboration would mean more than the mere joining of human energies. It required that the designer of a collaborative science think in civil terms, be attuned to the propensities of people — their strengths and weaknesses — and to the history of learning's failures. It required that the designers think not merely in terms of truth, but also in terms of power and that they be prepared not merely to exhort but to command.

THE NEED FOR ORGANIZATION

Having arrived at the idea that the inquiry into nature was a labor to be performed by people working in concert, it was important for Bacon to show the way in which the work could be organized. The idea that natural science could be presented as a single project, with differentiated and sequenced parts, is implicit in much of Bacon's writing from the first decade of the seventeenth century, but the clearest overview of the project as a whole came in 1620 with the publication of the *Great Instauration* preceding the *Novum Organum*. Here Bacon showed how the activity of scientific inquiry could be organized into parts, which taken together would yield certain and useful knowledge.

The plan to rationalize and direct the *activity* of scientific inquiry is also, of course, a plan to direct the *people* to whom the inquiry is entrusted. This might go without saying, were it not for the fact that Bacon was far from believing people to be naturally suited to the procedure which he advocated. It is this unsuitedness of the spontaneously acting human mind for science that throws the coercive intent of the Great Instauration into relief and reminds us that organizing humans and human works is no easier in the little commonwealth of learning than in the commonwealth of society as a whole.

In the "Proem" and "Preface" which precede the presentation of the plan of the Great Instauration, Bacon makes it clear that the organization of the project is designed to bridge the gap between the demands of nature and the liabilities of humans. On the one hand is the "labyrinthine" character of the natural order:

> *The universe to the eye of the human understanding is framed like a labyrinth, presenting as it does on every side so many ambiguities of way, such deceitful resemblances of objects and signs, natures so irregular in their lines and so knotted and entangled.*[19]

On the other, is the incapacity of the unaided intellect:

> *The entire fabric of human reason which we employ in the inquisition of nature is badly put together and built up. . . .*[20]
> *The human intellect left to its own course is not to be trusted. . . .*[21]
> *Neither the natural force of man's judgment nor even any accidental felicity offers any chance of success. No excellence of wit, no repetition of chance experiments, can overcome such difficulties as these.*[22]

It is not just an indictment of ratiocination that Bacon intends here, but also of the senses and even of experimentation and observation that are undertaken piecemeal. Thus he writes of "the uncertain light of the sense, sometimes shining out, sometimes clouded over, through the woods of experience and particulars"[23] and belittles the achievement of experimenters "who have committed themselves to the waves of experience and almost turned mechanics," yet whose efforts amount to a kind of "wandering inquiry" without profit or end.

It is quite wrong, as is so often done, to equate Baconian induction and Bacon's Great Instauration with unfettered observation and experimentation. Bacon reacted against experimentation which was not tightly directed ("wandering inquiry") quite as strongly as he did against whose overrational kinds of natural philosophy which were all notion and completely lacking in empirically derived substance. His Great Instauration, thus, was to be a cure not only for Aristotelian scholasticism but also for a variety of popular empirical and experimental approaches to knowledge.

What is most needed, Bacon is at pains to stress as he embarks on a presentation of the Great Instauration, is a new organization of inquiry. If the inquiry into nature were to succeed at all it must cease to be what it had formerly been: "a whirling round about, and perpetual agitation, ending where it began" (*in iis vero quae jam fiunt circa scientias, est vertigo quaedam et agitatio perpetua et circulus*).[24] It is not only that inquiry has proceeded without plan or reason, but that it exhibits as well all of the most lawless propensities of men themselves, and in introducing his plan for the Great Instauration Bacon invokes the most powerful language to make his point. Thus, he reiterates his condemnation of intellectual democracy which reduces all inquiry to anarchy:

> For however various are the forms of civil polities, there is but one form of polity in the sciences; and that always has been and always will be popular. Now the doctrines which find most favor with the populace are those which are either contentions and pugnacious, or specious and empty—such, I say, as either entangle assent or tickle it. And therefore no doubt the greatest wits in each successive age have been forced out of their own course: men of capacity and intellect above the vulgar having been fain, for reputation's sake, to bow to the judgment of the time and the multitude; and thus if any contemplations of a higher order took light anywhere, they were presently blown out by the winds of vulgar opinions. So that Time is like a river which has brought down to us things light and puffed up, while those which are weighty and solid have sunk.[25]

Men have sustained the anarchy and lawlessness of inquiry by their own love of "promiscuous liberty" which has undermined the "severity of inquiry" (*promiscua quaerendii licentia severitatem inquisitionis enervarunt*).[26] But, as Bacon repeatedly emphasizes, "the human intellect left to its own course is not to be trusted" (*intellectum humanum sibi permissim merito suspectum esse debere*).[27]

The work must be organized and the labor regulated. There is, Bacon says, "but one course left, therefore — to try the whole thing anew upon a better plan" (*melioribus praesidiis*).[28] For "wandering inquiry" must be substituted what Spedding translates as a "regular system of operations" but which is more literally rendered as "fixed law" (*in ipsa experientia erraticam quandam inquisitionem exercent, nec ei certa lege militant*).[29] Also note the contrast of the verbs in the Latin, *exerceo* connoting "being at work on" or "being busy with," while *milito* conveys the much more disciplined and regimented sense of "making war on." The whole project must be rationalized: "No excellence of wit, no repetition of chance experiments, can overcome such difficulties as these. Our steps must be guided by a clue, and the whole way from the very first perception of the senses must be laid out upon a sure plan."[30] Much of the language that Bacon uses to introduce his argument for planned inquiry is suggestive of political and military discipline, and it is quite clear from his prefatory remarks that the idea of organizing the *activity* of inquiry is closely tied to the idea of organizing the *inquirers themselves*.

We already know from our discussion of his political ideas that for Bacon any attempt to organize people for a given social activity involves elements of coercion and constraint, and it is reasonable to ask whether his ideas about organizing the inquiry into nature involves a similar dimension. Bacon sometimes refers to his plan as providing "helps" or *auxilia* to human inquiry[31] and to his method as an "organum," which is variously translated as "implement," "instrument," or "machine."[32] These terms emphasize that way in which the Great Instauration will increase human powers, but alongside them and balancing them is another set of terms which emphasize the element of constraint. In his prefatory remarks, as we have seen, Bacon explicitly condemns "promiscuous liberty" and invokes the idea of "fixed law." In a similar way, at the level of diction rather than of discursive argumentation, Bacon introduces suggestive pairings of words to describe the relationship which he intends to establish between his plan and those who carry it out. The following lines are a case in point: "[I ask men,] being now freed and guarded by the securities and helps which I offer from the errors and impediments of the way, to come forward themselves and take part in that which remains to be done."[33] Bacon's pairing of the terms "freed" and "guarded" (*liberati et muniti*) and "security and helps" (*praesidiis et auxiliis*) is surely intended to convey his belief that an augmentation of human power was dependent upon people accepting a new sort of discipline and new constraints, and this is particularly likely given the military connotations of *praesidium* and *muniti*.

Bacon's presentation of his plan for organizing the inquiry into nature is, in fact, filled with the language and imagery of constraint and discipline—of lawful order, one might say, in contrast to promiscuous liberty—much of it drawn from the language of civil and military life, and as we now turn to the plan itself we shall need to be as attentive to this aspect of the presentation as much as to the discursive arguments. Imagery and language alert us to the everpresent connections between Bacon's ideas about organizing scientific inquiry and his more general ideas on social and political organization, and they show the way in which the characterization of collective science in political terms introduced themes of discipline and authority into his reflections on inquiry and knowledge.

The Great Instauration was to consist of six sequenced parts, and these Bacon listed at the very beginning of his presentation:

  1. The Divisions of the Sciences
  2. The Novum Organum; *or Directions Concerning the Interpretation of Nature*
  3. The Phenomena of the Universe; or a Natural and Experimental History for the Foundation of Philosophy
  4. The Ladder of the Intellect
  5. The Forerunners; or Anticipations of the New Philosophy
  6. The New Philosophy; or Active Science.[34]

Let us examine each part or phase of the work in turn.

The work was to begin with an account of "the division of the sciences," that is, "a summary or general description of the knowledge which the human race at present possesses" in order that "the old may be more easily made perfect and the new more easily approached."[35] Likening this work to geographical exploration, Bacon suggested that, "We will therefore make a coasting voyage along the shores of the arts and sciences received."[36] The aim here is to discover which departments of learning had been well treated and which were lacking. Subjects that were well developed already were likened to gardens—an image already familiar to us from Bacon's political writings. But "there are found in the intellectual as in the terrestrial globe waste regions as well as cultivated ones [*culta*]."³⁷ When some desert area was discovered, Bacon said, he intended not only to note the deficiency but to indicate how the work was to proceed—either by directions [*praecepta*] or by an example "executed by myself as a sample of the whole."³⁸ At the end of this section, Bacon likens his program to a military occupation with himself as the commander. "I do not propose merely to survey these regions in my mind, like an augur taking auspices, but to enter them like a general [*dux*] who means to take possession."³⁹ This part of the Great Instauration was the subject of the *Advancement of Learning* and the later Latin expansion of this work, the *De Augmentis Scientiarum*.

The second phase of the Great Instauration was the *Novum Organum,* an inductive logic to supplant deductive logic and the older, faulty induction of antiquity. To this part belonged "the doctrine concerning the better and more perfect use of human reason in the inquisition of things, and the true helps of the understanding, that thereby (as far as the condition of mortality and humanity allows) the intellect may be raised and exalted, and made capable of overcoming the difficulties and obscurities of nature."⁴⁰ At every point along the way in this discussion, the characteristic features of the *Novum Organum* are developed as correctives to the characteristic failings of the old logic and of the undisciplined human mind. For all its highly formalized and abstract character, there is a sense in which for Bacon the most glaring weaknesses of traditional logic stemmed from the fact that it enshrined and legitimized rather than corrected the natural failings of the mind. Bacon's critique of traditional logic is thus also a critique of natural psychology. Bacon faulted traditional logic (or, as he calls it, "vulgar" logic) on three counts—the end aimed at, the "order of demonstration," and the "starting point of the inquiry"—and on each count presented his own Organum as a remedy.

Vulgar logic had been fashioned as a tool for disputation, and as such it reflected all the personal limitations of those who sought to establish "dictatorships" in the realm of opinion. The aim of Bacon's logic was quite different:

> For the end which this science of mine proposes is the invention not of arguments but of arts; not of things in accordance with principles, but of principles themselves; not of probable reasons, but of designations and directions for works. And as the intention is different, so accordingly is the effect; the effect of the one being to overcome an opponent in argument, of the other to command nature in action.⁴¹

Vulgar logic sanctioned and legitimized the mind's natural tendency to

leap from particulars to general propositions, an act which in a psychological context Bacon referred to as "anticipation." Bacon's attack here
focused mainly on the syllogism:

> *Hitherto the proceeding has been to fly at once from the sense and*
> *particulars up to the most general propositions, as certain fixed poles*
> *for the argument to turn upon, and from these to derive the rest by*
> *middle terms—a short way, no doubt, but precipitate and one which*
> *will never lead to nature, though it offers an easy and ready way to*
> *disputation.*[42]

The new logic is both constraining and enabling, curbing the natural
tendency of the mind to fly from particular to general and at the same
time substituting a more orderly, measured, and solid ascent:

> *Now my plan is to proceed regularly and gradually from one axiom to*
> *another, so that the most general are not reached till the last: but then*
> *when you do come to them you find them to be not empty notions, but*
> *well defined, and such as nature would really recognise as her first*
> *principles, and such as lie at the heart and marrow of things.*[43]

Interestingly, Bacon does not argue for scrapping vulgar logic entirely but invokes the legal and administrative idea of jurisdiction to
define the domains over which the old and the new logics will hold sway:

> *Although, therefore, I leave to the syllogism and these famous and*
> *boasted modes of demonstration their jurisdiction over popular arts*
> *and such as are matter of opinion (in which department I leave all as it*
> *is), yet in dealing with the nature of things I use induction throughout,*
> *and that in the minor propositions as well as the major.*[44]

The invocation of the concept of jurisdiction echoes Bacon's notion,
discussed already, that each domain of learning must be subject to its
own law.

Vulgar logic, in Bacon's view, took on trust and as its starting point
precisely those ideas it was most necessary to question, most particularly
ordinary experience and ordinary language, both of which reflected the
workings of the undisciplined, ungoverned mind.

> *I begin the inquiry nearer the sources than men have done heretofore,*
> *submitting to examination those things which the common logic takes*
> *on trust. . . .*[45]

> *Now what the sciences stand in need of is a form of induction which shall analyze experience and take it to pieces, and by a due process of exclusion and rejection lead to an inevitable conclusion.*[46]

Vulgar logic has implicated hitherto existing sciences in the vulgarity of the undisciplined mind. The new logic must be given a new *imperium* or authority.

> *I hold that true logic ought to enter the several provinces of science* [singulas scientiarum provincias] *armed with a higher authority* [imperio] *than belongs to the principles of those sciences themselves, and ought to call those putative principles to account until they are fully established.*[47]

What Bacon is suggesting when he proposes the establishment of a new *imperium* in the commonwealth of learning is something like an inquisition to root out the errors that have been intruded by the vulgar mind: "There is not one of the impressions taken by the intellect when left to go its own way, but I hold it as suspect and no way established until it has submitted to a new trial and a fresh judgment has been thereupon pronounced."[48]

If Bacon's new logic aimed at correcting the errors of traditional logic with its unwarranted incorporation of vulgar notions, it is not fair to characterize Bacon's method as empirical in any simple sense of the word, and his whole presentation is as much a critique of sensory knowledge as of the notions of the mind. "For the testimony and information of the sense has reference always to man, not to the universe; and it is a great error to assert that the sense is the measure of things."[49] It is true that Bacon relied heavily on experimentation as part of his inductive method but also true that his idea of experiment was elaborated almost in opposition to his idea of sensory knowledge. Even acknowledging that the power of the senses could be magnified by specially designed instruments, Bacon expressed a preference for experimental over sensory knowledge:

> *The subtlety of experiments is far greater than that of the sense itself, even when assisted by exquisite instruments — such experiments, I mean, as are skillfully and artificially devised for the express purpose of determining the point in question. To the immediate and proper perception of the sense, therefore, I do not give much weight; but I contrive that the office of the sense shall be only to judge of the experiment, and that the experiment itself shall judge of the thing.*[50]

Experimentation, in any case, was not itself the primary path to knowledge of nature but was rather a means of answering questions that had already been posed by the process of induction. Experiments are works of art, and art is to be substituted for the spontaneous workings of the senses. The senses are removed from the immediate process of acquiring knowledge and are made judges once-removed. They are to operate henceforth only within a prescribed routine or discipline which both curbs their spontaneity and delimits their role. The art that frames questions, designs experiments, and thus stands as a manager of the senses is the new logic that Bacon has sought to create.

In his effort to discipline the senses and define their place in the organization of inquiry, Bacon invoked another image drawn from outside the realm of learning, though this time neither civil nor military but sacerdotal. "I conceive that I perform the office of a true priest of the sense (from which all knowledge of nature must be sought, unless men mean to go mad) and a not unskillful interpreter of its oracles."[51] Against the background of religious struggle over the role of the priesthood, this is an interesting image indeed, particularly in view of the frequent attribution of a strong Puritanical element in Bacon's thought. In his relationship to nature, Bacon seems to say, humans cannot rely on a direct, spontaneous, and individual kind of knowing but must accept the "helps and guards" offered by the ministrations of a priest—a figure of enlightenment, elevation, and spiritual authority—to help them rise above the morass of vulgarity.

Bacon invokes a related image of sacramental blessing, again as part of his discussion of idols and what he sometimes called the "promiscuity" of the mind. In his doctrine of idols, Bacon provided one statement of the problems that beset the human mind when it set about inquiring into nature. The mind, Bacon thinks, is "strangely possessed and beset so that there is no true and even surface left to reflect the genuine rays of things,"[52] and it is as a remedy for this condition that his whole method and program are presented. Idols were for Bacon the deep-rooted, false notions of a general and pervasive sort, whose pernicious influence distorted the way the mind organized and interpreted all subsequent ideas and sensory data, and it is because of them, in Bacon's view, that "the mind . . . cannot be trusted."[53]

While Bacon's doctrine of idols has been much discussed and we do not need a complete review of it here, it will be useful to note just a few points. Bacon divides the idols which beset the mind into two classes: adventitious and innate. The adventitious idols "come into the mind from without—namely, either from the doctrines and sects of philosophers or from perverse rules of demonstration,"[54] and, though they may be extremely stubborn, these can be expelled with sufficient effort, to be supplanted by correct notions. The innate idols, on the other hand, are "inherent in the very nature of the intellect, which is far more prone to error than the sense is,"[55] and can never be permanently eliminated.

> *All that can be done is to point them out, so that this insidious action of the mind may be marked and reproved (else as fast as old errors are destroyed new ones will spring up out of the ill complexion of the mind itself, and so we shall have but a change of errors, and not a clearance); and to lay it down once for all as a fixed and established maxim that the intellect is not qualified to judge except by means of induction, and induction in its legitimate form.*[56]

It is the ultimate incorrigibility of the mind which renders necessary the imposition of a legitimate regimen of induction from without. Even if freed from the tyranny of the past and of past errors, on its own the mind would simply reproduce the old errors in new form. It is this actively error-producing quality of the mind which Bacon saw as illicit, wanton, and promiscuous, and he frequently invoked sexual imagery to characterize man's unwholesome intellectual desires and his fruitless intellectual pleasures. Here, however, as he concludes his description of the second part of the Great Instauration, Bacon suggests that marriage might serve as a cure for illicit relations between the mind and nature:

> *The explanation of which things, and of the true relation between the nature of things and the nature of the mind, is as the strewing and decoration of the bridal chamber of the mind and the universe* [thalamum mentis et universi], *the divine goodness assisting, out of which marriage let us hope (and be this the prayer of the bridal son) there may spring helps to man, and a line and race of inventions that may in some degree subdue and overcome the necessities and miseries of humanity.*[57]

Marriage is procreative, of course, but procreation is to take place within the framework of a legal and sacramental relationship which chastens, legitimizes, and blesses intercourse.

The new logic, to conclude, is a means for increasing the power of humans to find the truth, but it is at the same time a regimen or discipline which straitens the mind. Virtually every aspect of the new inductive logic is elaborated in part as a constraint on the inherent tendencies of the mind, and the images Bacon uses to drive home this regimenting side of the method are drawn largely from the political, legal, and military spheres.

The third part of the Great Instauration was the systematic and comprehensive compilation of natural and experimental history. If the aim of the new logic was "to keep the mind from going astray or stumbling,"[58] the aim of a systematically compiled natural history was to supply the matter on which method was to work. Sometimes Baconianism has been identified with undirected and open-ended experimentation and fact gathering, but this was certainly not what Bacon himself proposed. Existing natural histories and indeed all the matter with which science had been supplied in the past were faulted precisely on the haphazard and slipshod way in which they had been assembled. Bacon indicted virtually every sort of existing data: "The information of the sense itself, sometimes failing, sometimes false; observation, careless, irregular, and led by chance; tradition, vain, and fed on rumor; practice, slavishly bent upon its work; experiment, blind, stupid, vague, and prematurely broken off; lastly, natural history trivial and poor."[59] The poor quality of the materials with which science had worked in the past was inextricably bound up with the corruption of methods and modes of interpretation and, more generally, with the lack of any comprehensive plan. The new natural history should collect all the solid materials that were available from the past and should add the information that could be provided by directed experimentation. Natural histories should be compiled with the end of induction clearly in mind, and not randomly or in accordance with natural curiosity. The importance of experimentation lay in the fact that experiments were to be designed to answer questions that had already been posed.

> I mean it to be a history not only of nature free and at large (when she is left to her own course and does her work her own way), —such as that of the hevenly bodies, meteors, earth and sea, minerals, plants, animals, —but much more of nature under constraint and vexed; that is to say, when by art and the hand of man she is forced out of her natural state, and squeezed and moulded. Therefore I set down at length all experiments of the mechanical arts, of the operative part of the liberal arts, of the many crafts which have not yet grown into arts properly so called, so far as I have been able to examine them and as they conduce to the end in view. . . . The nature of things betrays itself more readily under the vexations of art than in its natural freedom. . . . I drag into light many things which no one who was not proceeding by a regular and certain way to the discovery of causes would have thought of inquiring after, being indeed in themselves of no great use; which shows that they were not sought for on their own account, but having just the same relation to things and works which the letters of the alphabet have

*to speech and words—which, though in themselves useless, are the
elements of which all discourse is made up.*[60]

As this passage makes quite clear, not only was nature not to be left
"free"; the inquiry itself and the inquirers were likewise to be subject to
rule.

Just as the method of induction was in part conceived as a means
for constraining the mind and checking its natural tendency to err, so too
Bacon's prescriptions for natural history are deployed to curb certain
inherent human propensities. While Baconianism has at times been identified with the search for useful knowledge, Bacon makes it quite clear
that the premature search for use can be one of the most damaging
influences on scientific inquiry. "That unseasonable and puerile hurry to
snatch by way of earnest at the first works which come within reach," he
wrote, "I utterly condemn and reject as an Atalanta's apple that hinders
the race."[61] The Great Instauration would be threatened, in other words,
by the error he discussed in relation to plantations: the impatience with
delayed gratifications and the tendency to choose present rewards, however illusory or small, over future rewards, however great. A second
danger lay in the natural human tendency to lose oneself in particulars.
"Knowing how much the sight of man's mind is distracted by experience
and history,"[62] wrote Bacon, it was important that the compiling of
natural history be accomplished under a strict guidance leading always in
the direction of legitimate induction and precluding the possibility of
being led away from the path. Yet a third danger was that in their collection of materials searchers would introduce into the history false or
confused notions which would taint the data. Bacon's organization of
inquiry into stages and his sharp separation of natural history from
induction was to be a cure for overactive minds, which were forever
projecting themselves into nature. If it were to be fit for induction the
factual material of the natural history must be free from insinuating
interpretations. These last two dangers are no more than restatements of
Bacon's criticisms of the failings of the two main traditions of science in
his own time—wandering empiricism on the one hand and rationalism or
the imaginative science of the alchemists on the other.

Just as Bacon had sought to give point to every preceding stage of
the Great Instauration by invoking images of legitimacy, law, and social
duty, so here he likened the new philosophy at the history-making stage
to a suckling infant receiving its first food[63] and called upon the inquirers to feel themselves constrained by the obligations of a nursemaid or
teacher:

It has been well observed that the fables and superstitions and follies which nurses instill into children do serious injury to their minds; and the same consideration makes me anxious, having the management of the childhood, as it were, of philosophy in its course of natural history, not to let it accustom itself in the beginning to any vanity.[64]

To the end of creating a sound natural history Bacon wished to create a moral and psychological sanction with all the force of a religious obligation: "I interpose everywhere admonitions and scruples and cautions, with a religious care (*religione*) to eject, repress, and, as it were, exorcise every kind of phantasm."[65] Bacon's sense of the dangers which the inquirers themselves posed to the inquiry was keen, and the comparisons he drew, invoking parental and religious obligation, were measured to the task.

The fourth and fifth parts of the Great Instauration represent way stations on the path leading from the beginning of induction to the completion of the long arduous process, and in proposing them at all Bacon seems implicitly to recognize how difficult the course would be. At nearly every point of the way, Bacon asked his inquirers to defer two kinds of gratification for which all people yearn: first, the gratification of an intellectual desire to escape the confusion of experience by the formulation of general, organizing ideas; second, the gratification of the desire to enjoy the material fruits of knowledge. Much of traditional learning had gone astray precisely by succumbing to one or both of these desires prematurely, and in one sense the whole program of the Great Instauration was designed to postpone premature satisfactions. Nonetheless, Bacon seems to have recognized that certain measured gratifications were necessary to retain support for the project and carry people along in their arduous labors.

The fourth part of the Great Instauration, which Bacon titled "The Ladder of the Intellect," would offer provisional intellectual gratification and encouragement by giving some successful examples of the process of induction from the compilation of natural history to the framing of more general and more truthful statements. The aim here was partly to show how the process of induction worked and partly to provide knowledge for present "use."[66] Didactic ends would be best served if subject areas were chosen that were "at once the most noble in themselves among those under inquiry, and most different one from another, that there may be an example in every kind."[67] These "anticipations" would serve as "actual types and models, by which the entire process of the mind and the whole fabric and order of invention from the beginning to the end, in certain subjects, and those various and remarkable, should be set, as it were, before the eyes."[68]

Similarly, the fifth part, which Bacon entitled "The Forerunners; or Anticipations of the New Philosophy," would make available such bits and pieces of useful and applicable knowledge as had emerged along the way:

I do not make so blindly for the end of my journey as to neglect anything useful that may turn up by the way. And therefore I include in this part such things as I have myself discovered, proved, or added — not, however, according to the true rules and method of interpretation, but by the ordinary use of the understanding in inquiring and discovering.[69]

Bacon invokes two comparisons to illustrate the function of this part. He likens it first to a "wayside inn" in which "the mind may rest and refresh itself on its journey to more certain conclusions."[70] Then, in language that emphasizes the similarities of the Great Instauration to economic enterprise in general, he compares it to a financial investment, in which consumption is deferred in the interests of long-run profit. "The fifth part," he wrote, "is for temporary use only, pending the completion of the rest, like interest payable from time to time until the principal be forthcoming."[71]

The last part of the Great Instauration was the stage in which induction led to a discovery of the most general and deepest laws of nature. Though Bacon believed that this stage would only be completed after his death, it was nonetheless the prize which justified the entire project.

The sixth part of my work (to which the rest is subservient and ministrant) discloses and sets forth that philosophy which by the legitimate, chaste, and severe course of inquiry which I have explained and provided is at length developed and established. The completion, however, of this last part is a thing both above my strength and beyond my hopes. I have made a beginning of the work — a beginning, as I hope, not unimportant: the fortune of the human race will give the issue, such an issue, it may be, as in the present condition of things and men's minds cannot easily be conceived or imagined. For the matter in hand is no mere felicity of speculation, but the real business and fortunes of the human race, and all power of operation. For man is but the servant and interpreter of nature: what he does and what he knows is only what he has observed of nature's order in fact or in thought; beyond this he

*knows nothing and can do nothing. For the chain of causes cannot by
any force be loosed or broken, nor can nature be commanded except by
being obeyed. And so those twin objects, human knowledge and human power, do really meet in one; and it is from ignorance of causes
that operation fails.*[72]

The culmination of the Great Instauration thus was to include the discovery of real causes and to lay the foundation for the practical transformation of the world. Bacon could necessarily say little about the body of
knowledge that would result from the procedure which he had outlined,
but this did not lessen his conviction that only an organized and systematic inquiry—one that was "legitimate, chaste, and severe"—would yield
a comprehensive knowledge of nature's laws to satisfy human intellectual and practical needs.

The desire to organize and systematize natural inquiry led Bacon to
conceptualize the Great Instauration as a succession of sequenced
phases, each building on its predecessor and each looking toward the
completion. This way of organizing inquiry was much more than a matter of method narrowly considered. It was a way of managing the entire
project from start to finish. Although the scheme is certainly in one
respect a means of augmenting the power of the inquirers to understand
and manipulate natural processes, it is equally a scheme for curtailing
some deep-rooted and persistent habits of mind.

The plan to organize the work of natural inquiry thus shows itself to
be likewise a plan for systematically controlling workers themselves, and
Bacon never ceases to emphasize the consequences for philosophy of the
lack of such control. His remarks on intellectual "Democratie," and
repeated variants on the same theme, which show, in Bacon's eyes, popular rule in the commonwealth of learning to be tantamount to anarchy,
argue strongly for the establishment of some kind of government in the
commonwealth of learning.

THE NEED FOR GOVERNMENT

Though the idea of governing scientific inquiry is one of the great
unifying themes of Bacon's lifework, though he continually uses
political and related imagery and language suggestive of this intention, and though his whole scheme unfolds as an analogue to his
political conception, there is no single place that I know of where he
expressly states that the founding of an intellectual government is one of

his primary intentions. There is, however, an extremely interesting passage in the *De Augmentis* where Bacon drew an explicit parallel between the political and philosophical realms and suggested generally that intellectual life required government quite as much as civil life.

In the *De Augmentis* Bacon called for a history of learning and the arts. Such a broad history would chronicle the historical conditions under which particular kinds of learning had arisen, flourished, spread, and decayed; the origin and character of each particular art; the great intellectual controversies of the past; and the institutional embodiments of various sorts of learning. And since Bacon would "wish events to be coupled with their causes," he would have this history inquire particularly into those factors which had advanced or retarded the progress of learning: the character of peoples; the role of historical accident; the effects of religions and of varying legal systems; and the role of important individuals. The history would be compiled not only from extant accounts but from primary sources as well—the learned works which made up the accumulated literary heritage of Europe. Bacon would justify this vast historical enterprise, not on the grounds of the delight which such a "profusion of images" would assuredly afford or out of any sterile antiquarianism, but by its use. Specifically, a history of learning "would greatly assist the wisdom and skill of learned men in the use and administration of learning; . . . it would exhibit the movements and perturbations, the virtues and vices, which take place no less in intellectual than in civil matters; and . . . from the observation of these the best system of government might be derived and established."[73]

The passage is interesting for its suggestion, first, that the dynamics of intellectual life—its "movements and perturbations" and "virtues and vices"—closely paralleled the dynamics of civil life and, second, that the concepts of "administration" and "government" were appropriate to the intellectual realm. As in the civil realm, so in the intellectual realm Bacon's ideas about the government of inquiry were set against the backdrop of the human inherent tendency to lawlessness. It will not be out of place to suggest the form that such anarchy took in Bacon's account of past learning, for it is only in conjunction with his account of the reasons for the failure of science in the past that his implicit call for order and government can be properly understood.

The analysis of past learning and its failures occupied a central place in Bacon's writings. Rhetorically it served to discredit past positions and methods and to wean people from intellectual tradition; analytically it served to ground Bacon's own positive prescriptions for the advancement of learning. Frequently accounts of Bacon's analysis of the failures of traditional learning focus on his doctrine of idols, which is set forth in one form or another in many places but most clearly and fully in the first book of the *Novum Organum,* and, though the focus on the idols has perhaps been unduly narrow, it is as good a place as any to start.

In Aphorism XXXVIII of the first book of the *Novum Organum* Bacon introduces the doctrine of idols in the following way:

> *The idols and false notions which are now in possession of the human understanding, and have taken deep root therein, not only so beset men's minds that truth can hardly find entrance, but even after entrance is obtained, they will again in the very instauration of the sciences meet and trouble us, unless men being forewarned of the danger fortify themselves as far as may be against their assaults.*[74]

Bacon recognized four classes of idols: idols of the tribe, idols of the cave, idols of the marketplace, and idols of the theater.

Idols of the tribe are those errors and false notions which "have their foundation in human nature itself, and in the tribe or race of men."[75] They result from the overactive character of the mind ("The human understanding is unquiet; it cannot stop or rest, and still presses onward, but in vain."[76]) and lead the mind to project itself onto, intrude itself into, and mingle itself with the world it seeks to know:

> *The human understanding is of its own nature prone to suppose the existence of more order and regularity in the world that it finds. And though there be many things in nature which are singular and unmatched, yet it devises for them parallels and conjugates and relatives which do not exist.*
>
> *The human understanding when it has once adopted an opinion (either as being the received opinion or as being agreeable to itself) draws all things else to support and agree with it.*[77]

Being ungoverned by any legitimate rule, the faculties of the mind run beyond their respective competencies. Here Bacon is particularly critical of the imagination, the senses, and the will and affections. The will and affections make the understanding the plaything of man's desires:

> *The human understanding is no dry light, but receives an infusion from the will and affections; whence proceed sciences which may be called "sciences as one would." For what a man had rather were true he more readily believes. Therefore he rejects difficult things from impatience of research; sober things, because they narrow hope; the deeper things of*

nature, from superstition; the light of experience, from arrogance and
pride, lest his mind should seem to be occupied with things mean and
transitory; things not commonly believed, out of deference to the opin-
ion of the vulgar.[78]

When measured against the intricacies of nature, the human senses are
plagued by "dullness, incompetency, and deceptions" and will not permit
the mind to extend itself to the subtler, yet unseen, parts and processes of
nature. "Hence it is that speculation commonly ceases where sight
ceases; insomuch that of things invisible there is little or no observation." Bacon once again distinguishes his own quest for knowledge from
simple empiricism:

The sense by itself is a thing infirm and erring; neither can instruments
for enlarging or sharpening the senses do much; but all the truer kind
of interpretation of nature is effected by instances and experiments fit
and apposite; wherein the sense decides touching the experiment only,
and the experiment touching the point in nature and the things itself.[79]

The imagination, too, misleads the understanding, for "it feigns and
supposes all other things to be somehow, though it cannot see how,
similar to those few things by which it is surrounded," and it can do great
harm to the quest for knowledge unless the intellect be forced to grapple
with the real "by severe laws and overruling authority." This last idea
justifies a formulation which Bacon gives toward the end of the first
book of the *Novum Organum:* "I do not slight the understanding, but
govern it [*sed regimus*]."[80]

Bacon's remarks on the idols of the tribe make it clear that he saw
the human mind as a microcosmic, boisterous polity, in which various
factions or faculties were forever threatening and often succeeding in
moving out of their proper place and appropriating power to themselves.
The solution was here the same as in his political thought per se: to
overawe the contenders with a severe governing authority and subject it,
in turn, to a law which would teach each mental function its proper place
and sphere.

The idols of the cave are those errors or false notions which "take
their rise in the peculiar constitution, mental or bodily, of each individual" and also in education, habit, and accident. Some minds, for example, are more attuned to "the differences of things," others to their re-
semblances; some minds love antiquity, others novelty. Some people
become so enamored of one of their intellectual creations that they let it
overshadow all the rest that they do, as Aristotle "made his natural

philosophy a mere bond servant to his logic, thereby rendering it conten-
tious and well-nigh useless" and as the alchemists let themselves be carried away by a few initial experiments. The danger here is always that of
letting some personal bent rob a mind of its capacity for balance. The
proper mind for science, according to Bacon, is one "so duly tempered
that [it] can hold the mean" and avoid "excess." "And generally let every
student of nature take this as a rule: that whatever his mind seizes and
dwells upon with peculiar satisfaction is to be held in suspicion."[81] Neither individual desire nor individual pleasure furnish good criteria in the
search for truth; both are more likely signs that the mind is gratifying its
particular wants rather than grappling with nature as it is.

The idols of the marketplace, which Bacon described as "the most
troublesome of all," were those which "crept into the understanding
through the alliances of words and names," or, to put it differently,
through the social medium of language.

> Now words, being commonly framed and applied according to the
> capacity of the vulgar, follow those lines of division which are most
> obvious to the vulgar understanding. And whenever an understanding
> of greater acuteness or a more diligent observation would alter those
> lines to suit the true divisions of nature, would stand in the way and
> resist the change.[82]

Even the careful definition of key terms cannot completely eliminate
these idols of the marketplace, "since the definitions themselves consist
of words, and those words beget others." What is needed is to create a
natural philosophy which does not begin with words and commonsense
notions but rather with "individual instances [of natural occurences] and
those in due series and order," which is the purpose of Bacon's whole
scheme for the Great Instauration, in which the procedure begins with
natural phenomena and rises artificially (rather than by the spontaneous
workings of the mind) to real (and not linguistic) categories and laws of
causality.

Finally, Bacon discusses the idols of the theater. These "are not
innate, nor do they steal into the understanding secretly, but are plainly
impressed and received into the mind from the playbooks of philosophical systems and the perverted rules of demonstration."[83] At one point,
Bacon refers to these as the idols "of Systems," or of philosophical sects.
Just as in the political sphere Bacon took the proliferation of political
factions to be a sign of political unhealth, so in the philosophical sphere
he found the multiplication of sects or systems to be the "external signs"
of philosophical sterility and error. For Bacon, virtually all preceding

philosophy falls under the rubric of sectarianism. He mentions three principal categories of such sects, each one flawed by a distinctive error or one-sidedness. First, there is the "Rational School" (which he also calls "Sophistical")—including the Aristotelians and also all those ancient philosophers like Anaxagoras, Leucippus, Democritus, Parmenides, Empedocles, and Heraclitus who built systems and attracted followers—who snatch "from experience a variety of common instances, neither duly ascertained nor diligently examined and weighed, and [leave] all the rest to meditation and agitation of wit."[84] Next is the "Empirical School"—including in his own time both the alchemists and Gilbert—who "having bestowed much diligent and careful labor on a few experiments, have thence made bold to educe and construct systems, wresting all other facts in a strange fashion to conformity therewith."[85] Finally, Bacon mentions a third class of sects, which he calls "Superstitious," made up of "those who out of faith and veneration mix their philosophy with theology and traditions; among whom the vanity of some has gone so far aside as to seek the origin of sciences among spirits and genii." In this latter group, Bacon includes Pythagoras and Plato, but also those "moderns" who "have with extreme levity indulged so far as to attempt to found a system of natural philosophy on the first chapter of Genesis, on the book of Job, and other parts of the sacred writings." Each of these sects, in any case, perpetually threatens to enslave and contaminate the understanding by intruding false notions from without and of all of them, Bacon warns, the mind must be "thoroughly freed and cleansed."[86]

In his doctrine of idols, Bacon shows how the inquiry into nature has previously been subverted by the failings of human nature and the spontaneously acting mind, the vicissitudes of individual constitution, the inadequacies of ordinary language, and the fallacies of existing doctrines. While some idols stem from universal human failings and others from causes that can broadly be described as social, it is nonetheless true that in the doctrine of idols Bacon is particularly concerned to show the manner in which the individual mind is perverted and led astray. Even at this level of psychological analysis, Bacon is able to call upon a political rhetoric, as when he calls for the imposition of "severe laws and overruling authority."[87] But while Bacon's doctrine of idols argues strongly for the imposition of regimen on the operations of the individual mind, it is perhaps not the best way to approach his idea of the necessity for a collective regimen or government.

Alongside his doctrine of idols, Bacon gave other analyses of the failings of traditional philosophy which were more social and even political in character and which serve as a better explanation for what he had

in mind in calling for the establishment of government in the commonwealth of learning. In his discussion of idols of the theater, Bacon had
discussed the sectarian character of preceding philosophy, but he had
been interested in this topic principally because of the way that sectarian
ideas intruded into the individual mind and distorted the inquiry into
nature. At the individual level, the solution was to "free and cleanse" the
understanding—so far as this was possible. The problem of sectarian
controversy, however, was much larger than the problem of the individual mind. It was the intellectual analogue of tumult and anarchy in the
political realm.

The analogy is clearly developed in the Preface to the Great Instauration and exemplifies one of the ways in which Bacon applied overtly
political categories in his analysis of the vicissitudes of traditional philosophy. Again we encounter two of the three sects which Bacon discussed
in connection with idols of the theater—the Rationalists and the Empiri-
cists—but here with a different focus. Now the emphasis is on the dynamics of the sects themselves considered as social entities, and the key
variables concern differing attitudes toward such elementary political
values as authority and liberty, law, and anarchy.

Although his discussion of the Rationalists in this context does
sometimes invoke epistemological and methodological considerations, it
hinges more centrally on Bacon's idea of intellectual dictatorship. Bacon
never tired of lamenting that so many men had given themselves over so
slavishly to the authority of the ancient Greeks, particularly Aristotle.
For in truth, he wrote, Greek wisdom was like the boyhood of knowledge and it had the "characteristic property of boys: it can talk, but it
cannot generate." How was it then that the Greeks had established such
a hold on the minds of men? "The truth is," wrote Bacon, "that this
appropriating of the sciences has its origin in nothing better than the
confidence of a few persons and the sloth and indolence of the rest."[88]
After the sciences had sprung up and many had worked diligently on
them, there would arise (in Bacon's account) "some man of bold disposition."

> *[He would be one] famous for methods and short ways which people*
> *like, who has in appearance reduced them to an art, while he has in fact*
> *only spoiled all that the others had done. And yet this is what posterity*
> *like, because it makes the work short and easy, and saves further in-*
> *quiry, of which they are weary and impatient.*[89]

Once a philosopher had set himself up as the leader of a sect, his
followers, in "servile" fashion, did all they could to bolster his reputation

and authority and to swell his "retinue." Bacon characterized these followers as men who had "made over their judgments to others' keeping"[90] and compared them to "those senators whom they call *pedarii,*" that is, the senators in ancient Rome who had not yet a vote of their own but could only assent to the vote of another. With such support, a philosopher might even win "general acquiescence and consent," though Bacon would have been the first to deny that such consensus had anything to do with truth. On the contrary, Bacon saw such consensus as the result of a kind of popular dictatorship (*"dictatura"*)[91] resting on the audacity of the leader and the mean submissiveness of the followers.

The illicit alliance of intellectual dictator and followers is intimately connected with what Bacon (as we have already seen) characterized as popular polity or "Democratie" in the intellectual realm. Would-be dictators courted the intellectual rabble and in turn became the captives of their followers:

The greatest wits in each successive age have been forced out of their own course; men of capacity and intellect above the vulgar having been fain, for reputation's sake, to bow to the judgment of the time and the multitude; and thus if any contemplations of a higher order took light anywhere, they were presently blown out by the winds of vulgar opinions. So that Time is like a river, which has brought down to us things light and puffed up, while those which are weighty and solid have sunk.[92]

Because his authority was founded only on his own boldness and the weakness of the people, the intellectual dictator was far from being able to produce the easy way to truth that he had promised. To cover the hollowness of his methods and theories he must therefore develop a rationale for philosophical failure if he were to preserve his hold on the minds of his followers or, as Bacon put it, "a device for exempting ignorance from ignominy." Acting as "judge in its own cause" the dictator's art would thus never allow itself to be called into question and typically laid the blame instead on "the common condition of men and nature."[93]

It was by this oft-repeated process, therefore, that the traditional but unholy alliances of great men, slavish followers, and acquiescent multitudes, embodying a kind of illicit and destructive authoritarianism, had brought learning to such a sorry pass — "barren of works, full of questions; in point of enlargement slow and languid; carrying a show of perfection in the whole, but in the parts ill filled up; in election popular, and unsatisfactory even to those who propound them; and therefore fenced round and set forth with sundry artifices."[94] And thus, "philosophy and the intellectual sciences [had come to] stand like statues, worshipped and celebrated, but not moved or advanced."[95]

Far from securing peace within the commonwealth of learning, however, the establishment of popular but illicit and fruitless intellectual dictatorships had inevitably given rise to further disorder. As Bacon proceeded with his account of the process, we see emerge something that might be called a dialectic of intellectual authoritarianism in which the exercise of illicit authority stimulated the forces which opposed and sought to topple it.

Out of the ranks of followers, Bacon said, there would arise some who chafed at the servitude in which they suffered. Most likely, however, they would discover themselves too enmeshed in the errors and deceptions of their servitude and likewise too weak-willed to break free. With luck they might become reformers who made small changes in the received system, but they would never make a new beginning.

> If there be any who have determined to make trial for themselves, and put their own strength to the work of advancing the boundaries of the sciences, yet have they not ventured to cast themselves completely loose from received opinions or to seek their knowledge at the fountain; but they think they have done some great thing if they do but add and introduce into the existing sum of science something of their own; prudently considering with themselves that by making the addition they can assert their liberty, while they retain the credit of modesty by assenting to the rest. But these mediocrities and middle ways so much praised, in deferring to opinions and customs, turn to the great detriment of the sciences. For it is hardly possible at once to admire an author and to go beyond him; knowledge being as water, which will not rise above the level from which it fell. Men of this kind, therefore, amend some things, but advance little; and improve the condition of knowledge, but do not extend its range.[96]

These "liberals" of the commonwealth of learning, attempting to steer a course between fundamental reform and acceptance of the status quo, wish to enjoy the illusion of liberty without relinquishing the security of servitude and fail to see that a choice must be made. They produce a ceaseless agitation in the commonwealth of learning and the appearance of change but no real progress.

There were others, bolder in spirit, who did succeed in accomplishing what might appear to be an act of intellectual liberation. Bacon was keenly aware, however, of the elusiveness of truly fundamental change and seems to suggest that it was considerably easier to overthrow a tyrant than to unlearn the habits of tyranny.

> *Some indeed, there have been who have gone more boldly to work, and taking it all for an open matter and giving their genius full play, have made a passage for themselves and their own opinions by pulling down and demolishing former ones; and yet all their stir* [tumultus] *has but little advanced the matter; since their aim has been not to extend philosophy and the arts in substance and value, but only to change doctrines and transfer the kingdom of opinions to themselves; whereby little has indeed been gained, for though the error be the opposite of the other, the causes of erring are the same in both.*[97]

"Stir" or "tumult" was, of course, an idea that appears frequently in Bacon's political writing in connection with civil disorder. The tumults created by shallow-minded and short-sighted intellectual revolutionaries did not produce fundamental change or bring productive peace to the commonwealth of learning any more than political tumults led to the establishment of sound political order. New dictatorships might be formed and new dictators come to power in what Bacon called the *"regnum opinionum,"* but this was all.

At the extreme of the spectrum of opposition Bacon recognized a group that might be called "libertarian," but in his remarks on these Bacon shows quite clearly that, however much he might oppose the deadening weight of illicit, dictatorial authority, he did not believe a wholesome commonwealth of learning could be erected on the principle of unrestrained individual liberty:

> *If there have been any who, not binding themselves either to other men's opinions or to their own, but loving liberty* [libertati faventes], *have desired to engage others along with themselves in search, these, though honest in intention, have been weak in endeavour. For they have been content to follow probable reasons, and are carried round in a whirl of arguments, and in the promiscuous liberty of search* [promiscua quaerendi licentia] *have relaxed the severity of inquiry.*[98]

In the intellectual realm (as in the political) the unrestrained love of liberty quickly leads to license and precludes the kind of regimen without which natural inquiry will ever fail.

Neither the possessors, followers, reformers, coveters, or libertarian rejectors of illicit authority in the commonwealth of learning had done much good in Bacon's view. None, for example, had dwelt "upon experience and the facts of nature as long as is necessary."[99] On the contrary, all had wasted themselves in endless, repetitive struggles for the possession or destruction of intellectual authority and had completely lost sight of the advancement of true learning which should be the real business of science.

All of the groups described above, however intense or bitter the struggles among them, constituted a single tradition. Bacon sometimes identified it as the "Rationalist" tradition, sometimes as the philosophy of the schools. But there was another tradition of learning which Bacon set alongside the Rationalist tradition as its equally one-sided opposite. This was the tradition of lawless experience or the Empirical tradition. "Some there are indeed who have committed themselves to the waves of experience, and almost turned mechanics; yet these again have in their very experiments pursued a kind of wandering inquiry, without any regular system of operations."[100] Though these have avoided the most important failings of the Rationalists by attending more closely to "experience and the facts of nature," they have not done so in any organized way— "nec ei certa lege militant."[101] The lawlessness of this group had two unfortunate consequences. First, individuals engaged in such "wandering inquiry" had tended to get lost in "petty tasks" because they worked without any guiding plan.[102] Second, they tended to rush too soon to application. Though Bacon is often closely identified with the idea of knowledge-for-use, he never tired of warning that the impatient and over-hasty wish to reap early fruits, born of natural impetuosity and desire for gratification, was one of the great enemies of true scientific progress.

> All industry in experimenting has begun with proposing to itself certain definite works to be accomplished, and has pursued them with premature and unseasonable eagerness; it has sought, I say, experiments of Fruit, not experiments of Light; not imitating the divine procedure, which in its first day's work created light only and assigned to it one entire day; on which day it produced no material work, but proceeded to that on the days following.[103]

The lack of plan was accompanied by a lack of regimen and a consequent inability to restrain the natural eagerness of these mechaniclike men for use and gratification.

Here Bacon reiterated his insistence on discipline, suggesting that the Empirics lacked precisely what the Rationalists had. Although Bacon frequently attacked received logic as heavily implicated in the sterility of traditional Greek-derived learning, he chose here to emphasize the necessity for a logic and discipline of some sort. The advocates of logic as a tool of science had "indeed most truly and excellently perceived that the human intellect left to its own course is not to be trusted."[104] It was logic — or rather the kind of ordered attack which traditional logic purported to provide — that was most notably lacking in the wandering inquiry of the Empirical tradition.

The Rationalist and the Empiricist traditions of learning were equally one-sided and incomplete. The strengths of each were the failings of the other. In this sense, the traditions might be seen as complementary, and part of what Bacon sought to do was to fashion a method which would join the strengths of both. What is most striking in the present context, however, is the manner in which Bacon brings a distinctly political outlook to bear in his analysis of these two traditions of inquiry.

Bacon's doctrine of idols, though it certainly reflected a concern with the social character of learning, was above all an account of the failings that beset the individual mind. To the extent that such an account is taken as the principal backdrop for the Great Instauration, Bacon's prescriptions for a new science are easily interpreted as falling into the familiar category of Renaissance and early modern methodological works and treated as guides for the conduct of mental operations. In this view, Bacon's method might be classed, for example, with that of Descartes, and references to government and laws (the idea discussed earlier in connection with the idols that the mind must be subjected to "severe laws and overruling authority") might be construed as metaphorical.

Bacon's account of the Rationalist and Empirical traditions, on the other hand, finds its focus precisely in the social character of science which was only incidental to the idols. Here it is the interaction of leaders and followers, the vicissitudes of ambition and envy, and the varying attitudes toward authority and liberty which shape his account. Here we find the same schemata and the same stereotyped accounts of disorder that we encountered in his political writings — from the earliest ones on religious discord to the late accounts of disorder under Henry VII. We find the language of politics used to account for the relations which bind together philosophers and followers and cause the intellectual realm to split into one-sided, opposing factions. But here it is quite clearly not just a matter of language. Political formulations are more than metaphors. People in groups, Bacon seems to say, behave similarly no matter what the nature of their activity, and this must surely be the meaning of the statement quoted at the beginning of this section that a history of learning would "exhibit the movements and perturbations, the virtues and vices, which take place no less in intellectual than in civil matters."

The sterility and vanity of past learning — its altogether unproductive character — were thus for Bacon indissolubly connected with the lack of order in its social organization. His insistence on the erection of authority and the imposition of law must be taken in a literal and not metaphorical sense. Bacon conceived of science, as we have already seen, in economic terms as a work to be organized and done, with its own technical character that called for organizational expertise, requiring an investment of labor and resources, and necessitating a postponement of consumption. The rationalization of inquiry must be collective, for only the labors of many working in concert and of many generations could see to its completion. Such collective rationalization, finally, could only be accomplished in Bacon's view by "severe laws and overruling authority," that is, by government.

The next chapters explore Bacon's conception of scientific organization. The idea of government in the intellectual realm will recur, particularly in the constraining and coercive aspects of the project. A strong authoritarian impulse lies at the very core of Bacon's project and in Bacon's philosophical thought just as in his political writings, this authoritarian conception of order not merely coexists with but is a logical prerequisite to his idea of progress.

It is sometimes suggested that Bacon envisioned the creation of a new scientific elite which would stand above the vulgar herd. There is some truth in this idea. But it is also true and interesting to note that even within the community of science Bacon seeks to replicate his vision of an ordered society as a whole: hierarchical, disciplined, and buttressed by the irrational bonds of authority and custom.

Precisely because Bacon thought of science not in terms of individual imagination, intuition, or genius but in terms of government and work, his philosophical thought bears the undeniable imprint of Elizabethan ideology. This is not to deny the epochal importance of his understanding that science must become collective and collaborative or the brilliance with which he developed his ideas. It suggests, however, a note of caution in linking Bacon too closely with modern liberal ideologies which belong much more to the eighteenth than to the sixteenth or early seventeenth centuries.

5

A Community of Scientists

Bacon failed to found a community devoted to natural inquiry, but much of what he wrote was an attempt to lay the groundwork for such an institution rather than an end in itself. Bacon believed that natural inquiry must be reestablished on a collaborative, organized basis and subjected to stringent government. The plan for the Great Instauration and much of his methodological writing was aimed at guiding the labors of such a collective enterprise. This chapter examines his ideas on the actual recruitment of personnel and the establishment of a new community — on the problematic position of the founder.

We have become habituated to employing the metaphor of revolution as a means for understanding the origins of modern science. But as I. Bernard Cohen has shown, the emergence of the concept of revolution as a creative political act and the subsequent adaptation of this concept to nonpolitical contexts are both themselves historical phenomena.[1] Far from being a neutral interpretive device, the idea of "revolution" in relation to science has itself become a problematic application requiring interpretation. Cohen makes one thing clear, however, that is relevant to our current inquiry, and this is the fact that Bacon "did not have at hand the word 'revolution', nor the concept that this word implies in its current usage."[2] It is not, as Cohen rightly points out, just a matter of words. The very idea of revolution (with its modern connotations of creative liberation through an act which destroys constituted authority and the existing order) is foreign to Bacon.

For men of Bacon's era, still so keenly attuned to classical antiquity, a much more potent cluster of connotations surrounded the idea of founding. One need only think of Livy's pregnant discussion of the founding of Rome, of Bacon's fascination with Henry VII as founder of a dynasty, or of his list of political heroes. Bacon's writings on plantations make clear the almost mystical sense of possibility that surrounded the founding of a new community. In the success of the founder the blessings of wisdom and fortune were found to coincide, and it is certainly by way of a rhetoric of foundation rather than of revolution that Bacon conceived and presented the tasks which he faced as the initiator of the Great Instauration.

To the extent that Bacon's philosophizing and philosophical projecting must be understood in political terms, the terms are those of order and not revolution. Bacon wanted learning to be integrated into the order of the existing state. Internally, he sought a restructuring of science which would imitate his vision of the general social order. He believed strongly that science would only progress if people worked collaboratively, that such collaboration would only take place if people worked according to a single organizing plan, and that, people being what they are, organized activity required government both to rationalize the activity itself and to enforce conformity to the organizing procedures. Bacon, in short, approached the problem of redirecting science in the same spirit as he approached the more general predicaments of Elizabethan England and invoked the same kind of policies to accomplish the redirection.

When Bacon analyzed the predicament of science in his own day in social and political terms, what he confronted was not the existence of a single illegitimate and burdensome order to be overthrown. Rather it was the lack of any order at all or rather, the fragmentation of the commonwealth of learning into petty, squabbling principalities – the competing partial orders of feudal anarchy. Despite the fact that Bacon has often been associated with an alleged modern revolt against authority in the intellectual realm, his analysis of intellectual "dictatorship" shows that the authority he opposed was that of factious warlords. He saw the most grievous result of such petty kingdoms as the lack of any overarching authority at all – certainly of any legitimate authority. The terms in which Bacon analyzed the learned world in his own day were not those in which the classic modern revolutionaries analyzed their respective "old regimes" but rather those in which the partisans of the rising national monarchies analyzed late feudal society. If Bacon-the-intellectual-reformer is to be compared to any political figure, it is not to Robespierre or Lenin, but to Caesar, Vespasian, Aurelianus, Theodoric, Henry VII of England, or Henry IV of France – these were the political heroes whose situations most closely corresponded to his own perceived situation as a would-be organizer of science.

If we accept the parallel that Bacon drew between the commonwealth of learning and the civil order as a whole and also the idea that much of his work may be seen as the result of his wish to impose a quasi-political order on the community of learning, we are immediately struck by one glaring gap in the analogy between the intellectual and the civil realms. When Henry Tudor defeated and killed Richard III at Bosworth Field in 1485, he may not have had an intact political order but at least he had a nation on which the imposition of order might begin. This is to say that civil government was always an order that was superimposed on an existing society, no matter how torn that society might be by anarchy and war. Before Bacon could begin the practical task of creating a government for the community of learning, he first had to create the community itself. His efforts to do this—to lay the foundations of the new community—are the subject of this chapter.

The task of constituting a community (as opposed to imposing a government) was not confined in Bacon's thought to the single case of science. We have already seen, for example, that in the context of political policy-making Bacon pondered the requirements of successful colony founding. The problem of founding a colony and making it productive resembled in many ways the problem of constituting a community of working scientists. Both involved the creation of a highly disciplined, hard-working group, dedicated to the accomplishment of a set of rather narrow ends. In both there would be hardships and a perpetual temptation to resist the requisite regimen and stray from the overarching purposes of the enterprise. In neither was the personnel naturally given and self-sustaining—at least at the outset—but must, on the contrary, be chosen with an eye to their special suitedness to the task and then welded artificially into a community.

Though the initial constitution of a community must conform to the ultimate purposes of that community and anticipate the manner in which that community would subsequently be governed, it is nonetheless an analytically separable phase in the process of organizing a communal enterprise. The problems implicit in this first phase were of great concern to Bacon in his attempt to organize science along new lines. The concern is registered and the problems explored in a number of Bacon's writings from the first decade of the seventeenth century. Before turning to these writings specifically, however, we shall examine some of the circumstances which, in Bacon's view, rendered the constitution of a community of scientists complex and difficult.

THE SEGREGATION OF SCIENCE FROM SOCIETY:
A NEW TRIBE OF LEARNERS

As we have already seen in discussing his idea of policy, Bacon clearly wished to make the advancement of learning an object of government attention. From the standpoint of the government, learning was one of those productive activities which promised improvement to society as a whole and which, moreover, was likely to advance only under the direction and with the support of the established governmental authority. Left to their own devices, the learned were likely to spend their energies in self-indulgent theorizing and disputation. Government could intervene as a higher authority (as when Bacon suggested a state-sponsored review of university curriculum) and provide the kind of resources required for serious natural inquiry (as with the provisioning of laboratories).

To say that Bacon wished to integrate learning into the gamut of productive social functions by way of coercive and rationalizing government policies is not, however, to say that he wished to make science a public activity in the sense of enlisting the broad public in scientific inquiry. After recognizing that Bacon wanted science to produce benefits for society at large, we must also acknowledge that he wished to effect a radical separation and segregation of scientific inquiry from public opinion and public discourse. Inquiry into nature along the lines of the plan for the Great Instauration was, in Bacon's view, a highly demanding activity with its own discipline and its own routines and an activity for which the masses were singularly unsuited. Because of its peculiarly innovating character, science could endanger the general social order if it were not severely hedged. It could, likewise, be threatened by the habits of the vulgar mind which reigned in public discourse at large. Bacon's desire to segregate science, therefore, must be understood as an effort to protect both science and society at large. In this respect, Rossi's suggestion that Bacon wished to bestow upon science a "public" and "democratic" character and other interpretations in a similar vein are quite misleading. I have alluded several times to Bacon's criticism of "Democratie" in the intellectual realm. While Bacon did seek to initiate certain changes in the general intellectual culture, for example, in his proposals for educational reform and remarks on general learning in the *Advancement,* this was not his strategy in his scientific work. There he sought to create a community of scientists to which access was carefully controlled, which constituted an elite and was self-consciously elitist, and which was bound together internally by both rational and irrational bonds. Science was emphatically not, for Bacon, a democratic or democratizing ideal, but rather the realm in which the vulgar desires, habits, and tendencies of the masses were to be overcome by a small group—he called them the "sons" (*filii*) of science—collectively submitting to a regimen that was "legitimate, chaste, and severe."

With respect to the society as a whole, Bacon hoped to constitute the community of scientists as a group apart, serving social ends but free from the corruption that afflicted the mass of society, and in this his approach to science bears a striking resemblance to his approach to government. We have already seen that Bacon conceived of government as a special activity, to be shrouded in secrecy and subject to its own rules. The masses were not capable of government, and Bacon's notions of political expertise and political wisdom were always developed in opposition to his characterization of "the vulgar," just as his scientific ideas were. Indeed the tendency to define especially demanding activities as the province of some elite and to isolate and insulate them from society at large is so pervasive in Bacon's writings as to constitute one of the key elements in his whole outlook, deriving as much perhaps from his psychological constitution as from his Elizabethan ideology.

The segregation of science from society at large had many aspects, not least among them the protection of the social order, based on authority and custom, from the unsettling effects of innovation in the intellectual sphere. There are places in his writing where Bacon seems to have been at pains to show that science and society could coexist even though the two orders necessarily called for different valuations of innovation. In Aphorism CX of the *Novum Organum,* Bacon appeared to offer a distinction according to which innovation in the intellectual and political realms could be differentiated in such a way that intellectual innovation was rendered legitimate and nonsubversive. The point of the aphorism was that the then-current arrangements for the "administration and government of learning" (*administratio et politia scientiarum*)—that is, "the customs and institutions of schools, academies, colleges, and similar bodies destined for the abode of learned men and the cultivation of learning"—worked against healthy innovation. If, within these institutions, there arose someone with fresh thoughts and a questioning spirit, that person was "straightway arraigned as a turbulent person and an innovator."

But surely there is a great distinction between matters of state and the arts; for the danger from new motion and from new light is not the same. In matters of state a change even for the better is distrusted, because it unsettles what is established; these things resting on authority, consent, fame and opinion, not on demonstration. But arts and

sciences should be like mines, where the noise of new works and further
advances is heard on every side.[3]

The passage is interesting for its double treatment of the problem of
innovation in learning. Bacon seems to say that innovation in the sciences is to be accepted because science is a matter of light not motion
and that only motion can disturb the ordered world of practical affairs.
That this solution is not completely compatible with Bacon's position as
a whole should be apparent from the fact that for him new light should
lead to new works — hence, to motion. Later in the paragraph, however,
Bacon offers another solution: science is a form of production (like
mining) and can be contained *within* the social-political order if (as with
other productive activity) it is subject to firm control by government.
The importance of the passage, in any case, lies not so much in the
solution but in the fact that Bacon clearly perceived the tension between
a customary political order and an intellectual order based on innovation. This perception forms one of the bases in Bacon's thought for
segregating scientific inquiry and the community of scientists from society at large.

Implicitly, Bacon recognized that traditional learning, however
much it might have failed to give a true understanding of nature, was
itself implicated in the body of social custom, formed an important
bulwark of the social order, and must therefore be handled with care.
For this reason, Bacon continually tempered his attacks on traditional
learning precisely because it was bound up with "authority, consent,
fame and opinion," and sought to differentiate his program for a new
science not only from social discourse at large but also from traditional
learning. In the *Refutation of Philosophies* Bacon posed a crucial question:

Infinite are the prejudices that have sprung up, the false opinions that
have been adopted, given lodging, passed on to others. The theolo-
gians, for instance, have borrowed freely from [traditional] philosophy
and have thus established a system of speculation in which the doc-
trines of both are combined. Men engaged in affairs of state, thinking it
helpful to their standing to pass for learned, liberally besprinkle their
writings and their speeches with wisdom from the same spring. Sayings
and terms have been coined under the influence of that same philoso-
phy and in agreement with its dictates and decrees. Nay, from the
moment you learn to speak you are under the necessity of drinking in
and assimilating what perhaps I may be allowed to call a hotch-potch
of errors. Nor do these errors derive their strength only from popular

usage. They are sanctioned by the institutions of academies, colleges, orders, and even states themselves. Can all this be renounced in a moment? Is this what I ask you to do?[4]

In the received scholarly portrait, Bacon is often depicted as a relentlessly uncompromising destroyer of idols, but in this passage we can see the way in which his political prudence tempers his campaign for the advancement of learning. A wholesale attack on error might threaten the social order. Bacon does not recommend it. As the above passage continues, Bacon writes:

My sons, that is not what I ask. I have no objection to your enjoying the fruits of your philosophy. I do not disallow them. I do not wish to hurry you into isolation. Use your philosophy; let your arguments be nourished at her breast; adorn your conversation with its jewels; profess it in public and increase your gravity thereby in the eyes of the masses. The new philosophy will bring you no such gains. It does not flatter the mind by fitting in with its preconceptions. It does not sink to the capacity of the vulgar except in so far as it benefits them by works. Therefore keep your old philosophy. Use it when convenient. Keep one to deal with nature and the other to deal with the populace. Every man of superior understanding in contact with inferiors wears a mask.[5]

The passage is richly suggestive. Here we see clearly that the public realm is to be decisively differentiated from the realm of science. The practice of scientific inquiry is not for the vulgar, who will be touched by science only to the extent that they enjoy its fruits. A certain conscious duplicity, moreover, is enjoined on scientists: outward conformity to the old forms of discourse, inward contempt for them. The masses are to be awed by false learning and cynically manipulated, while the true work of science is accomplished in isolation from the crowd. No passage expresses more eloquently or with greater power the complexity of the problems with which Bacon had to deal as he set out to found a new scientific community or the audacity of his solution, and none shows with greater clarity the sense in which it is fundamentally wrong to say that Bacon sought to organize science as a public and democratic activity.

Bacon would later put it differently, but to similar effect, in the *Novum Organum* when he wrote:

Be it remembered then that I am far from wishing to interfere with the philosophy which now flourishes, or with any other philosophy more correct and complete than this which has been or may hereafter be propounded. For I do not object to the use of this received philosophy, or others like it, for supplying matter for disputations or ornaments for discourse—for the professor's lecture and for the business of life. Nay, more, I declare openly that for these uses the philosophy which I bring forward will not be much available. It does not lie in the way. It cannot be caught up in passage. It does not flatter the understanding by conformity with preconceived notions. Nor will it come down to the apprehension of the vulgar except by its utility and effects.

Let there be therefore (and may it be for the benefit of both) two streams and two dispensations of knowledge, and in like manner two tribes or kindreds of students in philosophy—tribes not hostile or alien to each other, but bound together by mutual services; let there in short be one method for the cultivation, another for the invention of knowledge.[6]

It was clear to Bacon that public discourse and public order rested in large part on "preconceived notions" and on the "flattery" of common understanding, and Bacon was unwilling to disturb the body of opinion on which the peace of the realm depended. If science had a service to perform for the public at large, that service was not general enlightenment but "utility and effects." Falsehood was no argument against publicly-held opinions so long as they served to make people act as good subjects. For science to progress, however, it must recognize a sharp line of demarcation between the realm of opinion and the realm of natural inquiry. Scientists must likewise withdraw from the general community, which was built on opinion, and constitute themselves as a "tribe" apart from the masses.

In his desire to draw a sharp line of demarcation between science and public discourse and between the community of scientific initiates and the vulgar mass, Bacon shows how clearly his vision of science was informed by a characteristically Tudor political prudence. Attuned as ever to the fragility of the social and political order, to the feebleness and corruption of the masses, and to the necessity of confining power and (what is in some respects the same thing for him) dangerous knowledge to a carefully selected elite, Bacon sought to build his community of scientists in secrecy, upon the foundation of prudent dissimulation (or, in the literal sense, of duplicity) and to have it work in safe isolation from the order of authority and custom.

In calling for the segregation of scientific inquiry and scientists themselves from the general society, Bacon wrote that the separation would be "for the benefit of both," and it is quite clear that beyond wishing to protect the social and political order from science, Bacon also wished to protect the young science from the contamination of traditional and vulgar ideas, and this aim furnished a second rationale for the constitution of "two tribes or kindred." The masses are immersed in popular opinions and live by vulgar habits of mind. They are selfish and impulsive, incapable of governing themselves by reason, impatient of government from without, unable to delay gratification or think of the future. Bacon's frequent denunciations of intellectual "Democratie" are closely related to his view that most men are governed by their appetites and most minds under the sway of the imagination. At root, this is to say, Bacon's psychological and sociological analyses rest on the same perceptions of human fallibility. By proposing a withdrawal of scientific inquirers from the general life of society—the realm of opinion—Bacon hoped to create a condition in which their minds could be cleansed of vulgar tinctures, trained in new habits, and subjected to a new regimen.

The first fact with which we must deal as we explore Bacon's ideas about the founding of a new scientific community is the sharp line of separation he sought to establish between the community of natural inquirers and the society at large. It was this separation that would condition all that he wrote about organized science. It meant that scientists would constitute a distinct social order—a distinct society writ small. It meant likewise that, however carefully the personnel of the new science might have been selected for their personal aptitudes and virtues, Bacon could treat the new order as a microcosmic political community with its own requirements, necessities, and possibilities. In ordering this community, Bacon would apply the same analytic techniques and employ the kinds of policy-making strategies that he had already learned in his political career. Inevitably, he was to impress on his vision of organized science that same combination of conservative means and progressive ends that we have encountered in his political thought generally.

If society were to be transformed by the new science, the transformation would be of a conservative kind which did not alter the fundamental constitution of social and political life. Because of science, the vulgar would have more material comforts and longer, healthier lives. They would not think or behave differently. Bacon's was a doctrine of social transformation only in a carefully delimited sense, and in his vision of science no less than in his general vision of society and social progress, Bacon preserved the cautious prudence of the Tudor statesman that he always was.

THE RHETORIC OF THE FOUNDER

One prominent tendency among those Bacon commentators who are attuned primarily to ideas is to treat Bacon's lifelong campaign for the "advancement of learning" principally as an effort to formulate a new philosophy and to deliver this philosophy to the public in the form of published writings. Bacon is thus often seen as an advocate of a new kind of experimentalism or induction, and his contribution to the new science is evaluated on the basis of the long-term impact of the ideas which he set abroad.

This view of Bacon principally as a philosopher or ideologue is limited, insofar as it fails to treat Bacon's practical, organizational efforts as more than incidental to his philosophical and literary efforts. But Bacon's organizational effort cannot be understood merely as ancillary to his philosophy. It deserves treatment in its own right as a central element in Bacon's program. Bacon sought not merely to change the way people thought but also to change the way they behaved and to bring them into a new and more productive practical relationship to one another.

Commentators who are attuned to the arts of rhetoric and are prepared to treat Bacon not merely as a philosopher but also as a rhetorician are able to grasp his practical intentions more fully. They understand Bacon's writings not merely as an effort at formulating new ideas but also as an attempt to move people—to draw people into a new praxis. Rhetoric-minded commentators attribute to Bacon's writings an acutely active orientation to his audience with the end of persuading them not only to believe new ideas but to give themselves and their labors to a new activity and movement.

So far as it goes, the rhetorical treatment of Bacon's work furnishes an important means for understanding the practical ends of his enterprise, but it, too, fails to grasp the full dimensions of Bacon's organizational vision. In its simplest form the rhetorical model includes a speaker or writer addressing an audience and attempting to persuade at least some of that audience to believe or do a certain thing. The relationship between speaker/writer and audience, however, is still an open one; the choice to believe or do, that is, still remains on the side of the reader/auditor. The influence exercised by the speaker/writer still resides in the realm of opinion, and however much Bacon may have sought to shape opinion, his ultimate desire was to create a community of inquirers who were bound together not merely by opinion (which was shifting and unreliable) but by government and law. In a fully constituted and well-governed scientific organization, the labors of scientific inquirers would (as we have already seen) be subject to a strict discipline or regimen. Form and direction would be given not by suasion but, as Bacon sometimes said, by "command."

Implicit in Bacon's whole effort, therefore, we must recognize a level of intention and labor which is not fully comprehended in either the philosophical or the rhetorical approach — as something more than either the formulation of new ideas or the suasive manipulation of audiences — and this level I call the organizational. The presuppositions, the language, and the model which Bacon brings to the task of organizing science, as I have already suggested, are political and mark his ideas about collective, collaborative science as a distinctly Tudor product, and most of what he sought to accomplish for natural inquiry must be understood in terms of the imposition of government and laws.

There is one point, however, at which Bacon's organizational effort must be understood in rhetorical terms, and that is the phase in which he seeks to found the new community, for there it is not a question of commanding people but of persuading them to accept a regimen in which command would become possible. Even here, the organizational aim is always in the background and conditions the whole rhetorical enterprise. The problem Bacon faced was complex. In the first place, Bacon did not want to attract followers indiscriminately but only those who were specifically suited by ability and temperament to the arduous demands of scientific inquiry. In the second place and paradoxically, he had to make his appeals in terms of commonly understood goods — material abundance, social improvement, intellectual satisfaction, and even glory — which were likely to appeal to a broad mass, many of whom were not suitable for scientific work. Finally, though he wanted to attract a superior class of followers, people who were sufficiently free and independent-minded to reject the old, outworn traditions of learning, the requirements of research along the lines of the Great Instauration required precisely that scientific workers sacrifice their intellectual freedom and independence of judgement to accept the heavy yoke of intellectual government and laws.

Because Bacon was not simply a *buccinator* or propagandist for the new science but its would-be organizer as well, the rhetorical strategies which Bacon devised presenting his ideas and initiating his project must be understood in terms of organization and not just of philosophical exposition or general publicity. Selection for him involved a double strategy of enticement and incitement on the one hand and discouragement and exclusion on the other. Preparation of the select, likewise, involved a double strategy of stimulation and motivation coupled with a dampening of enthusiasm, a curbing of zeal, and an elevation of discipline.

Bacon has sometimes been credited with fostering a peculiarly modern kind of hedonism in his praise for material amenities and advancements, but this view overlooks the very real asceticism of his whole approach to science. Scientists would produce great gains for human beings at large, in Bacon's view, precisely to the extent that they were able to forego vulgar gratifications — material and intellectual — and learn to work for distant rewards. No line conveys more fully or eloquently the ascetic requirements of Bacon's program, the intellectual self-abnegation of the scientific inquirer, or the gravity of the decision to join the new community of scientists than his statement that "the understanding must not therefore be supplied with wings, but rather hung with weights."[7] But along with this weighting of the understanding went a parallel curbing of a host of appetites, for Bacon firmly believed that nothing had subverted science more disastrously in the past than the premature attempt to reap fruits. Bacon's rhetoric of recruitment clearly shows the extent to which he wished to weed out impulsive gratification-seekers at the outset.

People are impatient with authority — this was one of Bacon's cardinal principles not just in the political realm but in his thoughts on organizing science. Scientists must somehow be found who could be weaned from the old authorities and, at the same time, made to see the necessity for a new, more legitimate authority. Those chosen must be prepared to accept the burden of an intellectual law which left little to the individual understanding or judgment — workers who would toil with earnest industry and pious seriousness within the constraints necessitated by the labor itself.

Though Bacon requires a kind of religious devotion and ascetic self-denial from his men of science, he is never willing to trust the success of his enterprise to the faithfulness or goodwill of his followers and thus, while it sometimes portrays the decision to do Baconian science in terms resembling those of religious conversion, the rhetoric of recruitment never forsakes its essentially secular and political intent.

Bacon's rhetorical strategies may be seen further to include both rational and irrational appeals to his audience, just as the authority of government and the rule of law in society at large were bolstered by both rational and irrational means. Alongside the utilitarian and rational arguments for abandoning the old and joining the new order, therefore, we find Bacon experimenting rhetorically with figures of charismatic leadership who attract the new "sons" of science at least as much by patriarchal mystery and devotion-inspiring personal magnetism as by reason.

It is within the field of tensions indicated here, in any case, that Bacon's writings (dating principally from the first decade of the seventeenth century) on the founding of a new scientific community must be understood as having unfolded. Zeal and sobriety, liberation and constraint, material conquests and self-denial, reason and reverence — these and other polarities define the tensions which Bacon sought to create in his writings and by which he hoped to select and prepare his following. Traditional treatments, which emphasize Bacon's optimistic espousal of the goods which might flow from the Great Instauration have not generally devoted sufficient attention to the disciplining, sobering, ascetic, and, ultimately, exclusionary side of his thought, but it is precisely these that are thrown into relief as one begins to wrestle with his ideas about the selection of men for the new community of science.

THE *AD FILIOS* WRITINGS

Convinced that organized science would have to be separated from society at large and that scientists themselves would have to be selected from the vulgar mass by a kind of rhetorical winnowing, Bacon's writings in the first decade of the seventeenth century are specifically expressive of his aims as the founder of a new community and convey some of his preoccupations as he sought to select and prepare candidates for membership. The writings which are of special interest in this connection are *The Masculine Birth of Time* (1603), *Thoughts and Conclusions* (1607), and *The Refutation of Philosophies* (1608).

Benjamin Farrington, who translated these previously untranslated works, has interpreted these unpublished writings as rhetorical experiments signalling "a transitional period of his thought" during which Bacon ceased to hope for an "administrative" implementation of his schemes and set out to accomplish the Great Instauration by literary means:

> The germ of Bacon's philosophy obsessed his mind from boyhood. This is well known. What is not always remembered or perhaps realised, is that at first he thought of introducing his reform administratively. Administrative action was a natural line, considering his family position, for his ambition to take.[8]

Farrington interprets certain scattered remarks from the 1580s and 1590s to mean that Bacon hoped "to interest influential persons in his ideas and to achieve the means of putting them into execution."[9] Farrington also refers to the famous letter to his uncle, Burghley, in which Bacon

expressed his hope that he might be given a post that would give him
"commandment of more wits than of my own," presumably the headship
of some going institution. Farrington implicitly accepts the idea (which I
have criticized earlier) that Bacon's driving ambition from his youth was
philosophical and that he hoped for political advancement only as a
means toward the attainment of philosophical ends. When, despite Essex's efforts on his behalf, Bacon's bid for place met with repeated failure, he turned (in Farrington's account) to literary means; that is, to the
writing of works aimed at the general public.

Because Farrington believes that the essence of Bacon's thought was
an ethical reorientation of science and that his ideas on this matter were
relatively well-formed prior to 1603 (dubious contentions, both) he sees
the problems that Bacon faced in the writings of 1603–1609 as principally rhetorical. Failing an administrative initiation of the Great Instauration "from above," Bacon turned to a literary initiation "from below"
by means of persuasion aimed at the general public. In contrast to Roger
Bacon, who had sought to make science "the preserve of an elite of
initiates," Francis Bacon now began "to make the case for science as a
publicly organised collaboration."[10] While it is certainly true that these
are experimental writings and likewise true that Bacon seems to have
been torn between administrative and rhetorical means for initiating his
program, Farrington's account is beset by two major problems. In the
first place the proposed shift from administrative to rhetorical means is
not so clear as Farrington makes it seem. In the second place, it is not
permissible to identify the rhetorical mode with a popular vision of
science or with the idea that it should be a public enterprise. A moment's
reflection will show that these two qualifications are not unrelated. In
imagining that a new scientific community might be launched by rhetorical means, Bacon never supposed that it could be organized on other
than closed and tightly organized—even authoritarian—lines, and there
is much more continuity between the end results of an administratively
initiated and rhetorically initiated science than Farrington suggests. In
both cases Bacon sought a community which could be separated from
the vulgar mass and, to use his word, "commanded." Let us take these
points in turn.

When, sometime around 1603, Bacon turned to the serious development and elaboration of his schemes for scientific advancement, he was
acutely aware that he had no following. As early as the 1590s in his letter
to his uncle, Burghley, Bacon had expressed the hope that he might find
some position that would allow him to direct some already existing institution: "And I do easily see, that place of any reasonable countenance
doth bring commandment of more wits than of a mean's own; which is

the thing I greatly affect."[11] In the absence of an appointment to such a position, he complained, he would have to pursue his scientific ends by becoming, as he put it, "some sorry book-maker."[12] As things turned out, and as Farrington recognized, he never did attain the headship of a going institution and was forced to pursue his goals by "book-making" (i.e., rhetorically), but he never fully renounced the desire to preside over a ready-made community. Thus, one of the abbreviated memoranda in the *Commentarius Solutus* of 1607 read as follows:

> *Layeng for a place to command wytts and pennes. Westminster, Eton, Wynchester, Spec. Trinity College in Cambridg, St Jhons in Camb. Maudlin College in Oxford, and bespeaking this betymes, wth ye K. my L. Archb. my Treasorer.*[13]

A few years before he died, after he had fallen from power in disgrace, Bacon learned that the headship of Eton had fallen vacant and was still hoping that such an appointment might allow him to preside over a community of wits.[14] The hope for some appointment which would allow him to "command wits" — to assume leadership of a community which was already established and to then turn it to his own purposes — was never fully abandoned by Bacon. It is not, therefore, a case of administrative strategies having been superseded by rhetorical strategies.

Rather, I would suggest, it is a matter of one or the other strategy moving into greater prominence depending on Bacon's perception of external circumstances and possibilities. Bacon's strategies for organizing science in the first decade of James's reign might well be related to the role that he was coming to play in Parliament during these years. Still lacking a position of authority in James's government but at the same time fully committed to serving the Crown's ends in his capacity as a member of Commons — as one among many and without the leverage of any special office — Bacon sought to work in a loose sense "rhetorically" to serve the new King. There is a certain similarity between Bacon's political and intellectual situations during these years and between the ways in which he handled these situations. But just as his work in Parliament never led him to give up his hopes for a position in the King's government where policy was made for the nation as a whole, so his rhetorical and suasive efforts to initiate a new community of natural inquirers never led him to abandon the idea that in the end such a community would succeed only if it were tightly organized, subject to law and government.

That the three pieces which Farrington cites as evidence of Bacon's rhetorical strategy anticipate not a loose movement for the new science but rather a tightly controlled organization, separated from the rest of society and subject to its own internal regimen, is something that can be demonstrated only by a careful reading of the texts. Three pieces — *The Masculine Birth of Time, Thoughts and Conclusions,* and *The Refutation of Philosophies* — are a distinguishable group precisely because their aim seems to be something more than that of explicating Bacon's ideas about the shortcomings of past natural inquiry or the possibilities that science might offer in the future — more, that is, than philosophical explication. All three contain dramatic elements and a peculiar rhetorical stance which suggest that they are directed not to some public at large but to a narrower group, such as might actually be recruited for the new community and the new work.

In a colorful passage at the end of the first book of the *Advancement of Learning,* which belongs to the same period as these three writings, Bacon wrote:

> *I do not pretend, and I know it will be impossible for me by any pleading of mine, to reverse the judgment, either of Aesop's cock, that preferred the barleycorn before the gem; or of Midas, that being chosen judge between Apollo president of the muses, and Pan god of the flocks, judged for plenty; or of Paris, that judged for beauty and love against wisdom and power; or of Agrippina,* occidat matrem, modo imperet, [*let him kill his mother so he be emperor*] *that preferred empire with condition never so detestable; or of Ulysses,* qui ventulam praetulit immortalitati [*who preferred an old woman to immortality*] *being a figure of those which prefer custom and habit before all excellency; or of a number of the like popular judgments. For these things continue as they have been: but so will that also continue whereupon learning hath ever relied, and which faileth not:* Justificata est sapientia a filiis suis [*wisdom is justified by her children*].[15]

The passage vividly testifies to Bacon's opinion, already discussed in several contexts, that learning is not the work of the vulgar mass but rather of a select few. More particularly, I would like to note the designation of these few as *filii,* for this word — this idea of *sons* or *children* who constitute a specially bonded group — is a tag that occurs in many of Bacon's writings to signal the idea of selectness, chosenness. *The Masculine Birth of Time,* thus, takes the form of an address by an older man to a younger whom he calls "son." *The Refutation of Philosophies,* likewise, is in the form of an address to a group of men called "sons." Though the tag does not occur in *Thoughts and Conclusions,* the *Filum*

Labyrinthi, which is in part close to being an English version of the same and whose writing Farrington attributes to the year 1607, begins (in the manuscript from which Spedding took his text) with the inscription *"ad filios."*

In his *Commentarius Solutus,* the collection of memoranda from 1608, Bacon wrote: "Qu. of an oration ad filios, delightfull, sublime, and mixt wth elegancy, *novelty of conceyt and yet sensible.*"[16] It is interesting to see that in his notes to himself, Bacon seems to have regarded his writings *ad filios* as occupying a rhetorical category which was distinguished by its intended audience from other works of exposition.

Bacon gave what might be considered a statement of rhetorical strategy for these *ad filios* writings in his "Preface for *De Interpretatione Naturae,*" attributed by Spedding to the year 1603:

> *Now for my plan of publication — those parts of the work which have it for their object to find out and bring into correspondence such minds as are prepared and disposed for the argument, and to purge the floors of men's understandings, I wish to be published to the world and circulate from mouth to mouth: the rest I would have passed from hand to hand, with selection and judgment. Not but I know that it is an old trick of impostors to keep a few of their follies back from the public which are indeed no better than those they put forward: but in this case it is no imposture at all, but a sober foresight, which tells me that the formula itself of interpretation, and the discoveries made by the same, will thrive better if committed to the charge of some fit and selected minds, and kept private.*[17]

At the time that he wrote this passage, Bacon seems to have regarded his writings for the new scientific elite as consisting of two phases: first, the publication to a general audience of works designed to select and prepare the inquirers who would take part in the Great Instauration; second, the more guarded communication of esoteric knowledge—the "formula of interpretation"—to those who had been selected and prepared. This was not, of course, the actual course that Bacon followed, for the formula was actually published in 1620 as the *Novum Organum.* Nonetheless, it represents the scheme as Bacon conceived it in 1608 and provides a rationale for the *ad filios* writings of those years.

The point, however, is not the particular plan of publication and whether Bacon followed it. The idea that Bacon's collection of writings constitutes a single logical structure or unfolds according to a single preconceived plan is not tenable. Though there is a remarkable consistency of ideas within the Baconian corpus it is a consistency—even a redundancy—of substance rather than a consistent progression through a logical program of writings. The important point here is not that Bacon had a tight program of writing which was set in the first decade of James's reign and systematically pursued for the remainder of his life but rather that he always thought of science as an activity of insiders and that some of his writings at least were designed to make outsiders into insiders.

Taken together, the foregoing considerations suggest that the writings to which we now turn must be examined for more than their explication of Baconian ideas. They must be considered part of a practical effort to found a new community and launch a new enterprise. The human and dramatic situations in which the exposition of philosophical ideas is embedded may thus be considered as important as the ideas themselves, and the works may be interpreted as experiments in and harbingers of the social matrix Bacon sought to create for the new science.

THE MASCULINE BIRTH OF TIME

S pedding reports that one of the surviving manuscript fragments of *Temporis Partus Masculus* is preceded by an inscription which includes the phrase, "destined to be separate and not public."[18] The piece is written as already mentioned, in the form of an address to one designated *filius*. All of this suggests that somehow the work is intended for the select—the ones to whom the accomplishment of the Great Instauration is to be entrusted.

Farrington, who views this piece along with other works from this period as Bacon's experiments in "presenting his ideas to the public,"[19] notes the harshness of language of *The Masculine Birth of Time*—particularly the harshness of its attacks on traditional learning—and concludes that in the end Bacon judged the rhetoric of this piece too strident, too censorious, and that he went on to devise milder approaches. Granting, that all three of the pieces we are now considering must be judged in some sense experimental, it seems that Farrington, having committed himself to the idea that Bacon aimed at creating a public and popular science, has ignored what is most crucial to understanding the harshness of *The Masculine Birth of Time:* that is, its character as an esoteric piece directed to the select.

Bacon urged on his followers an outward (and duplicitous) deference toward traditional learning for largely political reasons. Traditional learning had come to form one of the important bulwarks of the civil order, so that it could not be publicly refuted without endangering the political and social status quo. Since church and state had adopted the language and arguments of traditional learning, a headlong attack on that learning would be tantamount to an attack on authority itself, and this could not be permitted.

The matter stood quite differently, however, when it came to the scientific elite. It was essential that they understand the bankruptcy of traditional learning—that their minds be "cleansed" and "purged" to use Bacon's words—for them to be ready to engage in the new project for natural knowledge unencumbered by the errors and vanities of the old. This, I think—and not some loose experimentation in the rhetoric of public presentation—is the reason that Bacon's attacks on traditional learning are so unrestrained in *The Masculine Birth of Time.*

All of this is to say that *The Masculine Birth of Time* is best understood as part of Bacon's program to constitute a new community. The piece is indeed an exaggeratedly harsh attack with the intent of showing how decisive the break must be, not merely with the past but with the ideas that would continue in the present and future to dominate the vulgar mind and public discourse. It is not a recanted effort to direct all of public opinion along new lines but an effort to draw a sharp line of demarcation between the community of scientists and public opinion and to demonstrate the true rigor of the new way.

In the opening and closing passages of *The Masculine Birth of Time,* where the speaker repeatedly addresses his listener as *filii,* sometimes as a teacher and sometimes with a kind of fatherly advice, Bacon makes clear some of what he demands of recruits to the new learning. Although much has been made (by Farrington, for example) of charitable motivation and ethical will in Bacon's vision of the new science, at the very outset of this piece Bacon seems to play down the importance of motivation, placing his emphasis instead upon the recruit's capacity for accepting a new kind of discipline and accepting it, moreover, for reasons whose complete vindication would lie only in the future:

> *I find, my son, that many men, whether in publishing or concealing the knowledge of nature they think they have won, fall far short of a proper standard of honour and duty. Others again, men of excellent character but poor understanding, produce, through no fault of their own, the same harmful result.*[20]

Whatever their character, men in the past have principally lacked a "legitimate method," and this is precisely what Bacon, "after prolonged examination both the state of nature and the state of the human mind" proposes to give them.[21] The problem is that people find it very difficult to see the necessity for adopting a new method, and this problem is aggravated by the fact that the new method (or regimen or law) that Bacon wishes to propose runs counter to many deeply ingrained and even natural mental habits and is bound to be uncomfortable. Sensing a certain impatience in the acolyte-listener, the speaker anticipates a question and seeks to lay bare the true predicament of the founder:

> But what, you ask, is this legitimate method. Please drop all arts and subterfuges, you say, and put the matter plainly before us, so that we may use our own judgment. Would to God, my dear boy, that your situation was such that this could be done. But do you suppose, when all the approaches and entrances to men's minds are beset and blocked by the most obscure idols — idols deeply implanted and, as it were, burned in — that any clean and polished surface remains in the mirror of the mind on which the genuine light of things can fall?[22]

Even the select, it would seem, remained the captives of the vulgar within each of them, and their judgment was not sufficiently chaste for them to judge rightly that to which they were being asked to commit themselves. Having suggested the problem, Bacon turned to the challenge he faced as the rhetorician of the new science and as the recruiter-teacher of the select:

> A new method must be found for quiet entry into minds so choked and overgrown. Frenzied men . . . may be beguiled by art. . . . The method must be mild and afford no occasion of error. . . . Then also science must be such as to select her followers, who must be worthy to by adopted into her family.[23]

The image of adoption into a family is interesting not only because it suggests the special bonds that will tie together the community of scientists and distinguish them from the mass of society at large but also for its intimation of the partly irrational nature of those bonds, like the bonds of sentiment and obedience which bind individuals to their natural families, and the partly irrational nature of the act by which acolytes commit themselves to an enterprise which they are not at the outset in a position to understand and judge. The kind of authority, moreover, which is suggested in the dramatic tone and structure of the piece is paternal, suggesting both the natural authority of the father within the family and the special wisdom of the elder.

The body of *The Masculine Birth of Time* is a relentless attack on the false intellectual authorities of the past. Aristotle is the "worst of sophists stupified by his own unprofitable subtlety, the cheap dupe of words."[24] Plato "took men's minds off their guard and weakened their mental sinews," and "taught us to turn our mind's eye inward and grovel before our own blind and confused idols under the name of contemplative philosophy."[25] Galen "deserted the path of experience and took to spinning idle theories of causation" and taught "ignorance and idleness" to the medical profession "by setting such limits to the art and duty of medicine as should suit their sloth."[26] Paracelsus, "conspicuous for his braggart air," gave way to his own imagination and fancies, indulged his own penchant for imposture, and filled his theories with "mutual imitations, correspondences, parallelisms."[27] Along with these, Bacon arraigned the lesser lights of traditional philosophy: Cardan, Ramus, the Arabian commentators on Galen, Fernel, Peter Severinus, Cornelius Celsus, and others.

Harsh as his criticism is, Bacon does not believe that his denunciation is excessive nor that the most vehement kind of attack is unwarranted when it is a question of freeing people to create the future: "Now I must do penance, for though my purpose was only to discredit it yet I have been handling what is unholy and unclean. What I have said against them all has been less that their monstrous guilt deserved."[28] The speaker notes that his acolyte might wish a fuller, more detailed refutation than he has given.

> *But verily that would be to sin on the grand scale against the golden future of the human race, to sacrifice its promise of dominion by turning aside to attack transitory shadows. The need is to set up in the midst one bright and radiant light of truth, shedding its beams in all directions and dispelling all errors in a moment.*[29]

At the end of the short piece, Bacon returns to the theme of the introduction and suggests again the paradox implicitly implied in launching a new intellectual community with men formed by old, corrupt traditions:

> *My son, if I should ask you to grapple immediately with the bewildering complexities of experimental science before your mind has been purged of its idols, beyond a peradventure you would promptly desert*

your leader. Nor, even if you wished to do so, could you rid yourself of idols by simply taking my advice without familiarising yourself with nature. On waxen tablets you cannot write anything new until you rub out the old. With the mind it is not so; there you cannot rub out the old till you have written in the new. Nay, though you might possible divest yourself of the idols of the inn, *there would be every fear of your falling victim to the* idols of the road, *unless you were prepared. You have become too accustomed to following a guide. At Rome, too, when tyranny was once in the saddle, the oath of allegiance to the Senate and the People became a vain thing. Take heart, then, my son, and give yourself to me so that I may restore you to yourself.*[30]

This, again, is one of those rich passages suggestive of the tension in Bacon's thought. Two of the comments I wish to make have to do with the difficulties Bacon perceived in new beginnings. First, there are the psychological difficulties. Bacon did not believe that people could easily free themselves of the shackles of past thought and past errors. Indeed, he seems to have assumed that inquirers would carry these errors with them even into the work of the Great Instauration and finally free themselves only as the new knowledge was accomplished. Thus, although in some places he seems to suggest that the mind must be cleansed and purged before it can come to know nature, here he suggests that the true and lawful inquiry into nature must necessarily be carried out by those whose minds were still beset by idols. An alternate and second formulation of the same paradox is suggested by his reference to decayed Rome. In a line replete with the affinities between himself and Machiavelli (whom he admired) Bacon drew an implicit parallel between political and intellectual corruption and thus between the difficulties inherent in both political and intellectual renewal. In both cases, renewal must be accomplished, paradoxically, by men who are still mired in the old.

My third comment concerns the conclusion of the passage in which a final paradox—that of the act by which the acolyte at once gives up and regains himself—which serves as a kind of answer to the riddle of renewal which Bacon has propounded. "Give yourself to me," Bacon's speaker says. What is required, in other words, of those who are chosen to join and work in the new community is not that they have freed themselves from the errors and vanities of the past and made their minds sound but more importantly that they be willing to suffer what Bacon elsewhere called the "humiliation of the spirit" and submit themselves to an authority without. For those who "have become too accustomed to following a guide," the proper alternative is not liberty but yet another guide—only now one who is authentic. Although Bacon's ideas about organized science are best understood in terms of his political thought, the tone and language of *The Masculine Birth of Time,* which is best understood as a work designed to initiate new members of the community of science, suggest the founding of a religious order as much as anything else. The paradox of submission and restoration and the plea of the closing to "give yourself to me" suggest that what Bacon wants is something like Christian humility and redemption through faith. The act by which the acolyte gives himself to the speaker as to a father is presented, in any case, as an essentially irrational act since the corrupt mind of the acolyte is as yet incapable of an unclouded rational choice.

There is another point to be made. The listener—the "son"—is obviously a curious young man who is ever impatient to know what he cannot yet know. The speaker—or "father"—anticipates his questions and acknowledges them but does not answer them. He cannot do so, for any answer he might give would be incomprehensible to the son. This says something of the nature of the initial commitment a recruit must make to the new science. There will be no immediate gratification, and the man of science must learn to labor patiently in spite of this. This is undoubtedly part of the self-denial and intellectual asceticism which Bacon believes must lie at the foundation of the community.

The voice of the father in this piece is capable of extreme variations in tone. If it is gentle and mild, patient and coaxing, in addressing the son, it is harshly judgmental in its denunciation of those past thinkers of admitted genius who have squandered and wasted their talents and labors. Perhaps there is a deliberate religious evocation in the movement between a voice of charity and a voice of righteousness, but it is certainly clear that the righteous voice which condemns Aristotle will be unyielding in the rigor with which it directs the new men of science. Bacon leaves no doubt that the loving father can nonetheless be an exacting taskmaster.

To the man who is able to join the new community by submitting himself to a new "father," Bacon promises the glory of participating in an unprecedented achievement—one which is more than great enough to compensate for the renunciation of the old.

I hear you put a last question: Do you think that you can supply the place of all those whom you reject? I shall give you a straight answer from my inmost heart. My dear, dear boy, what I purpose is to unite you with things themselves *in a chaste, holy and legal wedlock; and from this association you will secure an increase beyond all the hopes and prayers of ordinary marriages, to wit, a blessed race of Heroes or Supermen who will overcome the immeasurable helplessness and pov-*

erty of the human race, which cause it more destruction than all giants,
monsters, or tyrants, and will make you peaceful, happy, prosperous,
and secure.[31]

In the intellectual sphere, no less than the political, peace and prosperity
go hand in hand with lawful submission. In this piece at least the vehicle
for lawful submission is the charismatic figure of the father.

THOUGHTS AND CONCLUSIONS

I n rhetorical tone and structure *Thoughts and Conclusions* is quite
different from *The Masculine Birth of Time,* and Farrington is
surely right to suggest that Bacon is experimenting. Here, in contrast to the highly personal and irrational bond between "father" and
"son" portrayed in *The Masculine Birth of Time,* Bacon strives for a
studied impersonality. The piece is a collection of reflections, the first
beginning "Franciscus Bacon sic cogitavit," and each beginning "Cogitavit et illud."[32] The effect of this device is to create a chain of thoughts
whose cumulative argumentation is intended to lead the reader to a
recognition of the necessity of his scheme if natural knowledge is to
advance.

Although the weight of the argument here is discursive in the sense
that it derives from the unfolding of the ideas themselves and although
the piece lacks the dramatic dimension of either *The Masculine Birth of
Time* or *The Refutation of Philosophies,* it is not without a certain
artifice of presentation which draws our attention. What, one asks, is
the intention and the effect of framing the thoughts with the third-per-
son, perfect-tense reference to himself as thinker: "Francis Bacon
thought thus . . .?" One effect of the device is to render the author's
voice impersonal and reportorial, leaving the polemical voice to "Francis
Bacon" about whom the report is delivered. The implication of this
reportorial form and of the fact that the thoughts themselves are thrown
by the tense of the verb into the past is that these thoughts are important
and memorable. The device serves to single out "Bacon's" thoughts as if
retrospectively from the welter of inconsequential and unmemorable
thoughts and writings and to create the impression that they were preserved by history. Bacon often wrote prospectively about the Great Instauration in epochal terms. Here he writes about it in feigned retrospec-
tion. Although the general arguments he presents in this piece are
familiar enough from other of his writings, the peculiarity of this

form (whether I am right or not in my interpretation of it) is enough to suggest that Bacon was consciously experimenting with the effects he might create in his audience of *filii*.

The work is generally attributed to the year 1607. It reproduces and expands the ideas of the English *Filum Labyrinthi,* which is written in the same peculiar form, beginning "Francis Bacon thought in this manner."[33] Spedding is of the opinion that the English version came first, but there seems to be no way of dating this. As mentioned earlier, the English version begins with the inscription, *ad filios.*

Much of *Thoughts and Conclusions* deals with an analysis of the failings of past science. The medical practitioner, philosopher, alchemist, magician, and mechanic are arraigned in turn, though the denunciation is not so harsh as in *The Masculine Birth of Time.* Farrington thinks that the distinctive importance of the piece lies in its elaboration of a "sociology of knowledge," though in fact there are suggestions of a "doctrine of the sociological distortion of truth" as far back as the *Valerius Terminus.* It is true, in any case, that in this piece Bacon devotes considerable attention to the detrimental effect of mixing science with religion, of maintaining outmoded institutions of learning, of public opinion, and so forth. Also, among the grounds for optimism that a new kind of science is possible, Bacon gives a prominent place to what he calls "the special prerogative of our own age" and, more specifically, "the political conditions of Europe."[34]

> *England is stronger, France is restored to peace, Spain is exhausted, Italy and Germany are undisturbed. The balance of power is restored and, in this tranquil state of the most famous nations, there is a turning towards peace; and peace is fair weather for the sciences to flourish. Nor is the state of letters unfavourable. Rather, it has many auspicious aspects. By the Art of Printing, a thing unknown to antiquity, the discoveries and thoughts of individuals are now spread abroad like a flash of lightning. Religious controversies have become a weariness of the spirit, and men are perhaps more ready to contemplate the power, wisdom, and goodness of God in His works.*[35]

External circumstances, in other words, seemed to encourage "a hopeful view."[36] Or so it seemed; Bacon failed to discern the tensions and instabilities which would soon plunge Europe into the tragic horrors of the Thirty Years' War.

Much of Bacon's discussion of the failings of past learning and of the circumstances in the present which favored change was specifically intended to encourage optimism and a spirit of enterprise in prospective *filii.* Bacon's continual recurrence to the "distempers" of past and present learning was not analysis for its own sake but had the very practical goal of freeing men and preparing their minds to work for the future.

> *The surest ground of hope is in the mistakes of the past. When the affairs of a commonwealth had been mismanaged, there was comfort in the remark: The blacker the past, the brighter the hope for the future. In philosophy, too, if the old errors are abandoned (and to be made aware of them is the first step to amendment), things will take a turn for the better.*[37]

If the sterility of past learning could be shown to be due to specifiable and avoidable errors — and were not, for example, simply part of the human condition but rather susceptible to change and improvement — then men might truly believe, as he says, that "a new world beckons."[38] If the man of science might learn to turn his back on the past, then he might approach nature in a new way, naively and innocently: "One might say that the kingdom of nature is like the kingdom of heaven, to be approached only by becoming like a little child."[39]

Up to this point in the work, much of Bacon's effort has been to "kindle zeal" and "raise hope" — to stimulate and motivate his reader. Now, in the final pages of the piece, he turns to the more sobering questions of "the human mind and its management."[40] If the Great Instauration (though he has not yet come to this name) is deemed possible, it remains to consider the means by which the renewal of science might be accomplished. Bacon immediately identifies the first step as the assemblage of organized natural histories — the matter upon which the understanding must work — which would require the utmost in patience and restraint.

> *The understanding is endowed by nature with an evil impulse to jump from particulars to the highest axioms (what are called First Principles). This impulse must be held in check; but generalisations close to the facts may first be made, then generalisations of a middle sort, and progress thus achieved up the successive rungs of a genuine ladder of the intellect.*[41]

Men of science must be prevented from going their individual ways in dealing with the facts of nature, for that would be "to look for knowledge in one's private world."[42] Bacon repeats the idea "that the business in hand is not an opinion to be held but a work to be done."[43]

On one point, the strategy of *Thoughts and Conclusions* differs markedly from that of the earlier *Masculine Birth of Time* and the later *Refutation of Philosophies,* and that is on the questions of leadership. Here Bacon proposes to "effect a peaceable entry into the apprehensions of men" by offering "a work on the interpretation of nature and on nature itself" in such a way that people would be won over by the method itself and its fruits rather than by a charismatic leader. "He did not propose to put himself forward as leader or guide, but to elicit and spread light from nature herself, thus precluding for the future the need of a leader."[44] This is a point on which Bacon evidently felt some ambivalence, for before this (in *The Masculine Birth of Time*) and afterwards (in *The Refutation of Philosophies* and, much later, in the *New Atlantis*) father figures played an important role as an affective focus of the scientific group. Against the background of that larger pattern, the *Thoughts and Conclusions* is particularly notable for its studied impersonality and deliberate leaderlessness.

One statement near the end of *Thoughts and Conclusions,* however, is clearly consistent with the larger selective aims of the *ad filios* writings, and that is Bacon's desire, after having stimulated the "kindled the zeal" of his readers, to weed out those who were not prepared to accept the discipline required by his approach to natural inquiry. In *Commentarius Solutus,* his book of memoranda from 1608, Bacon wrote "Qu. of the Order and Discipline, to be mixt wth some poynts popular to invite many to contribute and joyne."[45] This suggests that Bacon was quite consciously intermingling messages of enticement with warnings of rigor. In proposing to give to selected readers (though not to publish) a sample of the new philosophy — "formulae of a legitimate mode of research, in certain fields, to serve as an example and to be a sort of visible embodiment of the work to be done,"[46] Bacon hoped not only to entice the fit but to discourage the unfit:

> *This seemed the best way to distinguish the true from the false path; to put it beyond doubt that what is proposed is as far as possible from being a matter of mere words; and so to frighten off, on the one hand, the man who has no confidence in the project, and, on the other, anyone who seeks to magnify it unduly.*[47]

Bacon sought to drive away those "feebler spirits" who were either unable to imagine the possibilities opened by the new method or incapable of the patience or discipline that it required.

> *For himself Bacon was minded not to yield to his own or to anyone's*

impatience, but to keep his eyes fixed on the ultimate success of the
project. He would therefore communicate his tables only to a few and
keep the rest back till after the publication of a treatise for popular
perusal. Looking ahead he could see that the stronger and loftier
minds, advised by what he now had to offer and without waiting for
greater aids, would not only aspire but succeed in achieving the rest for
themselves.[48]

At the very end of *Thoughts and Conclusions,* Bacon affects a kind of intellectual modesty and methodological permissiveness which, because it stands in such sharp contrast to his otherwise very rigid definition of the "legitimate, chaste, and severe," must be attributed to the rhetorical stance he adopts in the piece rather than to a genuine liberality. Referring to himself in the third person, Bacon writes:

He has no pretensions, like other teachers in the arts, of insisting on the
use of any particular formula of research. All he would claim is, that
after trying everything, he came, as the result of long experience and
(he thinks) some power of judgment, to the formula which he has
approved and offers to others as the most reliable and useful.[49]

Despite the fact that in overall tone the piece is mild and inviting rather than rigid and commanding, the themes which are the general focus of this chapter appear quite clearly here. Bacon was concerned with the selection and preparation of a select group. The historical and critical sections were intended to sever the minds of the *filii* from the world of past and present opinion and to make them fresh (as the minds of children). The prospective and constructive sections were intended to emphasize the ways in which the new methods—the new regimen—would need to curb certain habitual, and even natural, ways of thinking.

The most important variable with which Bacon appears to have experimented in this piece seems to have been that of leadership. At one level, Bacon seemed to minimize his own polemical presence in the piece by adopting a reportorial, pseudo-retrospective, and historical style. He tried to develop an approach to the problem of founding the new community which did not depend on the personal leadership of a father figure but relied instead on the power of a sample of the new science to win a following on its merits.

Whereas in *The Masculine Birth of Time,* Bacon demanded an act of submission on faith from the *filii* ("Give yourself to me," he said), here he seems willing to rely on men's rational faculties to bring them to an acceptance of the new way, and he accordingly makes his appeals to "men of sense" and "stronger and loftier minds." There is thus perhaps some ambivalence in Bacon's more general belief that the human mind and judgment are not to be trusted. Once we admit that Bacon was experimenting, however, and that his various writings are not so much parts of a single logical system of thought as they are rhetorical ventures and thought-trials of various strategies and organization models, we shift our attention from particular solutions to the axes of variation. The fact that he could build one piece around a charismatic leader and the irrational commitments of followers and another around leaderlessness and the rational choices of individual members, suggests precisely that Bacon was preoccupied by questions of authority and liberty, of rationality and irrationality in the new commonwealth of learning. To the extent to which he could envision the new community as an elite (and, therefore, exempt from the failings of the vulgar) he might imagine that it could be constructed along lines different from those of vulgar communities. But every new community had a way, in Bacon's scheme of things, of generating internally its own classes of vulgar and elite, directed and directors, and to this extent every community tended to be but a small version of society at large.

THE REFUTATION OF PHILOSOPHIES

If *Thoughts and Conclusions* represents a thought experiment in rational and leaderless community, in *The Refutation of Philosophies* one of the crucial variables is the age and sophistication of the audience to whom the appeal for a new science is addressed. In the *Commentarius Solutus,* tucked away among the hundreds of short memoranda, there is a line which reads, "Qu. of young schollars in ye Universities. *It must be the postnati.*"[50] Often when he writes about the personnel of the new science, Bacon quite clearly expresses a preference for the young, as being less corrupt, more childlike, more able, perhaps, to adapt themselves to the requirements and demands of the new methods. Here, he seems to pin his hopes on young men born after the accession of James I (the *postnati*). The *filius* of *The Masculine Birth of Time* would seem to be such a young man. The *Thoughts and Conclusions,* on the other hand, would seem to be directed to men of maturer judgment who do not need to submit themselves to a father-leader. In *The Refutation of Philosophies,* Bacon creates a situation in which an audience of older and wiser eminent men is addressed by a father figure who is old and wise himself. Here the aim is not so much to win over actual workers for the new science as to gain the endorsement of eminent people in public life who will be supporters of the new science.

Again, as with the other two works, *The Refutation of Philosophies* is no simple exposition of ideas, and it is the rhetorical and dramatic framework of the piece which first draws attention. The piece consists of a set of nested discourses or narratives, with three different voices. The outermost shell is a first-person account of the unnamed author's solitary efforts to prepare the way for a new philosophy. "I am preparing a refutation of philosophies but know not how to begin," the piece starts. He might begin, the author tells us, by presenting the new kind of natural knowledge and allowing "sense evidence and experience" to win his readers' agreement. (This was roughly the approach of *Thoughts and Conclusions*.) But this would be to ignore the disabilities that keep the mind from recognizing truth when it is encountered. The mind must, the author goes on, be prepared to encounter nature and truth "by opening up and levelling a special path on account of the inveterate prejudices and obsessions of our minds."[51] The first phase in the "levelling" of such a path must be the discrediting of past philosophies, which continue to exercise such a detrimental hold on the mind. What he required of his audience for this "refutation of philosophies" was only "the patience and fairness of lofty and resolute minds."[52]

The predicament of this solitary thinker must have embodied the sense of loneliness which Bacon himself felt as he pondered the difficulty of bringing others to understand his own position and of founding a new community dedicated to a common intellectual cause. While engaged in such a project, the narrator went on, "a surprising piece of good luck" came to his aid. He met a friend who had just returned from Paris. After exchanging greetings, the narrator told the friend about his project for the "refutation of philosophies" and lamented the fact that he was working "in complete isolation." The friend replied that there were others working along similar lines. "Would you like me to tell you what happened to me in France?" In this way the second narrative begins in the recounted voice of the friend.

While in Paris, the friend began, he was invited to a gathering which proved "the happiest experience of my life."

> There were some fifty men there, all of mature years, not a young man among them, all bearing the stamp of dignity and probity. He picked out among them officers of state, senators, distinguished churchmen, people from all ranks of life, and foreigners from various nations. At

this entry they were chatting easily among themselves but sitting in
rows as if expecting somebody. Not long after there entered to them a
man of peaceful and serene air, save that his face had become habitu-
ated to the expression of pity [oris compositio erat tanquam miseran-
tis]. *They all stood up in his honour, and he looked round and said with*
a smile: "It is more than I can understand, as I recognise you one by
one, how you can all be at leisure at the same time. How is it to be
explained?" Then one of the company replied, "You yourself are the
explanation, for we all put what you have to tell us above any other
business." "Then," said he, "I am incurring a heavy responsibility for
the total of time that will be lost here, during which you might all be
going about your several tasks serving I know not how many men. I
must not keep you waiting any longer." Which said, he took his seat,
not on a platform or pulpit, but on level with the rest and delivered the
following address.[53]

The figure here described is, of course, the sort of father figure encountered already in *The Masculine Birth of Time.* (He will reappear as the
Father of Salomon's House in *New Atlantis.*) The expression of pity is
the sign of his elevation above the common lot, the combination of
separateness and charitable solicitude that characterizes Bacon's vision
of science as a whole. Even his humility toward the notables whom he
addresses carries an implication of patient superiority and condescension
which the final gesture—deigning to sit on a level with them—does less
to efface than to emphasize.

As the father figure's address commences, the piece enters the third
and innermost of the nested discourses. At the very outset, the speaker
makes clear that his appeal will be to his listeners' rational faculty: "We
are agreed, my sons, that you are men. That means, as I think, that you
are not animals on their hind legs, but mortal gods [*non animantes
erecti, sed Divi mortales*]."[54] Indeed, throughout the address, the speaker
returned to the idea that within this select group of eminent elders it was
free reason to which he appealed and on which he depended to initiate
his program:

God did not give you rational souls [animas rationales] *in order that*
you should place in men the faith you owe to Him.[55]
     By no means can he [*Aristotle*] *who reduced so many splendid*
intellects [egregius ingenia], *so many free minds* [libera capita], *to men-*
tal slavery be called a benefactor of the human race.[56]
     There is in you a native spark of reason [lumen vobis innatum]

which I would blow upon and excite, if I could rescue you from the
dazzle of an alien and intrusive beam.[57]

 Undoubtedly, sons, there is in the human soul [animae humanae]
some portion of our understanding, however preoccupied and beset,
which welcomes truth [aliqua pars intellectus pura et veritatis hospita],
and there is a path which leads down thereto by a gentle incline.[58]

Whether the change was due to a shifting assessment on Bacon's part or
to the fact that he was now addressing an audience of older, wiser men,
the whole approach of *The Refutation of Philosophies* differs markedly
from that of *The Masculine Birth of Time* in its premise that the rational
faculties of the select are sufficiently strong to make them a feasible
opening for the new science.

 Along with the higher estimate here of human's rational faculty
goes a more optimistic assessment of their capacity for high-minded
goodness: "How am I to find a way to your understanding and your
senses? I do not anticipate a refusal, for you are kind [*vos enim
benevoli*]."[59]

 Even accepting the rational and moral capacities of his listeners,
however, the speaker did not neglect to point out the many disabilities
that would hamper their pursuit of sound knowledge:

From the moment you learn to speak you are under the necessity of
drinking in and assimilating what perhaps I may be allowed to call a
hotch-potch of errors. . . .[60]

 Your education, my sons, might be compared to a conducted tour
through a portrait-gallery of the ancients.[61]

Such disabilities required that even the lofty-minded select undergo a
process of preparation: "Your understandings must be prepared before
they can be instructed; your minds need healing before they can be
exercised; the site must be cleared before it can be built upon; and this is
the sole purpose of our being here today."[62]

 Commitment to the new program did not seem to require for these
men the same kind of complete submission which Bacon asked of the
filius in *The Masculine Birth of Time*. Here, instead of asking the *filii* to
give themselves to him, the leader makes a different sort of offer, notably
to the eminent and powerful, and though the difference may be mainly a
matter of rhetoric it is nonetheless remarkable: "How can I give myself
to you in such a way as to restore you to yourselves?"[63] Instead of
repeatedly emphasizing the gulf between himself and his listeners—a
gulf which precluded any direct and early communication of the secrets

of science to the recruits—the father figure here emphasizes the rule of candor. Recognizing that men were conditioned to esteem the ancients, the speaker suggests that he could easily turn this conditioning to his own advantage but did not choose to do so:

> *I know, if I wished to be insincere, that it would not be difficult to make men believe that among the sages of old, long before Greek times, philosophy and the sciences flourished with greater value and less noise. If I did this I could, by referring my present proposals to those ancient times, invest them with a certain solemnity, as self-made men do, who attach to themselves the nobility of some ancient stock by means of genealogical hints and conjectures. But my resolution is fixed, to rely on the evidence of facts and avoid any sort of imposture, however convenient or attractive.*[64]

Elsewhere, in discussing certain matters in the history of philosophy, the speaker promises, "I shall keep nothing back but frankly open up to you the whole of my thought."[65] It is perhaps impossible to know whether Bacon's profession of sincerity and candor marks a strategic or a rhetorical change. It is quite imaginable that what Bacon is doing here is fashioning a rhetoric of sincerity as an alternative to the rhetoric of esoteric, undisclosable knowledge that we encountered in *The Masculine Birth of Time.*

While the whole approach of *The Refutation of Philosophies* seems to be milder than that of *The Masculine Birth of Time* and more pitched to the rational capacities and good intentions of the audience, we should not imagine that the end product of recruitment was different from that suggested in other works. Neither the note of generous egalitarianism that was sounded as the speaker took his seat on a level with the others nor the praise of the rational faculties of the *filii* nor the ostentatious humility of the speaker should be taken to imply that the new community would be one of individual self-determination and liberty. If equality is indeed the proper word to describe what Bacon had in mind (many commentators have praised him as an intellectual leveller) then it was an equality of the Spartan sort in which, rather than all being equally free, all were equally enchained, and Bacon was at pains to make this clear to his listeners at the outset:

> *My system and method of research is of such a nature that it tends to equalise men's wits and capacities, like the holdings of the Spartans. If a man, relying only on the steadiness of his hand or the keenness of his eye, tries to draw a straight line or describe a perfect circle, then every-*

thing depends on hand or eye. But, give him a straight-edge or a com-
pass, and it is no longer so. Similarly, in that kind of natural philoso-
phy which rests solely on intellectual strength, one man may far
outdistance another. In the kind I recommend intellectual differences
between men count for little more than such differences as commonly
exist in their senses. For my part I am emphatically of the opinion that
men's wits require not the addition of feathers and wings, but of leaden
weights. Men are very far from realising how strict and disciplined a
thing is research into truth and nature, and how little it leaves to the
judgment of men.[66]

Having praised the ethical motivation and rational capacity of his listeners, Bacon nonetheless returns to the themes which have by now become
familiar to us: the ultimate incapacity of the human understanding and
the need for men of science to submit to the regimen embodied in Bacon's methodological and organizational prescriptions. If individual reason and goodness are not enough to guide the search for natural knowledge, however, why does Bacon have his speaker make such a point of
praising them in his address? The answer, I think, is that Bacon looked
to reason and goodness not because he thought they were sufficient for
the conduct of natural inquiry but rather because he thought that rational beings might be made to see the ultimate limitations of the ungoverned understanding and the necessity for submitting to the rule of some
directive law.

A large part of the father figure's address, in any case, is aimed at
showing, in ways already familiar to us, the shortcomings of traditional
learning. Again Aristotle and Plato are arraigned, the alchemists and
natural magicians, mechanics and theorizers. The aim, again, is to wean
his followers from the past and to convince them of the necessity for
taking up a new way. All of this is intended to produce what the speaker
finally calls "a true and proper humbling of the human spirit,"[67] for it is
only after such humbling that the spirit will submit itself to the way
which is "legitimate, chaste, and severe."

THE COMPLEX POSITION OF THE FOUNDER

We do not know whether or how these *ad filios* writings were circulated or the extent to which Bacon's schemes for selecting and preparing a new elite and founding a new community passed beyond the stage of imagination and experimental writing. Although the experimental character of much of Bacon's writing in this period means that some ideas are presented tentatively and that different pieces might seem to conflict on various points, certain facts emerge quite distinctly. The writings of the first decade of James's reign suggest that, though he never completely abandoned the idea of being installed as the head of an already-existing community which he might turn to his own ends, Bacon also expended considerable thought and energy in an attempt to discover the way that a community of learning might be founded. For a variety of reasons, not least among them the corrupt state of the human mind and the fact that humanity was already implicated in a variety of self-perpetuating vicious circles, he approached the task of founding such a community as problematic. Thus while his effort is sometimes presented as a simple attempt to publicize new ideas, such a characterization does not do justice to the prudence he believed was called for. To say this is already to say something important about the way that Bacon imagined his own role in the history of science. It is to recognize that the current discussion of scientific change — so closely tied to the question of the appropriateness of the model of revolution — is not adequate for grasping the way scientific change was perceived by at least one important Tudor philosopher of science. Bacon saw his task not so much as toppling an illegitimate order as founding an order where one did not yet exist. His language and conceptual framework attest to his commitment to order; his analysis of the state of learning is an analysis of anarchy.

As he set out to construct such a new community, Bacon was concerned not to jeopardize the existing civil order, to whose maintenance he was fully committed. Political caution urged him to refrain from headlong attacks on traditional learning in which he recognized a major bulwark of the existing order. If a new science required a body of scholars dedicated to innovation and disabused of any false reverence for the past, then this body must be radically segregated from society at large so as not to form a subversive or unintentionally disruptive nucleus. They must be taught, moreover, a kind of duplicity by which they might outwardly adhere to the old learning while inwardly and actually forsaking it. They would justify themselves to society at large only as the providers of new and more abundant goods, not as the apostles of new ideas.

The Great Instauration was above all a work to be done. The accomplishment of this work required that a small group be formed into a new kind of organization. The logic of ideas and the power of suasive argument would take people only so far. At some point, for the work to begin, people would have to accept new roles in a newly organized community and submit themselves to the authority and laws by which that community was defined and operated.

It is not precisely clear what Bacon meant when he wrote of letting his writings select the true sons of science, but there are indications in the writings themselves that what he hoped to do was to entice certain open minds by showing the fruits that might flow from the new method and then discourage the unfit by emphasizing the demanding, constraining nature of the regimen to which they would have to submit themselves. This construction would account for the fact that Bacon's rhetorical strategy in the *ad filios* writings is always two-fold and self-balancing: zeal is kindled; zeal is dampened; men are urged to imagine the wealth that might flow from a new science; men are cautioned that they must delay the gratification they might receive from the fruits of the new science and, in an ascetic spirit, look first to the light they might receive; men are asked to assert their liberty from traditional authorities; men are asked to humble their spirits by submitting to a new, more stringent authority and law. It is the perpetually self-balancing character of these *ad filios* writings that has left Bacon open to so many and such varying interpretations, but the apparently conflicting messages might be understood as part of Bacon's effort to select his followers by the winnowing effect of a kind of rhetorical cross fire.

In this first phase of his community building, when he was trying to determine a way of selecting appropriate personnel for the new science, Bacon seems to have felt some ambivalence about the motives that might lead people to commit themselves to the enterprise. In some writings, he seems to wish for young and malleable minds who, though they are not capable of understanding or appreciating the reasons which led Bacon to think the way he does, nonetheless are willing to commit themselves irrationally to the project. In other writings, he seems willing to rely on the rational capacities of his audience. Whether the path is one of reason or faith, however, the end point is the same: men must submit themselves to the new regimen. The mind must be weighted down and not allowed to fly forth.

Along with this ambivalence goes another. Bacon seems uncertain about the extent to which the new community will need to rely on a leader. His ideas about leadership vary, of course, with his ideas about the rationality of his audience. To the extent that people may be made to see the virtues of his way, they may function without a leader. To the extent that their commitment is irrational, they must be made to put their faith in someone. The father figure—rhetorical analogue to the idea that scientific inquirers are "sons" in a new family—never disappears from Bacon's thought.

The problem of selection is never completely separate from that of preparation, and the same writings which seem designed to select the sons of science likewise seem aimed at preparing their minds to commence scientific work. For Bacon preparation seems to have consisted of a number of related transformations. The inquirers must, in the first place, accept that what they are about has nothing to do with what philosophers have done in the past or what they have learned in school. They must accept a radical disjuncture in their intellectual lives. It is not merely a break with the past that Bacon demands, but a break as well with the kinds of thought that continue to dominate the public realm— the realm of vulgar opinion. Bacon wants people to accept membership in an elite and to cultivate a kind of doubleness, or duplicity, with respect to society at large. To the extent that it is possible they must clear their minds of idols and attitudes that will hinder the new inquiry into nature—scraping the wax tablet clean. Though Bacon is pessimistic that this can be done completely at the outset, it is certainly to be desired, and most of his most strident denunciation of past errors—the "refutation of philosophy"—undoubtedly aims at such a "cleansing" of the mind. But it is not on this cleansing that the Great Instauration will depend. Bacon never believes that people can be made so clear-sighted or good that they can do without law—in the intellectual sphere any more than in the civil sphere. It is the third part of preparation to bring people to understand this. Arguing sometimes historically—from the vanity of past learning— and sometimes psychologically—from the incorrigibility of the mind— Bacon always returns to the same conclusion. Even the best of minds cannot operate without constraint. The human spirit must be humbled and made subject to law. Bacon recognizes that this sort of submission will not be easy for individuals, who naturally love liberty to the point of anarchy and self-destruction. But this is what the Great Instauration will require.

It is to this intellectual law, this regimen, this government, that we now turn. We may think of it as *method* (for under this rubric it is usually discussed) if we keep in mind the fact that Bacon fashioned his method to accomplish a double aim. On the one hand, it was designed to increase human collective power to discover natural laws and manipulate natural processes. On the other (in the service of such power) it was intended, at virtually every step of the way, to curb the spontaneous tendencies of the mind. It is this constraining side of Bacon's method that has received least attention, and it is this side that most clearly links it to Bacon's political ideology.

6

Science Governed

FROM *BUCCINATOR* TO LORD CHANCELLOR

I n characterizing his approach to the problems of natural inquiry—
or the *production* of true and useful knowledge—Bacon relied
heavily on the language of government. "I do not slight the understanding," wrote Bacon, "but govern it."[1] It was in the "administration
and government of learning" that the past had failed so thoroughly.[2] The
intellect must be forced to accept "severe laws and overruling authority."[3]

Bacon's use of figurative language generally is so rich and varied
that one might be tempted to treat these particular political references
merely as one more set of figures, but as we have seen, the core problems
of science and society were substantively analogous for Bacon. Once he
defined scientific inquiry as a kind of labor to be pursued collectively in
an organized way, science had to be governed, and here, as everywhere in
Bacon's universe, government would prove problematic. Humanity's
corrupt and recalcitrant nature was as serious a problem for organized
science as for the commonwealth at large, and the task of government
was two-fold in intellectual society and society at large. On the one
hand, government must inhibit certain deep-rooted human propensities
in order to establish peace. On the other, it must organize and deploy
human labor constructively according to a comprehensive rational plan
so that work would yield fruit. In both intellectual society and society at
large, the constructive, rationalizing aims of government were forever
endangered by the destructive, irrational propensities of subjects, so that
collective production was deemed possible only under tight regulation
and supervision. Law and government in the intellectual sphere, as everywhere, would of necessity have a coercive function.

The *ad filios* writings of the first decade of James's reign were largely devoted to the persuasion of those people who were yet free, and the core problem was leading them to accept the yoke of intellectual law. These writings correspond to a time in his life when Bacon had not yet acquired a position of real political authority, but still operated as an ad hoc representative of the Crown in the Commons.

In the decade of the teens, however, Bacon's political position shifted as he became Attorney General in 1613, Privy Councillor in 1616, Lord Keeper in 1617, Lord Chancellor and peer in 1618. One might expect that a shift in his political position would produce a shift in the emphasis and tone of his philosophical writing. Such a shift does, in fact, occur.

While it would be a mistake to overemphasize discontinuities between the earlier and later writings, the *Novum Organum* does seem the work of a Lord Chancellor in a way that the earlier writings are not. If the earlier writings may be said to concern the problems of founding a community by suasive means, the later ones seem to be preoccupied with the task of governing such a community by one with the authority to command. The shift is psychological and rhetorical on Bacon's part, of course, rather than practical. Though he might write with a voice of authority, he did not in fact succeed either in founding or governing a community of natural inquirers. But the shift is unmistakable, and the *Novum Organum,* the *Parasceve,* and the *New Atlantis* — the three works principally discussed in this chapter — are different in rhetorical approach and tone from the earlier writings.

These three later works suggest that Bacon shifted his attention away from the problems of founding a scientific community to the problems of administering one. The *Novum Organum* and the *Parasceve* are both prescriptive works setting out certain regular procedures to be followed in the compilation of natural histories and the interpreting of the data thus assembled. The *New Atlantis,* however, is a descriptive work depicting an imagined society in which the centerpiece is an account of the scientific society called Salomon's House. All of these concern what might be called *policy* in the intellectual realm. They all show in varying ways the kind of rationalization of inquiry which Bacon sought to achieve by means of the institution of authority in the intellectual realm. The *New Atlantis,* moreover, suggests how an organized science would need to emulate society at large in the way both rational and irrational motives were mobilized to guarantee order and stability. Here we find Bacon projecting a scientific organization in which, in a thoroughly Tudor way, both authority and custom are employed as the bulwarks of order and stability.

NATURAL INQUIRY AS IF BY MACHINE

When, in the early writings, Bacon argued repeatedly that the human mind and human intellectual labors must be subjected to law and that little could be left to the ungoverned understanding or the individual judgment, he meant, among other things, that the natural inquiry must be reduced to a collective procedure which would both regulate and integrate individual labors and that the truth of the conclusions reached in the inquiry would be guaranteed by the procedure rather than by the intellectual virtues of the individuals participating in the enterprise. The prescriptions of Bacon's method constitute just such an intellectual law.

The general understanding of Bacon's method has been shaped by two usually unspoken assumptions. The first of these is that method is essentially a guide for the conduct of individual thought or, at most, a way of insuring that individuals working along parallel lines follow a standard procedure. The role of method as a means for coordinating and integrating the work of individuals to allow for division of labor and social production is generally ignored. The crucial opposition, for most Bacon commentators is thus between the inductive and deductive methods rather than between individual method and group regimen. While Bacon himself employs the inductive-deductive distinction for purposes of showing the divergence of his own approach from that of traditional learning, the parable of the obelisk shows quite clearly that Bacon's methodological innovation cannot be grasped at the level of individual mental activity.

It remains to point out that the way in which the "instruments and machinery" which he designed to "move the obelisk" served not only to join the labors of individuals but to constrain and direct them as well. "There remains but one course for the recovery of a sound and healthy condition," Bacon wrote in the same passage where he set out the parable of the obelisk, "namely, that the entire work of the understanding be commenced afresh, and the mind itself be from the outset not left to take its own course, but guided at every step; and the business be done as if by machinery [*res veluti per machina conficiatur*]."[4] This idea that organized science as a whole would operate as a kind of machine in which individual parts would be constrained to move in a specified manner, is central to Bacon's entire conception.

The intended function of the *Novum Organum*, to which the parable of the obelisk and these remarks on the machinelike character of natural inquiry were prefaced, can thus not be grasped, as is so often attempted, solely in the terms of traditional philosophy, of epistemology, of method. The domain of this philosophical tradition had always been the individual psyche. The function of "method" in the *Novum Organum* is broader and more ambitious than this. Like policy and law (the public part of policy) in the larger community the function of method — and, more generally, of all the "machinery" of organization — was to rationalize the social production of natural knowledge, and when Bacon states that his aim is to "govern" the understanding[5] the language should be taken to reflect quite literally his belief that what learning most requires is a collective regimen resembling that of society as a whole.

If the "new organon" should then be taken as an intellectual analogue of law in the civil sphere, one might ask whether and in what sense this intellectual law shows a constraining or coercive face, for surely inhibition is one of the distinguishing features of law as Bacon conceived it. This brings us to the second general notion that has guided Bacon commentators in their interpretation of Bacon's methodological innovations. There is a tendency among most commentators to treat Bacon's method as determined mainly, if not exclusively, by the challenge which nature set for man and to portray it principally as a means for increasing human power to know and to control natural processes. Surely Bacon gives good grounds for viewing his methodological innovations in this way, and it would be unfair to say that this idea of method as an instrument is incorrect. But it is certainly only part of the truth.

Bacon sometimes said that his methodological innovation was based on the study of both man and nature, and this formulation makes clear the double character of method. On the one hand, the method of natural inquiry had to be fitted to the supposed shape of nature, the way the blade of a tool had to be designed to do a particular job. On the other hand, it had to be designed with the user's strengths and weaknesses in mind, the way a handle must be designed with an eye to human anatomy. Bacon had a keen sense of the perversities and incompetencies of the unconstrained human mind, and his methodological thought was determined quite as much by his desire to inhibit the negative tendencies of the mind as by his wish to multiply the mind's legitimate powers.

One example, drawn from the opening pages of the *Novum Organum,* should suffice to illustrate this point. The entire negative or inhibitory import of Bacon's method is epitomized in his diatribe against what he calls "anticipations." The conclusions of human reason as ordinarily applied in matters of nature, I call for the sake of distinction *Anticipations of Nature* (as a thing rash and premature). That reason which is elicited from facts by a just and methodical process, I call *Interpretation of Nature.*"[6] Anticipations, in other words, are the ideas that are formed by the ungoverned mind as it operates spontaneously.

They represent, in a sense, the mind left free and not subject to government or law. They are powerful because they represent mental habits and patterns that are most congenial to the human mind. As Bacon says, "They straightway touch the understanding and fill the imagination."[7] But likewise, in Bacon's scheme of things, anticipations are made to serve as the polar opposite of legitimate interpretation, by which alone truth can be found. This is only to say what we have noted before in other contexts, for Bacon method must act as a bulwark against the natural tendencies of the mind just as law does in the civil sphere. The human mind will gain its power over nature, in other words, to the extent that it is prevented from following its own spontaneous impulses, for these can lead only to error, vanity, and intellectual strife.

The picture of the human mind which Bacon sketched in *The Advancement of Learning,* though not drawn specifically in relation to the problems of natural inquiry, makes clear that Bacon saw the mind itself, with its various conspiring and even warring faculties, as a kind of microcosmic warring commonwealth. The individual mind is not ruled by reason, as it should be. Reason is disturbed in its administration of the mind by false reasoning, by the affections, and by the imagination, just as people are led astray in their "negotiation with others."[8] The affections raise "continual mutinies and seditions."[9] Since it is reason's office to look toward future goods, uprisings of the imagination and the affections hold the mind captive to present ideas and desires. The unfettered mind is like a "popular state" in which the people were forever being stirred "into tumult and perturbation" by "seditious orators."[10] The factions of the mind must be mastered and, if necessary, played off against one another.[11] Political language runs through the portrait of the human mind that Bacon gives in the *Advancement,* but nowhere is the crucial tendency of the human mind more clearly disclosed than when Bacon speaks of "the natural hatred of the mind against necessity and constraint."[12]

But it is just such "necessity and constraint" that the *Novum Organum* is intended to impose on the mind of natural inquirers, and it is against the background of this portrait of the human mind that Bacon's methodological prescriptions must be understood. When Bacon's writings on method are read with this idea in view, it becomes clear that the desire to constrain or counter the innate tendencies of the mind is never far from Bacon's attention. However carefully men might have been selected to participate in the Great Instauration and however carefully their minds might have been cleansed and prepared, they were never beyond needing an externally imposed discipline or regimen.

In two ways then—rationalization and constraint—Bacon's writings on method, broadly construed, seem to echo his ideas about the role of law in society at large. Though a full consideration of Bacon's method does not lie within the scope of the present study, it will be useful to give a concrete example of the way he thought his scheme would operate as a kind of law for collaborative science. Bacon's methodological prescriptions are given mainly in two works. The *Novum Organum,* already mentioned, sets out Bacon's ideas (as far as he proceeded with them) on induction; and the *Parasceve ad Historiam Naturalem et Experimentalem (Preparative towards a Natural and Experimental History),* his ideas on the collection of natural histories, the data on which induction would work. It is to the latter that I now turn.

Though he attempted to point the way with his own labors, Bacon recognized that the collection of natural histories would have to be a major collaborative enterprise. The work would progress best if labor were divided among an army of specialized researchers, with Bacon himself doing some of the abstract and demanding mental work and otherwise acting as a general manager of the project. Among other things, the *Parasceve* gives a sense of the way that the rationalization of scientific inquiry would lead in the nature of things to a hierarchical organization among scientific workers themselves and, by implication, the concentration of governing authority at the top of the hierarchy. Not only these themes, but Bacon's own motives and his chosen place in the proposed hierarchy are suggested in the following passage:

> *It occurs to me therefore that it may not be amiss to try if there be any others who will take these matters in hand: so that while I go on with the completion of my original design, this part which is so manifold and laborious may even during my life (if it so please the Divine Majesty) be prepared and set forth, others applying themselves diligently to it along with me; the rather because my own strength (if I should have no one to help me) is hardly equal to such a province. For as much as relates to the work itself of the intellect, I shall perhaps be able to master that by myself; but the materials on which the intellect has to work are so widely spread, that one must employ factors and merchants to go everywhere in search of them and bring them in. Besides I hold it to be somewhat beneath the dignity of an undertaking like mine that I should spend my own time in a matter which is open to almost every man's industry.* [13]

Bacon is often praised for having broken down the social barriers within science and having removed the stigma from lowly and unprestigious work as long as it was productive of knowledge. It is quite clear from this passage, however, that Bacon saw a rationalized collaborative science very much in terms of rank and prestige, and he was as sure here as in his thoughts on political life generally that his place was at the top.

What is more to the point in the present context is the way in which Bacon would direct the compiling of histories and his ever-present sensitivity to the tendency of workers to stray from the prescribed regimen. The *Parasceve* is filled with prohibitive and corrective cautions, which, taken together, amount to a virtual catalogue of human philosophical failings. By far the most important of these is the never-ending tendency to rush ahead impetuously, whether in enthusiasm or greed, and to draw conclusions or form opinions prematurely. In *The Refutation of Philosophies* (and many other places) Bacon had criticized the alchemists for just this sort of thing.

> *The worth of their speculative philosophy is slight and deceptive. You have heard of the spoiled boy who found a plank on the strand and dreamed of building himself a ship. Such are the alchemists. They are in love with their art, possessed with the ambition to base a whole philosophy on a few experiments made in their furnaces.*[14]

This image is echoed and transformed in the *Parasceve,* where Bacon admonishes the compilers of his natural histories to restrain the desire to rush ahead and to discipline themselves to the task at hand. They are to work patiently to provide materials for others to use in the future.

> *No man who is collecting and storing up materials for ship-building or the like, thinks of arranging them elegantly, as in a shop, and displaying them so as to please the eye; all his care is that they be sound and good, and that they be so arranged as to take up as little room as possible in the warehouse.*[15]

Later in the *Parasceve,* Bacon invokes the warehouse image again to emphasize the partial and utilitarian character of the natural histories and to underscore the need for restraint in those who compile them, cautioning implicitly against the human tendency to look to one's own personal gratification rather than accepting a role in a larger order of activity:

> *It is always to be remembered that this which we are now about is only a granary and storehouse of matters, not meant to be pleasant to stay or live in, but only to be entered as occasion requires, when anything is wanted for the work of the* Interpreter, *which follows.*[16]

Bacon's admonitions here establish both his awareness of the need to hold in check the self-indulgent conclusion seeking of subjects and workers (for this is not a bad way to think of the researchers in the new commonwealth of science) and, more generally, the manner in which his vision of organized science may be seen to approach his vision of society at large.

In the tone which he adopts in addressing the lower orders of the commonwealth of science, Bacon shows an attitude of paternalistic solicitude and, at the same time, a clear sense that scientific workers will need detailed direction and guidance. Little leeway is to be left to those engaged in the compilation of histories. The list of his particular directions to these workers is revealing of the kind of government he thought them to need. They must avoid citing the authority of ancient authors to win credit for an idea. They must avoid becoming mired in vain disputes and controversies. They must learn to shun all that is merely "philological." They must avoid the temptations of eloquence and ornaments of speech. They must shun the delights of recording subtle differences of species and avoid the temptation to make science a "kind of sport." They must reject the temptation of "superstitions" and "old wives' tales" and all beliefs which are the fruit of human sloth and credulity. Above all, they must resist the temptation to usurp functions that are beyond their rank — most especially the forming of conclusions,[17] which must be left to the "interpreters." They must shun "things mean, illiberal, filthy."[18] They must become "as little children," suspending their own judgments and serving as good collectors.[19]

As in his vision of society as a whole, it is clear that for Bacon, the wisdom and rationality of the Great Instauration is to be embodied in its law, its organization, and its leadership, rather than in the individual workers in the enterprise. Though it clearly implies a kind of elite status in relation to the rest of the learned world, selection to participate in the Great Instauration does not thus mean that one is above the law. Rather, it means that one has accepted a new law and become a subject in a new order — an order in which, as in the Tudor commonwealth at large, obedience was taken to be the subject's cardinal virtue.

THE *NEW ATLANTIS*

The *New Atlantis* is one of Bacon's most interesting works, both for its account of a well-ordered society and for the portrait it gives of the scientific community which lies near the heart of that society. The work is frequently interpreted as a piece of futuristic imagination and sometimes over-interpreted as a piece of subtle, even devious thought, filled with hidden meanings and meaningful silences. It is made to serve as a pregnant emblem of modernity and of the wracking dilemmas presented by science and the power of knowledge in our own age. The account of the piece which follows is deliberately literal-minded, largely because I think the most important messages of the *New Atlantis* lie close to the surface.

Though aspects of the work are certainly relevant to Bacon's political thought and might have been discussed earlier, I have saved the *New Atlantis* for the end because there is some value in discussing the political and scientific elements of the work together. Indeed, New Atlantis is a society that has benefitted from the fruits of science and likewise accommodated an institutionalized science. But it is also a society which is remarkably traditional in many ways, or if not precisely traditional, rather what might have been made of a traditional society through enlightened policy. In his preface to this work, Rawley wrote that the political portraiture of the piece was incomplete. "His Lordship," wrote Rawley, "thought also in this present fable to have composed a frame of Laws, or of the best state or mould of a commonwealth; but foreseeing it would be a long work, his desire of collecting the Natural History diverted him, which he preferred many degrees before it."[20]

Incomplete or no, the partial portrait of the political and social life that we get in the *New Atlantis* is quite consistent with the main outlines of Bacon's political thought, save only that in this island utopia the kinds of policy that Bacon recommended for the England of his own day had been applied consistently for a long span of time and had re-formed it into something integrated and fully developed. This meant, among other things, that the policies which Bacon might have recommended for England as cautiously introduced innovations could appear in *New Atlantis* not as controversial and potentially disturbing novelties but in their happy effects only, and with all the sanctity and safety of long-hallowed traditions. I do not believe, in short, that the *New Atlantis* represented either a different order of political thought from that which is embedded in Bacon's historical and policy writings[21] or the prophetic vision of a distant future and thus somehow a prescient emblem of modernity. Rather, it is an indication at one level of the sort of society which might result if the blessings of fortune and wisdom of policy conspired.

The story recounts the experiences of a group of European sailors on route from Peru to the Orient, who are driven off course by a series of storms and end up discovering an island society somewhere in the north Pacific. From the beginning it is clear that the inhabitants of the island were different from the turbulent, overactive Europeans to whom the sailors were accustomed. It was also obvious that the society of these strange people was differently and more tightly ordered. The European sailors were prevented from landing immediately, being told that they could provision themselves on the condition that they leave in a specified period of time. The public official who delivered this message was self-confident yet aloof and careful to maintain a certain distance from the strangers. After they had agreed to the terms, the crew of the wayward ship was approached by a man of obvious importance who examined them as to their religious beliefs and seemed gratified to learn that they were Christians. This man made arrangements for the weary crew to stay at the Strangers' House during their time at Bensalem.

From the very beginning, Bacon tries to convey some of the values of the islanders in his description of the man who first acted as host:

> *There came towards us a person (as it seemed) of place. He had on him a gown with wide sleeves, of a kind of water chamolet, of an excellent azure colour, far more glossy that ours; under his apparel was green; and so was his hat, being in the form of a turban, daintilly made, and not so huge as the Turkish turbans; and the locks of his hair came down below the brims of it. A reverend man was he to behold.*[22]

In his dress the man gives a sense of restrained opulence and also of his rank in society. Thus *New Atlantis* is a place, generally, where symbolic behavior is much attended to as a form of social differentiation and expression and where visible signs betoken social order.

The Europeans remained in the Strangers' House for three days, resting and recuperating from their hardships, and at the end of that time were visited by another Bensalemite:

> *There came to us a new man that we had not seen before, clothed in blue as the former was, save that his turban was white, with a small red cross on the top. He had also a tippet of fine linen. At his coming in, he did bend to us a little, and put his arms abroad. We of our parts saluted him in a very lowly and submissive manner; as looking that from him we should receive sentence of life or death. He desired to speak with some few of us: whereupon six of us only stayed, and the rest avoided*

*the room. He said, "I am by office governor of this House of Strangers,
and by vocation I am a Christian priest; and therefore am come to you
to offer you my service, both as strangers and chiefly as Christians.
Some things I may tell you, which I think you will not be unwilling to
hear. The state hath given you licence to stay on land for the space of
six weeks: and let it not trouble you if your occasions ask further time,
for the law in this point is not precise; and I do not doubt but myself
shall be able to obtain for you such further time as may be convenient.
Ye shall also understand, that the Strangers' House is at this time rich,
and much aforehand; for it hath laid up revenue these thirty-seven
years; for so long it is since any stranger arrived in this part: and
therefore take ye no care; the state will defray you all the time you stay;
neither shall you stay one day the less for that."*[23]

The scene is reminiscent in some ways of the scene in *The Refutation of Philosophies,* when the father figure enters to address the assembled group, and, indeed, the figure of such a man forms a recurrent motif in this work. The image is one of superior knowledge and power which is exercised with gentleness and grace (but also with an awareness of elevated status) and in the text we are told that the sailors are struck by what is called the "gracious and parent-like usage" of the governor of the House of Strangers. We note also in this passage the sort of control that the wise islanders exercise over their intercourse with the outside world, a theme that we have already encountered in Bacon's writings on English trade and the importation of foreign fashions and which recurs in this work.

The education of the Europeans about the island to which chance has brought them begins with the governor's invitation. On the following day, the governor returns and sets to teaching the sailors about this place they had already come to believe was a "land of angels."[24]

*[He] said familiarly, "That he was come to visit us": and called for a
chair, and sat him down: and we, being some ten of us, (the rest were of
the meaner sort, or else gone abroad,) sat down with him. And when
we were set, he began thus: "We of this island Bensalem," (for so they
call it in their language,) "have this; that by means of our solitary
situation, and of this laws of secrecy which we have for our travellers,
and our rare admission of strangers, we know well most part of the
habitable world, and are ourselves unknown. Therefore because he that
knoweth least is fittest to ask questions, it is more reason, for the
entertainment of the time, that ye ask me questions, than that I ask
you."*[25]

Here in Bensalem, we find the same preference for elites, the same belief in the necessity for secrecy, the same sense of the danger of uncontrolled knowledge that we have already encountered in Bacon's other writings.

Noting that "there was no worldly thing on earth more worthy to be known than the state of that happy land,"[26] the Europeans were most interested to know how Bensalem had come to be Christian. The governor happily recounted how Christianity had been brought to them some twenty years after the ascension of Jesus by the miraculous appearance off their coast of a small boat containing the scriptures and a letter from Bartholomew calling them to the new faith.

As the sailors were to learn when the governor returned to them the next day, however, the happiness and prosperity of the island was not due to their Christianity. The seamen asked their host how it was that the New Atlantans seemed to know everything about the rest of the world while themselves remained unknown, and this question opened the way for a narration of the pre-Christian history of the remarkable society.

The governor began by recounting a golden age of commerce which flourished "about three thousand years ago" in which all the great civilizations of antiquity had extensive fleets that sailed the seas. Among them were the great peoples of the Americas, including Atlantis, Coya (Peru), and Tyrambel (Mexico). It was these latter two who launched great military expeditions—Coya against the society of Bensalem and Tyrambel against Europe. The expedition against Europe was so decisively defeated that not a man returned. That against Bensalem was defeated by the military skill of a great Bensalemite king, Altabin. During the following century the civilizations of the continental Americas were destroyed by what the governor calls "the Divine Revenge" in the form of a flood which obliterated the lowland centers and left only the uncivilized remnants of mountain dwellers to repeople the land. "As for the other parts of the world, it is most manifest that in the ages following (whether it were in respect of wars, or by a natural revolution of time,) navigation did every where greatly decay; and specially far voyages . . . were altogether left and omitted."[27] By implication the golden age of commerce witnessed the flourishing of other human activities in which people preserved the highly developed knowledge which Bacon and others commonly attributed to pre-Greek antiquity. In describing the survivors of the Atlantan (rather than Noachian) flood, the governor pointed out that the mountain dwellers lost the wisdom of Noah:

For the poor remnant of human seed which remained in their mountains peopled the country again slowly, by little and little; and being simple and savage people, (not like Noah and his sons, which was the chief family of the earth,) they were not able to leave letters, arts, and civility to their posterity. [28]

Bensalemite society, on the other hand, did not lose continuity with Noachian knowledge, and it seems to be the preservation of this heritage that spared Bensalem the fate of the peoples of the Americas. While the continuity with ancient learning was undoubtedly important to the development of New Atlantan civilization, however, it was not this that accounted for the special wisdom of Bensalem's laws and institutions.

As we have already seen in his political ideas, Bacon believed that the rationalization of society must take place from the top down, and his great political heroes were the founders of states, the repairers of civil strife, and the givers of laws. So, too, in the *New Atlantis.*

The governor turned now to a description of the work of the island's great lawgiver, Salomona, whose fateful innovations — particularly the society's rigidly enforced isolationism and the organized, state-supported pursuit of scientific knowledge — provide the key to understanding the peculiar virtues of Bensalemite civilization.

There reigned in this island, about nineteen hundred years ago, a King, whose memory of all others we most adore; not superstitiously, but as a divine instrument, though a mortal man; his name was Salomona: and we esteem him as the lawgiver of our nation. This king had a large heart, *inscrutable for good; and was wholly bent to make his kingdom and people happy. He therefore, taking into consideration how sufficient and substantive this land was to maintain itself without any aid at all of the foreigner; being five thousand six hundred miles in circuit, and of rare fertility of soil in the greatest part thereof; and finding also the shipping of this country might be plentifully set on work, both by fishing and by transportations from port to port, and likewise by sailing unto some small islands that are not far from us, and are under the crown and laws of this state; and recalling into his memory the happy and flourishing estate wherein this land then was, so as it might be a thousand ways altered to the worse, but scarce any one way to the better; thought nothing wanted to his noble and heroical intentions, but only (as far as human foresight might reach) to give perpetuity to that which was in his time so happily established. Therefore amongst his other fundamental laws of this kingdom, he did ordain the interdicts and prohibitions which we have touching entrance of strangers; which at that time (though it was after the calamity of America) was frequent; doubting novelties, and commixture of manners.* [29]

Motivated by charity and guided by a prudent fear of innovation, sensing rightly that the world had entered a period of turmoil and decline, Salomona thus cut off his island society from promiscuous and unregulated foreign intercourse. The governor-narrator is careful to show that in contrast to the Chinese pattern this Bensalemite isolationism is a piece of wise statecraft rather than foolish xenophobia. China's withdrawal into itself, he claims, had made that people "a curious, ignorant, fearful, foolish nation."[30] Bensalem's isolationism differed in two respects. In the first place, the New Atlantans felt bound to treat strangers with charity when they were thrown up onto its shores by chance. In the second, in addition to preventing, so far as possible, the visits of strangers to New Atlantis, Salomona also sought to prohibit the travels of New Atlantans themselves to foreign parts. There was one exception only to this rule, and this was travel by members of Salomon's House, the island's scientific establishment.

The establishment by the state of an institution for the discovery of natural knowledge and the production of natural works was the second great achievement of Salomona.

> This restraint of ours [upon travel] hath one only exception, which is admirable; preserving the good which cometh by communicating with strangers, and avoiding the hurt; and I will now open it to you. And here I shall seem a little to digress, but you will by and by find it pertinent. Ye shall understand (my dear friends) that amongst the excellent acts of that king, one above all hath the preeminence. It was the erection and institution of an Order or Society which we call Salomon's House; the noblest foundation (as we think) that ever was upon the earth; and the lanthorn of this kingdom. It is dedicated to the study of the Works and Creatures of God.[31]

One of the equivocations which runs through all of Bacon's thought and which is present here in his discussion of the name of this scientific order concerns the extent to which true civil and philosophical wisdom is an outgrowth of Judeo-Christian revelation or of purely natural and secular thought. Salomona's innovations belong to the pre-Christian era of Bensalem, but Bacon often resorted to the figure of Solomon as an emblem of wise, religiously-ordained kingship and natural inquiry. The historical origins of Salomon's House in this narrative are left uncertain.

> Some think [the House] beareth the founder's name a little corrupted, as if it should be Solamona's House. But the records write it as it is spoken. So as I take it to be denominate of the King of the Hebrews,

which is famous with you, and no stranger to us. For we have some
parts of his works which with you are lost; namely, that Natural His-
tory which he wrote, of all plants, from the cedar of Libanus *to the*
moss that groweth out of the wall, *and of all* things that have life and
motion. *This maketh me think that our king, finding himself to sym-*
bolize in many things with that king of the Hebrews (which lived many
years before him), honoured him with the title of this foundation. And
I am rather induced to be of this opinion, for that I find in ancient
records this Order or Society is sometimes called Salomon's House and
sometimes the College of the Six Days Works; whereby I am satisfied
that our excellent king has learned from the Hebrews that God had
created the world and all that therein in within six days; and therefore
he instituting that House for the finding out of the true nature of
things, (whereby God might have the more glory in the workmanship
of them, and men the more fruit in the use of them,) did give it also
that second name.[32]

In the end, of course, it does not matter, for throughout his writings we
find Bacon justifying his scientific ideas in both religious and secular
terms, a point which seems underlined by the fact that he leaves the
Judaic roots of Salomon's House a matter of speculation among the
New Atlantans themselves.

What is more interesting is the fact that at the very beginning the
Bensalemites sought to strike a controlled balance between custom and
innovation by drawing a hard-and-fast line between science and public
knowledge. The public order was to be shielded from "novelties" and the
"commixture of manners" by the general ban on foreign intercourse. The
quest for new knowledge, in addition, was entrusted to a closed order
within the larger society, established by the state and, as we shall see,
surrounded with its own safeguards.

Yet even the community of scientists were not allowed to have free
intercourse with the world. Scientific expeditions were rigidly controlled
as well as supported by the state:

When the king had forbidden to all his people navigation into any part
that was not under his crown, he made nevertheless this ordinance;
That every twelve years there should be set forth out of this kingdom
two ships, appointed to several voyages; that in either of these ships
there should be a mission of three of the Fellows or Brethren of Salo-
mon's House; whose errand was only to give us knowledge of the af-
fairs and state of those countries to which they were designed, and
especially of the sciences, arts, manufactures, and inventions of all the

world; and withal to bring unto us books, instruments, and patterns of
every kind; that the ships, after they had landed the brethren, should
return; and that the brethren should stay abroad till the new mission.
These ships are not otherwise fraught, than with store of victuals, and
good quantity of treasure to remain with the brethren, for the buying
of such things and rewarding of such persons as they should think fit.[33]

Like so many features of Bensalemite society, these laws reveal the privileged place of science and the fact that, privileges notwithstanding, scientists are also subject to restraint and regulation by the state.

Following his recounting of the reforms of Salomona, the governor
left the Europeans, and in the days following they went out from the
House of Strangers to acquaint themselves with the society of the New
Atlantans. The remainder of the work is an account of certain aspects of
the society which they discovered and comprises three main topics: the
Feast of the Family, a ceremony designed to confirm the patriarch and
the patriarchal family; the marital and sexual customs of the New Atlantans as recounted by Joabin, a Jewish merchant of Bensalem; and, finally, what Rawley claimed to be the principal purpose of the fable, "a
model or description of a college instituted for the interpreting of nature
and the producing of great and marvellous works for the benefit of men,
under the name of Salomon's House, or the College of Six Days'
Works."[34]

The Feast of the Family is interesting on many counts, but its importance in the present discussion is, first, as an illustration of the manner in which highly ritualized social behavior may be made to lend support to the social order by reinforcing the family as the principal social
unit and by using the family to strengthen the "natural" order. It's addi-
tional significance is in showing the way that Bacon sought to integrate
scientists into this established social order by locating them in the hierarchy of ranks. In Bacon's account of the feast, it is often the detail that
conveys the message.

One day there were two of our company bidden to a Feast of the
Family, as they call it. A most natural, pious, and reverend custom it is,
shewing that nation to be compounded of all goodness. This is the
manner of it. It is granted to any man that shall live to see thirty
persons descended of his body alive together, and all above three years
old, to make this feast; which is done at the cost of the state. The
Father of the Family, whom they call the Tirsan, *two days before the*
feast, taketh to him three of such friends as he liketh to choose; and is
assisted also by the governor of the city or place where the feast is

celebrated; and all the persons of the family, of both sexes, are sum-
moned to attend him. These two days the Tirsan sitteth in consultation
concerning the good estate of the family. There, if there be any discord
or suits between any of the family, they are compounded and appeased.
There, if any of the family be distressed or decayed, order is taken for
their relief and competent means to live. There, if any be subject to
vice, or take ill course, they are reproved and censured. So likewise
direction is given touching marriages, and the courses of life which any
of them should take, with divers other the like orders and advices. The
governor assisteth, to the end to put in execution by his public author-
ity the decrees and orders of the Tirsan, if they should be disobeyed;
though that seldom needeth; such reverence and obedience they give to
the order of nature. The Tirsan doth also then ever choose one man
from amongst his sons, to live in his house with him: who is called ever
after the Son of the Vine. The reason will hereafter appear. On the
feast-day, the Father or Tirsan cometh forth after divine service into a
large room where the feast is celebrated. . . . The Tirsan cometh forth
with all his generation or lineage, the males before him, and the females
following him; and if there be a mother from whose body the whole
lineage is descended, there is a traverse placed in a loft above on the
right hand of the chair, with a privy door, and a carved window of
glass, leaded with gold and blue; where she sitteth, but is not seen.
When the Tirsan is come forth, he sitteth down in the chair; and all the
lineage place themselves against the wall, both at this back and upon
the return of the half-pace, in order of their years without difference of
sex; and stand upon their feet. When he is set; the room being always
full of company, but well kept and without disorder; after some pause
there cometh in from the lower end of the room a Taratan *(which is as*
much as an herald) and on either side of him two young lads; whereof
one carrieth a scroll of their shining yellow parchment; and the other a
cluster of grapes of gold, with a long foot or stalk. . . . This scroll is
the King's Charter, containing gift of revenew, and many privileges,
exemptions, and points of honour, granted to the Father of the Family.
. . . This charter the herald readeth aloud; and while it is read, the
father or Tirsan standeth up, supported by two of his sons, such as he
chooseth. Then the herald mounteth the half-pace, and delivereth the
charter into his hand: and with that there is an acclamation by all that
are present in their language, which is thus much: Happy are the people
of Bensalem. *Then the herald taketh into his hand from the other child*
the cluster of grapes, which is of gold, both the stalk and the grapes.
But the grapes are daintily enamelled; and if the males of the family be
the greater number, the grapes are enamelled purple, with a little sun set

> *on the top; if the females, then they are enamelled into a greenish*
> *yellow, with a crescent on the top. The grapes are in number as many as*
> *there are descendants of the family. This golden cluster the herald de-*
> *livereth also to the Tirsan; who presently delivereth it over to that son*
> *that he had formerly chosen to be in his house with him: who beareth it*
> *before his father as an ensign of honour when he goeth in public, ever*
> *after; and is thereupon called the Son of the Vine. After this ceremony*
> *ended, the father or Tirsan retireth; and after some time cometh forth*
> *again to dinner, where he sitteth alone under the state, as before; and*
> *none of his descendants sit with him, of what degree or dignity soever,*
> *except he hap to be of Salomon's House. He is served only by his*
> *children, such as are male; who perform unto him all service of the*
> *table upon the knee; and the women only stand about him, leaning*
> *against the wall. . . . Towards the end of the dinner (which in the great-*
> *est feasts with them lasteth never above an hour and an half) there is an*
> *hymn sung, varied according to the invention of him that composeth it*
> *(for they have excellent poesy), but the subject of it is (always) the*
> *praises of Adam and Noah and Abraham; whereof the former two*
> *peopled the world, and the last was the Father of the Faithful: conclud-*
> *ing ever with a thanksgiving for the nativity of our Saviour, in whose*
> *birth the births of all are only blessed. Dinner being done, the Tirsan*
> *retireth again; and having withdrawn himself alone into a place where*
> *he maketh some private prayers, he cometh forth a third time, to give*
> *the blessing; with all his descendants, who stand about him as at the*
> *first. Then he calleth them forth by one and by one, by name, as he*
> *pleaseth, though seldom the order of age be inverted. The person that is*
> *called (the table being before removed) kneeleth down before the chair,*
> *and the father layeth his hand upon his head, or her head, and giveth*
> *the blessing. . . . And withal delivereth to either of them a jewel, made*
> *in the figure of an ear of wheat, which ever after they wear in the front*
> *of their turban or hat. This done, they fall to music and dances, and*
> *other recreations, after their manner, for the rest of the day. This is the*
> *full order of that feast.*[35]

The Bensalemites are clearly (as Ruth Benedict said of the Zuni Indians)
a ceremonious people, for whom social relations and the social order are
symbolized and cemented in elaborate and meticulously prescribed rit-
uals.

We have already seen in the context of discussing his political
thought generally, what an important role Bacon gave to custom as a
bulwark of social order, but it is in an account such as this, with its
almost compulsive attention to detailed prescription, rather than in his

general statements on this matter, that we get a full sense of the way customary ritual might work continually to repair nascent conflict and reaffirm the traditional relationships and institutions of social life. While the narrow purpose of this Feast of the Family was to honor the prolific patriarch, the larger purpose was to reconfirm the larger "natural" order of society in which age takes precedence over youth and males take precedence over females. The rewards offered by the state to the honored patriarchs—"gift of revenue, and many privileges, exemptions, and points of honour"—depend, moreover, on the "dignity" of the family, and one imagines (though Bacon does not emphasize the point) that this ritual also serves to bolster the hierarchical order of society.

As interesting as the evidence it provides of the traditionalism of the Bensalemites is the fact that this ritual shows how men of science will be integrated into a system of ranks and orders. Note the privileged place of the son of Salomon's House. He is given preference in the ritual over all other children of the Tirsan "of what degree or dignity soever." It is likewise clear that he does not stand outside the order but is fitted into it. To be a member of Salomon's House is to belong to a recognized social category. He, too, has a place in the order of ranks, which is by no means disturbed by the innovating order of science. Privilege is, after all, a mark of place in this social system, and the privileges of the member of Salomon's House are made to confirm rather than delegitimize the social hierarchy.

After recounting the Feast of the Family, the narrator tells of making the acquaintance of Joabin, a Jewish merchant, from whom he learns the sexual and marital arrangements of Bensalem. At the outset the European narrator pays special attention to the place of Jews in this society:

> By that time six or seven days were spent, I was fallen into strait acquaintance with a merchant of that city, whose name was Joabin. He was a Jew and circumcised: for they have some few stirps of Jews yet remaining among them, who they leave to their own religion. Which they may the better do, because they are of a far differing disposition from the Jews in other parts. For whereas they hate the name of Christ, and have a secret inbred rancour against the people amongst whom they live: these (contrariwise) give unto our Saviour many high attributes, and love the nation of Bensalem extremely. Surely this man of whom I speak would ever acknowledge that Christ was born of a Virgin, and that he was more than a man; and he would tell how God made him ruler of the Seraphims which guard his throne; and they call him also the Milken Way, and the Eliah of the Messiah; and many other

high names; which though they be inferior to his divine Majesty, yet
they are far from the language of other Jews.[36]

If relations between Christians and Jews in Bensalem differ from those
in Europe, the difference owes something to the difference in the carriage
here of Jews themselves, but something, too, to the sophisticated wisdom of Bensalem. As we have already seen in the discussion of the
etymology of the name "Salomon's House," this is a society that is able
not merely to tolerate but perhaps even to value a certain ambiguity in its
historical and spiritual roots. Joabin, at any rate, interprets the distant
origins of Bensalemite civilization as derivative from Mosaic Law:

> *And for the country of Bensalem, this man would make no end of*
> *commending it: being desirous, by tradition among the Jews there, to*
> *have it believed that the people thereof were of the generations of*
> *Abraham, by another son, whom they call Nachoran; and that Moses*
> *by a secret cabala ordained the laws of Bensalem which they now use;*
> *and that when the Messiah should come, and sit in his throne at Hieru-*
> *salem, the king of Bensalem should sit at his feet, whereas other kings*
> *should keep a great distance. But yet setting aside these Jewish dreams,*
> *the man was a wise man, and learned, and of great policy, and excel-*
> *lently seen in the laws and customs of that nation.*[37]

It is left to this man, a Jew, who sees in the social order of Bensalem a
cabbalistic transmission of Mosaic wisdom, and likewise a man "of great
policy," to espouse the Bensalemite conception of sexual chastity and to
explain the laws and customs by which this chastity is maintained by the
state.

It is worth remembering, before we move to an account of these
laws and customs, that throughout Bacon's writings, at the level of figurative language at any rate, sexual license is closely associated not merely
with disorder but also with procreative failure, while the chaste union of
wedlock is seen as leading to fertility and productivity. Such figurative
associations arise constantly in Bacon's philosophical discussions, as, for
example, when he presents the Great Instauration as inaugurating a
fruitful marriage of the mind with nature. "Chaste," moreover, is an
adjective that Bacon applied to the rigorous inquiry into nature. But this
is really only a special case of Bacon's more general conviction that
production requires an ascetic denial of immediate gratification. From
the discussion of Bensalemite sexual practices and beliefs, at any rate, it
is clear that sexual law and sexual license are believed to touch on the

very foundations of the social order and are, for that reason, of special concern to the state.

Joabin presents the sexual laws and customs of Bensalem as the counterpart of the Feast of the Family in providing for the peace and prosperity of the island society.

> *You shall understand that there is not under the heavens so chaste a nation as this of Bensalem; nor so free from all pollution or foulness. It is the virgin of the world. . . . For there is nothing amongst mortal men more fair and admirable, than the chaste minds of this people. Know therefore, that with them there are no stews, no dissolute houses, no courtesans, nor any thing of that kind. Nay they wonder (with detestation) at you in Europe, which permit such things. They say ye have put marriage out of office: for marriage is ordained a remedy for unlawful concupiscence; and natural concupiscence seemeth as a spur to marriage. But when men have at hand a remedy more agreeable to their corrupt will, marriage is almost expulsed.*[38]

As is so often the case in Bacon's writings, it is unclear whether the chaste sexual morality of the Bensalemites is being offered as a cause or a sign of their generally happy and well-ordered existence. Is Bacon suggesting that to control the libidinous desires of men is to control these men themselves entirely? Or, on the other hand, that we can measure the ordering power of law in Bensalem by seeing its success in regulating this one, particularly troublesome aspect of life? It is clear, in either case, that the function of law and custom is to make it both possible and desirable for men to lead chaste, well-ordered lives, and that bad laws allow men to indulge natural impulses at the expense of public virtue and well-being. It is the "libertine and impure single life," in any case that is here rejected in favor of the "yoke" of marriage.

Bacon makes quite clear his belief that the stability of social institutions rests on the control of the individual's impulses and desires. Sexual license, in particular, undermines not only the institution of marriage but also that of parenthood:

> *There are with you [Europeans] seen infinite men that marry not, but chuse rather a libertine and impure single life, than to be yoked in marriage; and many that do marry, marry late, when the prime and strength of their years is past. And when they do marry, what is marriage to them but a very bargain; wherein is sought alliance, or portion, or reputation, with some desire (almost indifferent) of issue; and not the faithful nuptial union of man and wife, that was first instituted.*

*Neither is it possible that those that have cast away so basely so much
of their strength, should greatly esteem children, (being of the same
matter,) as chaste men do.*[39]

For the "natural" pleasures of marriage and parenthood, are substituted
the false pleasure of innovation and the quest for endless variety—"the
depraved custom of change, and the delight of meretricious embrace-
ments."[40] Men come to crave "advoutries [adulteries], deflouring of vir-
gins, unnatural lust"[41] and "masculine love."[42] The psychodynamic theory which lies behind the prohibition of such desires is the one which
runs through all of Bacon's thought: "unlawful lust being like a furnace
. . . if you stop the flames altogether, it will quench; but if you give it
any vent, it will rage."[43]

As with the Feast of the Family, we see here again the intervention
of the state to uphold the power of the family over its individual members and to insure so far as possible that marriage is entered upon so-
berly rather than by impulse. None may marry, we learn, before a month
has passed from the time of the couple's first meeting. Parental consent
to marriage and the marriage choice is strongly encouraged: "Marriage
without consent of parents they do not make void, but they mulct it in
the inheritors: for the children of such marriages are not admitted to
inherit above a third part of their parents' inheritance."[44] As in the case
of some social and economic legislation actually proposed by Bacon, the
law is intended to work here not by express prohibition or command but
by way of indirect pressures and incentives.

It is quite clear, at any rate, that in Bensalem the power of the state
is forever actively involved in upholding the "natural" order of sexual
relations and family. It is likewise clear that disorder in these areas is
seen as closely implicated—as a cause or as a sign—of general social
disorder, and that the kind of regulation imposed by the state is not mere
meddlesomeness but an aspect of its true responsibility. Individual liberty carries none of the positive connotations for a true Bensalemite that
it does in the modern liberal ideology, but is viewed as a rupture of the
natural bounds upon which society must be built and without which it
will fall into chaos.

On the day following his account of the sexual and marital institutions of Bensalem, Joabin returned to the Europeans to make an announcement which introduces the final portion of the work, the description of Salomon's House:

*There is word come to the governor of the city, that one of the Fathers
of Salomon's House will be here this day seven-night: we have seen*

none of them this dozen years. His coming is in state; but the cause of his coming is secret. I will provide you and your fellows of a good standing to see his entry.[45]

The very announcement of the visit tells us something important about the place of science in Bensalemite society. In *The Refutation of Philosophies,* the father figure told his audience that the new science "does not sink to the capacity of the vulgar except in so far as it benefits them by its works."[46] Now we see a society in which appearances by the leaders of science are exceedingly rare and, even then, shrouded in secrecy. This is not a society in which science has infused or enlightened public discourse but one in which a great gulf separates the science from the public and in which the masses know science only through the material benefits that it provides them.

This initial impression is born out by the description of the Father of Salomon's House and of his entry into the city where the European sailors are staying:

He was a man of middle stature and age, comely of person, and had an aspect as if he pitied men. He was clothed in a robe of fine black cloth, with wide sleeves and a cape. His under garment was of excellent white linen down to the foot, girt with a girdle of the same; and a sindon or tippet of the same about his neck. He had gloves that were curious, and set with stone; and shoes of peach-coloured velvet. His neck was bare to the shoulders. His hat was like a helmet, or Spanish Montera; and his locks curled below it decently: they were of the colour brown. His beard was cut round, and of the same colour with his hair, somewhat lighter. He was carried in a rich chariot without wheels, litter-wise; with two horses at either end, richly trapped in blue velvet embroidered; and two footmen on each side in the like attire. The chariot was all of cedar, gilt, and adorned with crystal; save that the fore-end had pannels of sapphires, set in borders of gold, and the hinder-end the like of emeralds of the Peru colour. There was also a sun of gold, radiant, upon the top, in the midst; and on the top before a small cherub of gold, with wings displayed. The chariot was covered with cloth of gold tissued upon blue. He had before him fifty attendants, young men all, in white sattin loose coats to the mid-leg; and stockings of white silk; and shoes of blue velvet; and hats of blue velvet; with fine plumes of divers colours, set round like hat-bands. Next before the chariot went two men, bare-headed, in linen garments down to the foot, girt, and shoes of blue velvet; who carried the one a crosier, the other a pastoral staff like a sheep-hook; neither of them of metal, the crosier of balm-wood, the pastoral staff of cedar. Horsemen he had none, neither before nor behind his chariot: as it seemeth, to avoid all tumult and trouble. Behind his chariot went all the officers and principals of the Companies of the City. He sat alone, upon cushions of a kind of excellent plush, blue; and under his foot curious carpets of silk of divers colours, like the Persian, but far finer.[47]

Bacon's attention to details of ceremony and garb is once again striking and can only signal his own belief that such things are significant to the Bensalemites themselves as well as being impressive in their opulence to the Europeans. The overall effect is of a kind of ecclesiastical (rather than, for example, military) splendor, in which the motive is not one derived from battle but from spiritual elevation. As in the Feast of the Family, we learn that Bensalemite urban society is organized corporately into Companies and that in precedence of rank the Father of Salomon's House leads the way.

The expression of pity which shows on the face of the Father is a sign that we have seen before in Bacon's writing. Pity is for Bacon the affective face of the virtue he calls "charity," and it signals both the bond and the distance between the philanthropic benefactor and the vulgar beneficiaries. The expression, the distance, and the bond are fitting emblems of the relation between science and society in Bensalem.

As interesting as the spectacle of the procession is the response of the assembled multitude. In Bacon's day, of course, urban crowds were energetic and raucous when treated to a show; not so those of Bensalem. Like a high churchman, the Father "held up his bare hand as he went, as blessing the people, but in silence," and like grateful children the crowds received his benediction: "The street was wonderfully well kept: so that there was never any army had their men stand in better battle-array, than the people stood. The windows likewise were not crowded, but every one stood in them as if they had been placed."[48] It was with something like a military discipline, then, that the people paid homage to the Father of Salomon's House, and the suggestion that they stood where they were "as if they had been placed" is an indirect but telling suggestion that in Bensalem, as in his own state of England, Bacon would have the people be well-disciplined and obedient.

Like the other accounts of social behavior and social events in Bensalem, the account of the procession echoes themes that are already familiar to us from Bacon's other political writing. The people here (for so the affluence of Bensalem tells us) are the beneficiaries of science and gratefully recognize themselves to be so, but neither their thought nor behavior seems to be troubled or vexed by the nontraditionalism of the scientific quest for knowledge. As subjects they remain obedient tradi-tionalists. Indeed, the outward face of science is one of ceremonious pomp and lofty removal. The Father of Salomon's House is given a place in the framework which here also includes the various Companies of the city. His dress and bearing symbolize his position to the people. His whole outward being accommodates itself to the framework of a cus-tomary society and lends support to its stability.

The final vignette making up Bacon's portrait of the *New Atlantis* is of Salomon's House. Rawley suggests that this sketch was really Bacon's principal motive in composing the whole fable, his purpose being "that he might exhibit . . . a model or description of a college instituted for the interpreting of nature and the producing of great and marvellous works for the benefit of men, under the name of Salomon's House, or the College of the Six Days' Works."[49] Whether or not this is an adequate statement of his goal, it is clear that in this last section of the piece Bacon shifts his attention from the customary society which wise policy has created for the Bensalemites and from the way science is accommodated to that society toward the institutionalized structure of organized science itself.

SALOMON'S HOUSE

The happiness of Bensalem was the work of two men. Altabin had defended the island against the Coyan expedition and rescued it from the era of devastation which swept away so much of the civilization of the Western Hemisphere. Salomona, "whose memory of all others we most adore," had given it wise laws. Salomona's decision to interdict unregulated commerce between Bensalem and the rest of the world had made it a closed and largely static (or apparently static) soci-ety in which policy could work to create and maintain good order free from the disturbing effects of "doubting novelties and commixture of manners." To the extent that change might be sought and fostered — that is, in the sphere of natural knowledge — it was confined to a small group of men working apart from society at large and as part of a tightly organized institution. Alongside his decision to isolate Bensalem from the outside world, Salomon's House was the second great innovation of Salomona.

It would be a mistake to regard Bacon's portrait of Salomon's House as his only, or even his principal statement on organized science. As I have tried to suggest, virtually every aspect of his scientific thought and writing was tied in one way or another to his effort to establish a new order among natural inquirers. Thus the portrait of Salomon's House must take its place alongside the *ad filios* pieces and the writings on method as evidence for his ideas about organized science. Nonetheless, the portrait of Salomon's House is interesting for its vision of a scientific community that is long-established and fully formed and also for its attention to the ancillary provisions for such a community—the customs and institutional structure which surround and bolster organized inquiry.

What is most impressive in this portrait is a kind of paradox which we have already seen foreshadowed in the *ad filios* writings. In relation to the rest of society, the men of Salomon's House are seen to constitute a kind of elite, distinguished by their high intelligence and high character and clearly set apart from the mass of the vulgar. In this perspective they might seem different from ordinary men—perhaps (as Bacon sometimes seemed to suggest when he likened the scientist to Adam himself) quintessentially men. But from another perspective—that of the internal order of the House—they are again only men, in need of the same sort of externally imposed disciplines, the same cautious handling, the same system of *praemium* and *poena,* and, in short, the same sort of government as other societies. In this perspective they are, once again, the vulgar.

The most interesting fact, therefore, about Bacon's vision of organized science is the extent to which it mimics his vision of society at large and thus serves as an expression of his most Tudor views on human nature and collective life. The men of Salomon's House are like the learned men of Bacon's own day except that they have been subjected to good government and good laws, just as the silent, obedient populace at the procession are like the commonality of Elizabethan England only well-ordered and obedient. As Rousseau was to do in the eighteenth century, Bacon takes "man as he is and the laws as they might be," and the *New Atlantis* is the result.

The Europeans' discovery of this most unusual institution begins when they are invited by the Father to visit Salomon's House. While the whole company was invited to see the establishment only one of the group—the narrator of the tale—was permitted an interview with the Father, reiterating the ever-recurring theme of selection. In the following words the Father began his account of Salomon's House:

> *God bless thee my son; I will give thee the greatest jewel I have. For I will impart unto thee, for the love of God and men, a relation of the true state of Salomon's House. Son, to make you know the true state of Salomon's House, I will keep this order. First, I will set forth unto you*

*the end of our foundation. Secondly, the preparations and instruments
we have for our works. Thirdly, the several employments and functions
whereto our fellows are assigned. And fourthly, the ordinances and
rites which we observe.*[50]

The first item of presentation was easy to state: "The End of our Foundation is the knowledge of Causes, and secret motions of things; and the
enlarging of the bounds of Human Empire, to the effecting of all things
possible."[51] This, of course, was the goal that Bacon had always set for
science.

Almost as if to confirm Bacon's own idea that the vulgar understanding would be most immediately drawn to the magnificent works of
science, most commentators have made the second item of the Father's
presentation the center of their discussion of Salomon's House, and
indeed this second part does occupy the bulk of the Father's narrative.
Among the research works possessed and used by Salomon's House for
the discovery of knowledge and the enrichment of Bensalem were the
following: deep caves for experiments with "coagulations, indurations,
refrigerations, and conservations of bodies," for the production of artificial metals, and for the curing of certain diseases; burials in "several
earths" for the making of porcelains and agricultural composts; high
towers for "insolation, refrigeration, conservation" and for the observation of atmospheric phenomena; large lakes for the production of fish
and fowl and for various chemical experiments; artificial wells and foun-
tains for the production of chemicals which are used, among other
things, to improve health and prolong life; large buildings in which
atmospheric phenomena can be reproduced; rooms where the air can be
specially treated to cure illnesses along with baths for the same purpose;
gardens and orchards for the improvement of strains with respect to
quality and yield and for the production of herbal medicines; animal
laboratories for the improvement of breeds, the creation of hybrids, and
animal experimentation; special places for breeding fish and insects like
silkworms and bees; "brew-houses, bake-houses, and kitchens" for the
discovery of new foods and drinks especially conducive to nutrition and
health; "dispensatories or shops" for medicines, which are of great variety; places for the exercise and improvement of the mechanical arts by
which various materials ("as papers, linen, silks, tissues; dainty works of
feathers of wonderful lustre; excellent dyes, and many others") are made
for "vulgar use"; a great variety of furnaces for the production of chemical and physical effects; "perspective-houses" for the investigation and
production of optical effects, the use of optical devices, the exploration
of optical illusions and appearances; places for the production of vari-

ous jewels and loadstones both for beauty and use; "sound-houses" for the investigation of various audio-effects, musical instruments, imitations of natural sounds, hearing-aids; "perfume-houses" in which are produced a wide variety of scents and tastes for food and drink; "engine-houses" for the production of all sorts of motions, especially those of subtlety, velocity, or force exceeding the normal, for the production of weapons, for fireworks, for flying-machines, for submarines, for clocks, for perpetual-motion machines; a "mathematical-house" for the production of mathematical and geometric instruments; "houses of deceits of the senses" for "all manner of feats of juggling, false apparitions, impostures, and illusions; and their fallacies."[52]

Even a cursory reading of this condensed list of works pursued by Salomon's House gives an indication of the overall scientific and technological superiority of Bensalemite learning and of the material comfort and security it could provide to the population of the island society. Prominent among these works are those which will enrich agriculture and animal husbandry and those relating to the medical arts.

Although the power of this listing comes largely from its fullness and richness and from the fact that many of its items must have seemed only barely imaginable in Bacon's time, there are certain arresting details which call for comment. In the first place, it becomes clear as Bacon recounts the works of Salomon's House that the continuing existence of the scientific institution is not inconsistent with the claim that the Great Instauration would be a finite procedure. At the point in its history when we are permitted to glimpse Salomon's House, its main activity seems to be the application of natural knowledge rather than what we would now call "basic research." In his discussion of the production of hybrid strains, Bacon makes an interesting and telling point. "Neither do we this by chance," he has the Father of Salomon's House say, "but we know beforehand of what matter and commixture what kind of those creatures will arise."[53] It seems clear from this that the basic combinatorial structure of nature is already known to the Bensalemites, as indeed Bacon seems to suggest it would be upon the completion of the Great Instauration. The main business now is the ongoing application of this knowledge.

A second point has to do with the manner in which useful products are offered to the public. Without reading too much into the piece it is legitimate to note that the House of Salomon runs its own "dispensatories" for certain kinds of products like medicines.[54] We know further that not all products produced by Salomon's House are permitted to reach the public, for Bacon writes that one "dispensatory" carries products which "are not brought into vulgar use amongst us" in addition to "those that are."[55] This suggests that somewhere decisions are made about which products are fit for the vulgar and which are not. It is a tantalizing detail, and it would be interesting to know where the power of regulation lay: with the king and his government or with Salomon's House itself. We know little at all about the relationship between Salomon's House and the government, except that it was King Salomona who originally established the scientific institution and (presumably) set its basic institutional structure. The larger point in all this is that the separation of science and society (a point we have seen Bacon make repeatedly) required some sort of regulation of the way in which knowledge and goods would flow from the community of technology-minded scientists out into the public sphere.

One last point may be made before leaving this account of the works of Salomon's House, and this is a point that really looks ahead to the internal order of the institution and the system of *praemium* and *poena* by which that order was maintained. In his discussion of the production of "deceits of the senses" Bacon has the Father make an interesting comment:

> *And surely you will easily believe that we that have so many things truly natural which induce admiration, could in a world of particulars deceive the senses, if we would disguise those things and labour to make them seem more miraculous. But we do hate all impostures and lies: insomuch as we have severely forbidden it to all our fellows, under pain of ignominy and fines, that they do not shew any natural work or thing, adorned or swelling; but only pure as it is, and without all affectation and strangeness.*[56]

The words "imposture," "swelling," and "affectation" are closely associated in Bacon's writing with distempers which afflicted learning in his own day and, more specifically, with the alchemists. The significance of the passage lies first in the fact that a tendency toward these intellectual sins — one might almost say crimes — does not disappear with the inauguration of a new science. Rather, it lives on as a continuing danger precisely because it is rooted in the darker recesses of human nature. It cannot be cured but only curbed. This leads to the second significant feature of the passage. In Salomon's House, apparently, there is a system of coercive sanctions of both the formal and informal kinds. The reference here to "ignominy" suggests that the values and collective judgement of the group are so cohesive and so powerful as to form one important deterrent to wrongdoing. Beyond this, however, there would seem to be a formal system of sanction which includes, at very least, fines. Again, the textual details here are few and tantalizing rather than fully explanatory, but they are clear enough as far as they go. This is a community in which law is enforced and the breaking of law punished.

As the Father moves to the third part of his account, he shows us something of the internal organization and social differentiation of the scientific community. Like Bacon's conception of English society in his own day (and like Tudor social conceptions more generally) the social structure is compounded of both functional and hierarchical differentiations. And like many sixteenth-century social theorists Bacon allowed a degree of mobility to be combined with an otherwise fixed and unbreakable system of strata.

> *For the several employments and offices of our fellows; we have twelve that sail into foreign countries, under the names of other nations (for our own we conceal); who bring us the books, and abstracts, and patterns of experiments of all other parts. These we call Merchants of Light.*
>
> *We have three that collect the experiments of all mechanical arts; and also of liberal sciences; and also of practices which are not brought into arts. These we call Mystery-men.*
>
> *We have three that try new experiments, such as themselves think good. These we call Pioners or Miners.*
>
> *We have three that draw the experiments of the former four into titles and tables, to give the better light for the drawing of observations and axioms out of them. These we call Compilers.*
>
> *We have three that bend themselves, looking into the experiments of their fellows, and cast about how to draw out of them things of use and practice for man's life, and knowledge as well for works as for plain demonstration of causes, means of natural divinations, and the easy and clear discovery of the virtues and parts of bodies. These we call Dowry-men or Benefactors.*
>
> *Then after divers meetings and consults of our whole number, to consider of the former labours and collections, we have three that take care, out of them, to direct new experiments, of a higher light, more penetrating into nature than the former. These we call Lamps.*
>
> *We have three others that do execute the experiments so directed, and report them. These we call Inoculators.*
>
> *Lastly, we have three that raise the former discoveries by experiments into greater observations, axioms, and aphorisms. These we call Interpreters of Nature.*
>
> *We have also, as you must think, novices and apprentices, that the succession of the former employed men do not fail; besides a great number of servants and attendants, men and women.*[57]

Many things about this account are striking, but none more so than the smallness of the organization, or at least of its upper ranks: twelve Merchants of Light plus three each for the other eight categories for a total of thirty-six full-fledged fellows. These thirty-six command a good many more, it is true, but it is with this small core-group that the whole responsibility for the transmission and growth of science and technology would seem to rest. Given the fact that Bensalem was a substantial civilization (large enough in the golden age to hold its own against a major empire) the diminutive size of the scientific community is astounding. It testifies to Bacon's sense of the finitude of the natural order and consequently of the realm of technological possibility.

Below this elite of thirty-six men were two other groups. One was the collection of "novices and apprentices," some of whom would one day become fellows. The other was a "great number of servants and attendants, men and women."[58] These presumably would never rise to the status of fellows but were destined to do the menial work of science. We have already seen from comments that he made in the *Parasceve* that Bacon believed much of the work of collecting and compiling to be beneath him. The fellows of Salomon's House were undoubtedly provided with servants to relieve them from working on tasks which were demeaning or which constituted, in Bacon's view, a poor use of their intelligence and skill. This was the only group that Bacon mentions including women. It also seems to have been a permanent underclass in the community of learning, since it was distinguished from the novices and apprentices.

At the end of this description of the ranks and orders of the House of Salomon, the Father makes an interesting comment on their manner of proceeding:

> *We have consultations, which of the inventions and experiences which we have discovered shall be published, and which not: and take all an oath of secrecy, for the concealing of those which we think fit to keep secret: though some of those we do reveal sometimes to the state, and some not.*[59]

(In the Latin translation, one of the clauses in this passage reads, *"interdum Regi aut Senati revelemus,"* which adds just a bit to the little that we know about the government of Bensalem.) The point here is that, just as it controls the flow of new products into society at large, so does it control the flow of information. Whether the importance of such regulation is a result of the belief that knowledge is power and must be held by the elite or the idea that new knowledge simply poses a threat to a static social order based upon custom—this is left unclear. What is equally important about this brief passage—though, again, tantalizing rather than really explanatory—is the fact that the members of Salomon's House have it in their power to withhold knowledge even from the state. At very least this provision suggests a certain autonomy of the scientific community vis-à-vis the political authorities. Whether it should be taken to mean that in any vital respects the scientific establishment was in fact superior to the civil government is an open question.

In the fourth part of his account of Salomon's House, the Father turns to what he calls the "ordinances and rites" of the institution, and here we find indications that Bacon wanted the community to develop its own subculture. The first of these customs concerns the honoring of men who make important contributions:

> We have two very long and fair galleries: in one of these we place patterns and samples of all manner of the more rare and excellent inventions: in the other we place the statua's of all principal inventors. There we have the statua of your Columbus, that discovered the West Indies: also the inventor of ships: your monk that was the inventor of ordnance and of gunpowder: the inventor of music: the inventor of letters: the inventor of printing: the inventor of observations of astronomy: the inventor of works in metal: the inventor of glass: the inventor of silk of the worm: the inventor of wine: the inventor of corn and bread: the inventor of sugars: and all these by more certain tradition than you have. Then we have divers inventors of our own, of excellent works; which since you have not seen, it were too long to make descriptions of them; and besides, in the right understanding of those descriptions you might easily err.[60]

In *The Masculine Birth of Time*, Bacon had invited the young acolyte to join in initiating "a blessed race of Heroes or Supermen who will overcome the immeasurable helplessness and poverty of the human race."[61] That was part of the rhetoric of recruitment and community-founding. Now, with the establishment of organized science a long-accomplished fact, the cult of the inventor, as embodied in the gallery of statues, must have been intended to function in a slightly different way. It must have been intended to give the group its own sense of subcultural identity, its own history, its own scale of values. Even here, however, we must note something of a paradox. In all of his critical writings and all of his prescriptions of method, Bacon condemned the individual, no matter how brilliant or good, as a fit instrument for true science. The individual mattered not for the distinctive features of his mind or personality but rather to the extent that he could accept the common discipline and work as a member of the group. Organized science should work something like a machine in which each individual functioned as an integral part of the whole. Against the background of this analysis, the gallery of inventor-heroes might seem a little puzzling if it is taken as a true history of natural inquiry. It is less puzzling, however, if it is not intended to be such a history but rather part of the body of belief which guides and orients the science inquirers — part of the scientific subculture.

The cult of the inventor is surely part of the motivational system of Salomon's House, and it is not the only incentive offered to members: "Upon every invention of value, we erect a statua to the inventor, and give him a liberal and honourable reward."[62] Such are the *praemia* which, together with the *poena* mentioned above, work to regulate the work of the fellows of Salomon's House, and the conclusion that we draw from this is that in Bacon's vision of organized science the community can be made to respond to the same sorts of inducements and sanctions as operate in society at large.

Bacon also suggests that the collective life of this community is invested in ritualized practices. He has the Father mention "certain hymns and services, which we say daily, of laud and thanks to God for his marvellous works: and forms of prayers, imploring his aid and blessing for the illumination of our labours, and the turning of them into good and holy uses."[63] It is not enough to note that these men are good Christians, which, of course, in Bacon's view they are. What is important is that they have a special set of hymns, services, and prayers that bind them together as a group and set them apart from society in general. For Bacon religion was generally one of the important sources of social cohesion and stability, and this is no different in the smaller society of scientists.

Finally, the contacts between members of Salomon's House and the population of Bensalem are regulated by custom.

> We have circuits or visits of divers principal cities of the kingdom; where, as it cometh to pass, we do publish such new profitable inventions as we think good. And we do also declare natural divinations of diseases, plagues, swarms of hurtful creatures, scarcity, tempests, earthquakes, great inundations, comets, temperature of the year, and diver other things; and we give counsel thereupon what the people shall do for the prevention and remedy of them.[64]

Aside from showing us that even with a fully developed natural science humanity's control of nature is incomplete, the passage suggests that just as from the side of the public at large the appearance of scientists is a serious and ceremonious event. So too from the side of the scientists these excursions are regarded as part of the customary order of things — part, that is, of the "ordinances and rites" which govern the doings of Salomon's House.

The incompleteness of the portrait of Bensalem as a whole is echoed in the incompleteness of the portrait of Salomon's House. That is to say in the Father's account of the scientific institution we see the effects of good government in the commonwealth of learning without being told much at all about the governing authority itself. When the Father was introduced in the context of the description of his procession through the city, he was described as "one of the Fathers of Salomon's House." Who were these Fathers? Was it to them that the government of Salomon's House was entrusted? Did they rise from the ranks of the fellows or did they come to their positions by some other path? To what extent were they associated with the state itself? Bacon answers none of these questions. We do know that when the Father gives an account of the classes of men and women who do the work of Salomon's House, he makes no explicit mention of his place in it. We also know (because he says as much) that he is revealing only certain things about the House to the European narrator of the tale because only certain things are within his listener's understanding.

It is impossible to be quite satisfied with the *New Atlantis,* and it is tempting to read more meaning into its silences than is actually there.[65] Many of the attempts to coax esoteric messages from Bacon's utopia strike one as overartful and strained, implicitly imputing to Bacon a kind of esoteric cunning for which there is little independent evidence.

For our purposes, however, what is present at the surface of the piece is quite sufficient. Bacon's account of the internal order of the scientific community shows how closely it conforms to what we already know of his views on organized science and, more generally, to his deep-rooted convictions about the possibility of collective labor. In Salomon's House, men are organized into orders and ranks, each with its own functions, responsibilities, and expectations. Some men stand at the top; others serve obediently. Some may hope to climb if they are men of talent, but not all. The community has its law. Those who obey will be rewarded; those who disobey will be punished. Salomon's House is a customary society in which ceremony and ritual play a large part in solidifying and stabilizing the social order. However much it may constitute an elite in some respects, the society of Salomon's House is thus in many ways a microcosm of Bensalemite society as a whole and Bensalemite society, in its turn, is very much a well-governed England.

GOOD GOVERNMENT AND THE RATIONALIZATION OF LEARNING

In his article, "Science and Rule in Bacon's Utopia: An Introduction to the Reading of the *New Atlantis*," J. Weinberger writes that "the *New Atlantis* depicts a society formed by the rule of science."[66] In terms of the arguments developed in the preceding chapters, I think it is more correct to say almost the reverse—that it depicts a science formed by the application of sound and prudent social principles to the labor of learning.

In an ultimate sense, the Father and indeed the whole of Salomon's House are creatures of Salomona, a wise and good king. Salomon's House exists within the context of a well-ordered and prosperous society and is itself a well-ordered and prosperous society. In its internal organization it reflects the same prudent management that characterizes Bensalem as a whole. Both the microcosm of Salomon's House and the macrocosm of Bensalemite society reflect the fruits of good policy that was the aim of Tudor statesmen and political thinkers like Bacon.

Here scientific activity is governed (as Bacon all along said it should be) by the same principles which govern civil society. The fellows of the establishment remain the fallible creatures that they always were, subject to all the temptations which, as Bacon saw it, led learning astray in Tudor England. The difference was that they had been made to accept a regimen which held their perverse tendencies in check. Discipline was maintained by the creation of disciplining habits and customs and by the application of a system of *praemium* and *poena*.

While human power to manipulate nature was sufficiently great to assure overall abundance, nature was by no means completely subdued in Bensalem. Bensalemites remained subject to "diseases, plagues, swarms of hurtful creatures, scarcity, tempests, earthquakes, great inundations, comets, temperatures of the year, and divers other things." This is to say that the change wrought by science in the human predicament was marginal rather than radical. There is no direct textual evidence that science or scientists "rule" in Bensalem, or that the control of nature is so nearly complete as to reverse the curse which God laid upon sinful Adam.

As a statesman, of course, Bacon knew that marginal changes were important. It was significant that science had made Bensalem a society of abundance even if it did not radically transform the human relationship to nature, which remained forever postlapsarian in its "reluctation." Abundance was one of the keys to the stability and happiness of the society but only one. In his essay "Of Seditions and Troubles" Bacon had suggested that political disorder was a result of poverty or discontentment. Salomona was credited with two major innovations: Salomon's House and Bensalemite isolationism. Salomon's House provided a cure for poverty. The insulation of the island from the disturbing effects of foreign intercourse allowed the effective application of good policy and the development of a customary and ceremonious society in which discontentment, which was at root a psychological rather than a physical dissatisfaction, would not grow. Both of Salmona's decisions were important and consequential for the island society and together they indicate what good policy should be. Together, moreover, they would produce the happy effects which Bacon describes.

I do not mean to belittle the vision which Bacon embodied in his account of *New Atlantis* when I say that what Bacon wanted to show was simply a society and a learned community that were well-administered, well-governed, well-run. In many respects the principles underlying this government were those which guided Bacon's policy recommendations to Elizabeth and James I. The vision of a well-governed commonwealth—or commonwealth of learning—though less dramatic perhaps than modernist prophecy, should not seem unimportant to us, even if it occasionally appears quaintly time-bound.

The remarkable thing about Bacon's approach to learning is not that he discerned prophetically some future dilemma that would stem from the power of science to overwhelm politics but rather that, like many political thinkers of the Tudor age, he recognized the enormous power of government itself to provide peace and to rationalize social process and that, as a corollary to this general recognition, he boldly sought to extend the rationalizing potential of authority to the domain of learning. Having once conceived of scientific inquiry as a collective, collaborative, and social enterprise, it became for Bacon an activity accessible to the techniques of rationalization and control that were evolving in the political sphere. This is to say that he came to see it as an activity requiring government. In Bacon's account of method we can see the way in which he sought to regulate in detail the process of inquiry itself. In his depiction of Salomon's House he provided an imagined view of the institutional structure of organized science, complete with laws, penal system, social incentives, ritual and ceremonial, and social structure. Surely this is a remarkable conceptualization for a man whose intellectual tradition allowed the opposition between *vita comtemplativa* and *vita activa* and had drawn a sharp line of demarcation between thought and routinized labor. But if this conceptualization demonstrates anything, it is not the power of science to change politics (which in the *New Atlantis* it did not do in any radical way) but rather the power of politics to change science.

CONCLUSIONS

It was Bacon's distinction to have conceptualized the intellectual challenges of his age in terms of social production, to have analyzed the problem of producing natural knowledge in terms of principles drawn from the general social realm, and to have sought improvement in natural inquiry through the founding of a new community and the subjection of that community to stringent government. This entire strategy falls under the rubric of "scientific organization."

In the matter of organization, however, we must posit a profound discontinuity separating Bacon not only from the radical forms of Baconianism which flourished in the mid-century revolutionary period but even from the much more staid and conservative Baconianism of the postrevolutionary period. Throughout the seventeenth century, many would adopt Baconian slogans. His name has been variously associated with an attack on the illicit authority of the ancients and even on authority itself in the domain of learning, with a defense of unfettered and wide-ranging observation and experimentation, with collaboration and the exchange of scientific information, with the quest for socially useful knowledge. But none of those groups which called themselves "Baconian," adopted his vision of a tightly-organized, authoritarian science.

The reason for this discontinuity is not difficult to find. While there may indeed be aspects of scientific inquiry that can legitimately and profitably be discussed as "internal" issues and traced historically in isolation from the "external" contexts, this is most assuredly not true of those aspects which concern scientists themselves in their human dimensions and social being. Here the would-be organizer or philosopher or rhetorician of science had to draw on prevailing notions of human nature and prevailing conceptions of wisdom and prudence, and the historian of science who attempts to trace these organizational efforts must be prepared to seek outside the realm of science itself to find the roots of their ideas.

Bacon lived in a time when social and political ideas generally were entering a period of transformation. The early Stuarts did not sustain the order they had inherited from Elizabeth. English society did not stabilize as Bacon hoped it would, and prevailing ideologies were challenged radically by those who opposed the existing order. New principles were proposed and contested; new paradigms were put forward. The ideological world in which Bacon's vision of organization made sense and, indeed, seemed quite natural—this world passed.

The organizational paradigms which rose to the surface in the mid-century or during the Restoration were different. Although this is clearly a matter for further study, much of what Charles Webster has to say about the scientific aspirations of mid-century radicals suggests that one of the important paradigms for many of these groups was that of the brotherhood or religious fraternity. While elements of this ideal of spiritual solidarity are present in Bacon's writings, it is clearly not the central and pivotal conception. Likewise, the situation had altered again by the time the Royal Society was being organized. For one thing, the organizers of this body had lived through the revolutionary period with its harrowing vicissitudes and many of them were eager to establish science as something above politics and political bickering and, above all, as something apolitical. But to the extent that they still accepted a political paradigm to guide the internal orientation of the Society, it seems to have been parliamentary rather than monarchist. Indeed, at one point in his *History,* Sprat suggested that just as in Parliament, so in the Royal Society conflicting opinions could be debated, radical or one-sided errors could cancel one another out, and in the end public debate would lead to the truth. The idea that such an organizational shift took place by the time of the Restoration accords well with Barbara Shapiro's suggestion that a major epistemological shift had occurred in which a more open-ended and probabilistic ideal of knowledge replaced the quest for certainty.

It is not enough, in short, to assume that seventeenth-century Baconianism is one and homogeneous, and certainly in the matter of organization there would appear to be major internal discontinuities which demand exploration and explanation. I hope that the account of Bacon's organizational ideas will open such a plane of inquiry and allow us to begin to draw certain important distinctions between varieties of Baconianism and to understand some of the specific variables whose alteration allowed Baconianism to be adapted to a political and social world which was changing dramatically.

The history of ideas about scientific organization generally in seventeenth-century England and of the influence of political ideology on science has yet to be written. The recognition that on this point "Baconianism" was a highly variegated movement, in which the differing political outlooks and ideologies of succeeding generations of Baconians played an important role, will need to be the starting point. The history of organizational ideas and approaches will form one phase of that larger study which Robert Merton sketched out in the following series of questions:

> What are the modes of interplay between society, culture and science? Do these vary in kind and extent in differing historical contexts? What makes

for those sizable shifts in recruitment to the intellectual disciplines – the various sciences and humanities – that lead to great variations in their development? Among those engaged in the work of science, what makes for shifts in the foci of inquiry from one science to another and, within each of the sciences, from one set of problems to another? Under which conditions are changes in the foci of attention the planned results of deliberate policy, and under which the largely unanticipated consequences of value commitments among scientists and those controlling the support of science? How did these matters stand while science was being institutionalized and how do they stand since its thoroughgoing institutionalization? And once science has evolved forms of internal organization, how do patterns and rates of social interaction among scientists affect the development of scientific ideas? How does a cultural emphasis upon social utility as a prime, let alone an exclusive, criterion for scientific work variously affect the rate and direction of advance in science?[67]

Merton has interpreted the emergence of seventeenth-century English science as heavily influenced by religious ideas and ideals, and the long-argued connection between Puritanism and science has come in for a great deal of criticism in recent years. I have chosen as my focus a case in which not religious but political ideas appear to have exercised a decisive influence over one important phase in the history of science. In the case of Bacon, the influence was not so much on the practice of science as on its ideology. But as an ideology Baconianism played an important part in legitimating science for the seventeenth century by relating it to the broader value commitments of English society.

The desire to discover points of convergence and nexus between scientific thought and the broader social-cultural milieu (or thought and society generally) though closely associated with Marxist theory over the past century, should not be understood and judged – either positively or negatively – in narrowly ideological or sectarian terms. In one sense, what is at issue is much smaller and more particular than the grand, "totalizing" animus of materialist philosophy – and much more accessible to empirical inquiry. In this sense, particular questions of influence can not be judged on a priori grounds but are the continuing concern of any historian or biographer. In another sense, however, what is at issue is much larger that the "materialism" of Marx. For better or for worse, it seems to be part of the human intellectual fate to search for larger and more embracing patterns of order in place of smaller, fragmented ones. Bacon himself recognized this impulse as an infirmity of the human mind, and so it may be. But it is likewise part of the rationalizing drive of thought itself. The desire to relate important shifts in the history of thought to other aspects of the world in which the thinkers live, in any case, must not be interpreted only in terms of the categories of Marxism and anti-Marxism. Rather, it must be seen as part of the rationalizing quest which is deep-rooted in the human spirit.

The sociological approach of Merton may now have something of an outdated sound (though to the unbiased, tolerant reader it will still be immensely provocative), but the questions he posed will not be put to rest. In an interview given in 1977 Michel Foucault shed light on the impulse behind some of his own work in a way that is both historically and theoretically interesting:

> When I was studying during the early 1950s, one of the great problems that arose was that of the political status of science and the ideological functions which it could serve. It wasn't exactly the Lysenko business which dominated everything, but I believe that around that sordid affair—which had long remained buried and carefully hidden—a whole number of interesting questions were provoked. These can all be summed up in two words: power and knowledge. I believe I wrote *Madness and Civilization* to some extent within the horizon of these questions. For me, it was a matter of saying this: if, concerning a science like theoretical physics or organic chemistry, one poses the problem of its relations with the political and economic structures of society, isn't one posing an excessively complicated question? Doesn't this set the threshold of possible explanations impossibly high? But on the other hand, if one takes a form of knowledge (*savoir*) like psychiatry, won't the question be much easier to resolve, since the epistemological profile of psychiatry is a low one and psychiatric practice is linked with a whole range of institutions, economic requirements and political issues of social regulation? Couldn't the interweaving effects of power and knowledge be grasped with greater certainty in the case of a science as "dubious" as psychiatry? It was this same question which I wanted to pose concerning medicine in *The Birth of the Clinic:* medicine certainly has a much more solid scientific armature than psychiatry, but it, too, is profoundly enmeshed in social structures. What rather threw me at the time was the fact that the question I was posing totally failed to interest those to whom I addressed it. They regarded it as a problem which was politically unimportant and epistemologically vulgar.[68]

Foucault's quest (which proved so provocative and so fruitful) to investigate the points at which the domains of knowledge and power could be seen to intersect and mutually condition one another is not unrelated to the present study. Bacon's conception of science, his work on scientific organization, and his vision of Salomon's House are virtual emblems of the modern quest to achieve power through knowledge and—no less certainly—knowledge through power.

If Bacon's thought offers the possibility of exploring what Foucault called "the interweaving effects of power and knowledge," it likewise directs our attention more specifically to what has become in our own century a dominant trend in natural science: the management of scientific inquiry in the context of a community organized under a rationalizing authority. From the later seventeenth century until the early twentieth century science presented itself as free and open — a collaboration of autonomously directed individuals, each submitting ideas to public scrutiny, criticism, and debate, which process in turn became the ultimate arbiter of scientific truth. This liberal image of science may not always have been consistently born out by the actual behavior of the scientists, but it was widely accepted as expressing something essentially true about the scientific enterprise as a whole. Although such liberal science consistently looked to Bacon as an originating and guiding spirit, I hope I have succeeded in showing that his conception of science was anything but liberal.

Before dismissing Bacon as the prophet he has long been taken to be, however, we might consider twentieth-century science with its tightly organized and managed research institutions often operating in closely guarded secrecy. These (rather than the Royal Society or other "liberal" communities of science) are perhaps the true descendants of Salomon's House. Here power in the service of profit or national advantage seeks the careful management of personnel and resources to establish that true Baconian "empire" over nature. Here is that close union of "light" with "fruits" of which Bacon spoke. And here, sometimes for better and sometimes for worse, is the government of intellectual inquiry in the fullest, truest sense.

Notes

INTRODUCTION

1. The task of mapping the varieties of seventeenth-century Baconianism has not been systematically pursued. One extremely interesting and suggestive approach to the problem has been made, however, by Theodore M. Brown, who, acknowledging the influence of Kuhn, seeks to analyze Baconians into sociological groupings and to show that different groups tended to seize on different aspects of the thought of Bacon himself. See Theodore M. Brown, "The Rise of Baconianism in Seventeenth-Century England: A Perspective on Science and Society during the Scientific Revolution," in *Science and History: Studies in Honor of Edward Rosen,* Studia Copernicana 16 (Wroclaw: The Polish Academy of Sciences Press, 1978), 501–22.

2. Charles Webster treats the radical Baconianism, deeply imbued with millenarian and eschatological elements, which flourished in the politically turbulent middle decades of the seventeenth century under the inspiration and guidance of men like Samuel Hartlib and under the banner of the Lord Chancellor Bacon. See Charles Webster, *The Great Instauration: Science, Medicine and Reform, 1626–1660* (New York: Holmes & Meier, 1975).

3. Paolo Rossi, *Francis Bacon from Magic to Science,* trans. Sacha Rabinovitch (Chicago: University of Chicago Press, 1968), 9, 27. The relevant passages are quoted and discussed in the opening of Chapter 4.

4. Benjamin Farrington, *The Philosophy of Francis Bacon: An Essay on Its Development from 1603 to 1609 with New Translations of Fundamental Texts* (Chicago: University of Chicago Press, Phoenix Books, 1966), 22, 54. For discussion see opening of Chapter 4.

5. Christopher Hill, *Intellectual Origins of the English Revolution* (Oxford: Clarendon Press, 1965), 89f., 110, 112. See the opening of Chapter 4.

1. THE FORMATIVE PERIOD

1. Jonathan Marwil, *The Trials of Counsel: Francis Bacon in 1621* (Detroit: Wayne State University Press, 1976), 64. Although it is concerned almost exclusively with Bacon's political career, Marwil's study provides a fine introduction to Bacon-the-man and shows the virtues of a properly directed skepticism.

2. "Of Simulation and Dissimulation," Francis Bacon, *The Works of Francis Bacon,* ed. James Spedding, Robert Leslie Ellis, Douglas Denon Heath, 14 vols. (London: Longmans & Co. *et al.,* 1857–90), 6:388. The "Spedding edition" is still the standard edition of Bacon's works. The first seven volumes are devoted to Bacon's writings; the second seven to Bacon's "Life and Letters" by Spedding. All fourteen volumes will henceforth be cited as *Works,* whether the reference is to the first seven volumes or to the "Life and Letters."

265

3. Bacon, "Of Followers and Friends," *Works,* 6:495.

4. Robert Tittler, *Nicholas Bacon: The Making of a Tudor Statesman* (Athens: Ohio University Press, 1976), 10.

5. William Rawley, "The Life of the Honourable Author," in Bacon, *Works,* 1:4.

6. Bacon, *Works,* 8:4.

7. Ibid., 8:4f.

8. Epstein, *Francis Bacon: A Political Biography* (Athens: Ohio University Press, 1977) 24.

9. Tittler, *Nicholas Bacon,* 188.

10. Bowen, *Francis Bacon: The Temper of a Man* (Boston: Little, Brown, 1963); this phrase is the title of her chapter on Bacon's childhood.

11. Epstein, *Political Biography,* 26.

12. Robert C. Johnson, Francis Bacon and Lionel Cranfield," *Huntington Library Quarterly* 23, no. 4 (August, 1960): 301–20.

13. Epstein, *Political Biography,* 27; see also Bacon's letter to Burghley, May 6, 1586, *Works,* 8:59.

14. Epstein, *Political Biography,* 29.

15. Ibid., 30.

16. Ibid., 29.

17. Ibid., 30f.

18. Ibid.

19. Bacon, "To My Lord Treasurer Burghley," *Works,* 8:108.

20. Ibid., 109.

21. Bacon, *Works,* 8:107.

22. Marwil, *Trials of Counsel,* 63f.

23. Ibid., 70f.

24. Ibid.

25. Ibid.

26. S. R. Gardiner, "Francis Bacon," *Dictionary of National Biography* (Oxford: Oxford University Press, 1959–60), 1:802.

27. Ibid., 1:803.

28. J. E. Neale, *Elizabeth I and Her Parliaments, 1584–1601* (New York: W. W. Norton, 1966), 309.

29. Epstein, *Political Biography,* 41.

30. Ibid., 38.

31. Ibid., 48.

32. Ibid., 43f.

33. Ibid., 52.

34. Ibid.

35. Ibid., 53.

36. Bacon, "Certain Observations Made upon a Libel Published This Present Year, 1592," *Works,* 8:146–208.

37. Bacon, *The Essayes or Counsels, Civill and Morall, Works,* 6:375–518.

38. Ronald S. Crane, "The Relation of Bacon's *Essays* to His Program for the Advancement of Learning," in Brian Vickers, ed., *Essential Articles for the Study of Francis Bacon* (Hampden, Connecticut: Archon Books, 1968), 272–92.

39. Gardiner, "Francis Bacon," 1:807.

40. Ibid.

41. Alexander Balloch Grossart, "Ann Bacon," *Dictionary of National Biography* (Oxford: Oxford University Press, 1959–60), 1:795–96.

42. Bacon, *Works,* 10:5f.

2. THE PRODUCTIVE YEARS

1. James Spedding, "Preface to *The Advancement of Learning,*" Bacon, *Works,* 3:255f.

2. Bacon, *The Two Bookes of Francis Bacon of the Proficience and Advancement of Learning Divine and Humane, Works,* 3:263.

3. Ibid., 3:324.

4. Ibid., 3:325–29.

5. Epstein, *Political Biography,* 71.

6. Bacon, *Works,* 9:123.

7. Epstein, *Political Biography,* 73.

8. Ibid., 73f.

9. Ibid., 23.

10. Bacon, "A Speech of the King's Solicitor, Persuading the House of Commons to Desist from Farther Question of Receiving the King's Messages by Their Speaker, and from the Body of the Council, as well as from the King's Person. In the Parliament 7 Jacobi," *Works,* 11:177–80.

11. Epstein, *Political Biography,* 78.

12. Ibid., 79.

13. Ibid., 84.

14. Ibid.

15. Ibid., 86.

16. Gardiner, "Francis Bacon," 1:811.

17. Epstein, *Political Biography,* 90.

18. Ibid., 93.

19. Ibid.

20. Ibid., 95.

21. Ibid., 90.

22. Ibid., 95.

23. Farrington, *Philosophy of Francis Bacon,* 12.

24. Bacon, "On the Interpretation of Nature. Proem," *Works,* 10:84.

25. Ibid., 10:85.

26. Bacon, *Works,* 3:507f.

27. Gardiner, "Francis Bacon," 1:811.

28. Bacon, "Commentarius Solutus," *Works,* 11:63f.

29. Ibid., 11:64.

30. Ibid., 11:64–67.

31. Gardiner, "Francis Bacon," 1:811.

32. Epstein, *Political Biography,* 120–21.

33. Ibid., 102.

34. Ibid., 104.

35. Gardiner, "Francis Bacon," 1:813.

36. Ibid.

37. Epstein, *Political Biography,* 115.

38. Ibid., 123.

39. Ibid., 130.

40. Robert C. Johnson, "Francis Bacon and Lionel Cranfield," *The Huntington Library Quarterly* 23, no. 4 (August, 1960): 302f.

41. Quoted by Epstein, *Political Biography,* 135.

42. Ibid., 133.

43. Gardiner, "Francis Bacon," 1:820.

44. Bacon, *Works,* 14:293.

45. Bowen, *Temper of a Man.*

46. Benjamin Farrington, "Francis Bacon after His Fall," *Studies in the Literary Imagination* 4, no. 1 (April, 1971): 158.

47. Bowen, *Temper of a Man,* 213f.

48. Bacon, "To the Marquis of Buckingham," *Works,* 14:281.

49. Bacon, "To the King," *Works,* 14:282.

50. Bacon, Ibid., 14:303.

51. Thomas Meautys, "To the Lord Viscount St. Alban," *Works,* 14:325.

52. Bacon, "Memorial of Access" (Notes for an Interview with the King), *Works,* 14:351.

53. Bacon, "To the Right Honourable His Very Good Lord, the Lord Marquis of Buckingham, High Admiral of England," *Works,* 14:356.

54. Bacon, "To the King," *Works,* 14:382.

55. Ibid., 14:505.

56. Ibid., 14:518f.

57. Farrington, "Bacon after His Fall," 143–58.

58. Bacon, "To the Right Reverend Father in God, Lancelot Andrewes, Lord Bishop of Winchester, and Counsellor of Estate to His Majesty," *Works,* 14:371f.

59. Ibid., 14:372f.

60. Ibid.

61. Ibid.

62. Bacon, "To Father Redemptus Baranzan," *Works,* 14:377.

63. Ibid.

64. Ibid.

65. Ibid., 14:378.

66. William Rawley, Preface "To the Reader" to Bacon's *Sylva Sylvarum: or Natural History. In Ten Centuries,* Bacon, *Works,* 2:335f.

67. Ibid.

68. William Rawley, "Life of Bacon," in Bacon, *Works,* 1:15.

69. Bacon, "To the King," *Works,* 14:436.

70. Bacon, "Epistola ad Fulgentium," *Works,* 14:532f.

3. ORDER AND PRODUCTIVITY IN THE LARGER COMMONWEALTH

1. G. P. Gooch, *Political Thought in England from Bacon to Halifax* (London: Williams and Norgate, 1923), 23. Gooch's famous study was first published in 1914–15.

2. Ibid., 22.

3. Ibid., 32.

4. Ibid., 33.

5. Ibid., 33f.

6. Quentin Skinner, *The Foundations of Modern Political Thought,* 2 vols. (Cambridge: Cambridge University Press, 1978).

7. Ibid., 1:212.

8. Ibid., 1:217f.

9. Ibid.

10. Ibid., 1:222.

11. Ibid., 1:235.

12. Ibid., 1:239.

13. Whitney R. D. Jones, *The Tudor Commonwealth, 1529–1559* (London: University of London, The Athelone Press, 1970).

14. Ibid., 2f.

15. Ibid., 4.

16. Ibid., 226.

17. J. H. Hexter, *Reappraisals in History,* 2d ed. (Chicago and London: University of Chicago Press, 1979), 106.

18. Ibid.

19. Ibid., 109.

20. Ibid.

21. Ibid.

22. Christopher Morris, *Political Thought in England, Tyndale to Hooker* (Oxford: Oxford University Press, 1953), 72.

23. Ibid., 72f.

24. M. M. Knappen, *Tudor Puritanism: A Chapter in the History of Idealism* (Chicago and London: University of Chicago Press, Phoenix Books, 1966), 293.

25. Ibid., 294.

26. Ibid., 295.

27. Bacon, "To the Queen" ("Letter of Advice to Queen Elizabeth"), *Works,* 8:47.

28. Ibid., 8:49f.

29. Ibid., 8:50.

30. Ibid.

31. Ibid., 8:51.

32. Bacon, "An Advertisement Touching the Controversies of the Church of England," *Works,* 8:74.

33. Ibid, 8:75.

34. Ibid.

35. Ibid.

36. Ibid., 8:77f.

37. Ibid., 8:82.

38. Ibid., 8:86.

39. Ibid., 8:87.

40. Ibid., 8:88.

41. Ibid., 8:93.

42. Ibid., 8:94.

43. Bacon, "The Beginning of the History of Great Britain," *Works,* 6:276f.

44. Ibid.

45. Ibid.

46. Bacon, "Of Seditions and Troubles," *Works,* 6:406.

47. Ibid., 6:407.

48. Ibid., 6:408.

49. Ibid.

50. Ibid.

51. Ibid.

52. Ibid., 6:409.

53. Ibid.

54. Ibid., 6:410.

55. Ibid.

56. Ibid., 6:409.

57. Ibid., 6:411.

58. Ibid.

59. Ibid.

60. Ibid.

61. Ibid., 6:411f.

62. Ibid., 6:412.

63. Ibid.

64. Ibid.

65. Hill, *Intellectual Origins,* 97f.

66. Bacon, "Of Innovations," *Works,* 6:433.

67. Ibid., 6:433f.

68. Bacon, "Of Custom and Education," *Works,* 6:470.

69. Ibid., 6:471f.

70. Bacon, *Of the Wisdom of the Ancients, Works,* 6:702.

71. Ibid., 6:703.

72. Ibid.

73. Ibid.

74. Ibid., 6:718.

75. Ibid., 6:718f.

76. Ibid., 6:721.

77. Ibid., 6:722.

78. Ibid.

79. Ibid., 6:722.

80. Bacon, *Of the Advancement of Learning, Works,* 3:473ff.

81. J. W. Allen, *English Political Thought, 1603–1660.* 2 vols. (London: Methuen, 1938), 1:49.

82. Ibid., 1:50.

83. Bacon, "To the King," *Works,* 14:290.

84. Bacon, "A Copy of a Letter Conceived To Be Written to the Late Duke of Buckingham When First He Became a Favourite to King James; Containing Some Advices to the Duke for His Better Direction in that Eminent Place of Favourite: Drawn at the Entreaty of the Duke Himself. From Sir Francis Bacon," ("Advice to Villiers – The Second Version"), *Works,* 13:38f.

85. Bacon, "A Letter of Advice, Written by Sir Francis Bacon to the Duke of Buckingham, When He Became Favourite to King James("Advice to Villiers – The First Version"), *Works,* 13:14.

86. Ibid.

87. Bacon, "A Letter to Sir George Villiers, Upon the Sending His Patent for Viscount Villiers to Be Signed. Aug. 12 1616," *Works,* 13:6f.

88. Hexter, *Reappraisals in History,* 109.

89. Bacon, "Certain Observations Made upon a Libel Published this Present Year, 1592. Entitled, *A Declaration of the True Causes of the Great Troubles, Presupposed to be Intended against the Realm of England,*" *Works,* 8:153.

90. Ibid., 8:154.

91. Ibid., 8:159.

92. Ibid., 8:158f.

93. Ibid., 8:159f.

94. Ibid., 8:160.

95. Ibid.

96. Ibid., 8:173.

97. Ibid., 8:175.
98. Ibid.
99. Ibid., 8:176f.
100. Bacon, "Advice to Villiers — The First Version," *Works,* 13:17.
101. Ibid.
102. Ibid., 13:19.
103. Ibid., 13:21.
104. Ibid., 13:21f.
105. Ibid., 13:22.
106. Ibid.
107. Ibid., 13:22f.
108. Ibid.
109. Ibid.
110. Ibid., 13:24.
111. Ibid.
112. Bacon, "Advice to Villiers — The Second Version," *Works,* 13:47ff.
113. Bacon, "Of Plantations," *Works,* 6:457.
114. Ibid., 6:458f.
115. Ibid., 6:457f.
116. Ibid., 6:457.
117. Ibid.
118. Ibid., 6:458.
119. Ibid., 6:459.
120. Ibid.
121. Ibid., 6:457.
122. Ibid., 6:459.
123. Bacon, *Of the Advancement of Learning, Works,* 3:321f.
124. Ibid., 3:322f.
125. Ibid., 3:323.
126. Ibid., 3:324.
127. Ibid.
128. Ibid., 3:325.
129. Ibid., 3:326.
130. Ibid.
131. Ibid.
132. Ibid., 3:327.
133. Ibid.
134. Ibid.
135. Ibid., 3:328.
136. Farrington, *Philosophy of Francis Bacon,* 38.

4. COLLABORATION, ORGANIZATION, AND GOVERNMENT

1. Jeffrey Barnouw, "Active Experience vs. Wish-Fulfillment in Francis Bacon's Moral Psychology of Science," *The Philosophical Forum* 9, no. 1 (1977), 78.
2. Rossi, *Magic to Science,* 9, 27; Benjamin Farrington, *Philosophy of Francis Bacon,* 22, 54; Christopher Hill, *Intellectual Origins,* 89f., 110, 112.
3. Mary Hesse, "Francis Bacon's Philosophy of Science," in Vickers, *Essential Arti-*

cles for the Study of Francis Bacon (Cambridge: Cambridge University Press, 1968), 123.

4. Hesse, in Vickers, *Essential Articles,* 124.

5. Bacon, *The New Organon; Or, True Directions Concerning the Interpretation of Nature, Works,* 1:152; 4:40f.

6. Bacon, *Valerius Terminus of the Interpretation of Nature: With the Annotations of Hermes Stella, Works,* 3:219.

7. Ibid., 3:220.

8. Ibid., 3:220ff.

9. Ibid.

10. Ibid.

11. Ibid.

12. Ibid., 3:225.

13. Ibid.

14. Ibid., 3:225f.

15. Ibid., 3:226.

16. Shapiro, *Probability and Certainty in Seventeenth-Century England* (Princeton, N.J.: Princeton University Press, 1983), 90.

17. Bacon, *Valerius Terminus, Works,* 3:227f.

18. Ibid., 3:231.

19. Bacon, *The Great Instauration, Works,* 4:18.

20. Ibid., 4:7.

21. Ibid., 4:17.

22. Ibid., 4:18.

23. Ibid.

24. Bacon, *The New Organon, Works,* 1:121.

25. Bacon, *The Great Instauration, Works,* 4:15.

26. Ibid., 1:128.

27. Ibid., 1:129.

28. Ibid., 1:121.

29. Ibid., 1:128.

30. Ibid., 4:18; *"certa ratione menienda";* note that the verb, for *munio,* carries the meaning of fortifying or defending, with clear military connotations.

31. Ibid., 1:121.

32. Ibid., 1:124.

33. Ibid., 4:21; *"ac ab erroribus viarum atque impedimentis, nostris praesidiis et auxiliis, liberati et muniti, laborum qui restant et ipsi in partem veniant," Works,* 1:132f.

34. Bacon, *The Great Instauration, Works,* 4:22.

35. Ibid.

36. Ibid.

37. Ibid., 4:22f.; 1:134.

38. Ibid., 4:23.

39. Ibid., 4:23; 1:135.

40. Ibid., 4:135.

41. Ibid., 4:24.

42. Ibid., 4:25.

43. Ibid.

44. Ibid., 4:24.

45. Ibid., 4:24.

46. Ibid., 4:25.

47. Ibid., 4:25f.; 1:137.

48. Ibid., 4:26.

49. Ibid.

50. Ibid.

51. Ibid.

52. Ibid., 4:27.

53. Ibid.

54. Ibid.

55. Ibid.

56. Ibid., 4:27; ". . . *intellectum nisi per inductionem ejusque formam legitimam judicare non posse*," 1:139.

57. Ibid.

58. Ibid., 4:28.

59. Ibid.

60. Ibid., 4:29f.

61. Ibid.

62. Ibid.

63. Ibid.

64. Ibid., 4:30.

65. Ibid., 4:30; 1:143.

66. Ibid., 4:31.

67. Ibid.

68. Ibid.

69. Ibid.

70. Ibid., 4:32.

71. Ibid.

72. Ibid., 4:32.

73. Bacon, *Of the Dignity and Advancement of Learning* (*De Augmentis*), *Works*, 4:301.

74. Bacon, *The New Organon, Works,* 4:53.

75. Ibid., 4:54.

76. Ibid., 4:57.

77. Ibid., 4:55–56.

78. Ibid., 4:57.

79. Ibid., 4:58.

80. Ibid., 4:57; 4:112; 1:219.

81. Ibid., 4:59–60.

82. Ibid., 4:60–61.

83. Ibid., 4:62.

84. Ibid., 4:64.

85. Ibid., 4:65.

86. Ibid., 4:65; 4:66; 4:69.

87. Ibid., 4:57.

88. Bacon, *The Great Instauration, Works,* 4:14.

89. Ibid.

90. Ibid., 4:14.

91. Ibid., 1:127.

92. Ibid., 4:15.

93. Ibid., 4:16; *"disceptet et judicet,"* 1:127.

94. *Works,* 6:16.

95. Ibid., 4:14.

96. Ibid., 4:16.
97. Ibid., 4:16f.; 1:128.
98. Ibid., 4:17; 1:128.
99. Ibid., 4:17.
100. Ibid.
101. Ibid., 1:128.
102. Ibid., 4:17.
103. Ibid.
104. Ibid.

5. A COMMUNITY OF SCIENTISTS

1. See I. Bernard Cohen, *Revolution in Science* (Cambridge, Mass., and London, England: The Belknap Press of Harvard University Press, 1985).
2. Ibid., 86.
3. Bacon, *The New Organon, Works,* 4:89f.
4. Bacon, *The Refutation of Philosophies,* in Farrington, *The Philosophy of Francis Bacon,* 108. A number of important works from the first decade of the seventeenth century, though given in Latin, were not translated in Spedding's edition. Passages from certain of these works — *The Masculine Birth of Time, Thoughts and Conclusions,* and *The Refutation of Philosophies* — are quoted from the translations which Farrington provided in *The Philosophy of Francis Bacon.*
5. Ibid.
6. Bacon, *The New Organon, Works,* 4:42.
7. Ibid., 4:97.
8. Farrington, *The Philosophy of Francis Bacon,* 12.
9. Ibid.
10. Ibid., 22.
11. Bacon, "To My Lord Treasurer Burghley," *Works,* 8:109.
12. Ibid.
13. Bacon, *Commentarius Solutus, Works,* 11:66.
14. Bacon, "To Mr. Secretary Conway," *Works,* 14:408.
15. Bacon, *Of the Advancement of Learning, Works,* 3:319.
16. Bacon, *Commentarius Solutus, Works,* 11:64f.
17. Bacon, "Preface for *De Interpretatione Naturae,*" *Works,* 10:87.
18. Bacon, *Works,* 3:523.
19. Farrington, *The Philosophy of Francis Bacon,* 39.
20. Bacon, *The Masculine Birth of Time,* in Farrington, *The Philosophy of Francis Bacon,* 61.
21. Ibid., 62.
22. Ibid.
23. Ibid.
24. Ibid., 63.
25. Ibid., 64.
26. Ibid.
27. Ibid., 65.
28. Ibid., 70.
29. Ibid.

30. Ibid., 72.

31. Ibid.

32. Bacon, *Cogitata et Visa, Works,* 3:591.

33. Bacon, *Filum Labyrinthi, sive Formula Inquisitionis, Works,* 3:496.

34. Bacon, *Thoughts and Conclusions,* in Farrington, *The Philosophy of Francis Bacon,* 94.

35. Ibid., 94f.

36. Ibid., 98.

37. Ibid.

38. Ibid.

39. Ibid., 99.

40. Ibid.

41. Ibid.

42. Ibid.

43. Ibid., 100.

44. Ibid.

45. Bacon, *Commentarius Solutus, Works,* 11:66.

46. Bacon, *Thoughts and Conclusions,* in Farrington, *The Philosophy of Francis Bacon,* 100f.

47. Ibid., 101.

48. Ibid.

49. Ibid.

50. Bacon, *Commentarius Solutus, Works,* 11:66.

51. Bacon, *The Refutation of Philosophies,* in Farrington, *The Philosophy of Francis Bacon,* 103.

52. Ibid.

53. Ibid., 104f.

54. Ibid., 106; for Latin see Bacon, *Works,* 3:560.

55. Ibid., 106f.; for Latin see *Works,* 3:561.

56. Ibid., 107; for Latin see *Works,* 3:561.

57. Ibid.; for Latin see *Works,* 3:562.

58. Ibid., 109; for Latin see *Works,* 3:563.

59. Ibid., 107; for Latin see *Works,* 3:562.

60. Ibid., 108.

61. Ibid., 120.

62. Ibid., 108f.

63. Ibid., 107.

64. Ibid., 120f.

65. Ibid., 116.

66. Ibid., 118f.

67. Ibid., 133.

6. SCIENCE GOVERNED

1. Bacon, *The New Organon, Works,* 4:112.

2. Ibid., 4:90.

3. Ibid., 4:57.

4. Ibid., 4:40; 1:152.

5. Ibid., 4:112.

6. Ibid., 4:51.

7. Ibid.

8. Bacon, *Of the Advancement of Learning, Works,* 3:409.

9. Ibid., 3:410.

10. Ibid., 3:437.

11. Ibid., 3:438.

12. Ibid., 3:440.

13. Bacon, *Preparative towards a Natural and Experimental History* (*Parasceve*), *Works,* 4:251f.

14. Bacon, *The Refutation of Philosophies,* in Farrington, *The Philosophy of Francis Bacon,* 122.

15. Bacon, *Parasceve, Works,* 4:254f.

16. Ibid., 4:255.

17. Ibid., 4:254f.

18. Ibid., 4:258.

19. Ibid.

20. Rawley, Preface "To the Reader" to *New Atlantis* in Bacon, *Works,* 3:127.

21. See, for example, the distinction which Howard White seeks to draw between Bacon's provisional and definitive politics in *Peace among the Willows* (The Hague: Martinus Nijhoff, 1968).

22. Bacon, *New Atlantis, Works,* 3:131.

23. Ibid., 3:135.

24. Ibid., 3:136.

25. Ibid.

26. Ibid.

27. Ibid., 3:143.

28. Ibid.

29. Ibid., 3:144.

30. Ibid.

31. Ibid., 3:145f.

32. Ibid., 3:146.

33. Ibid.

34. Ibid., 3:127.

35. Ibid., 3:147–51.

36. Ibid., 3:151.

37. Ibid.

38. Ibid., 3:152.

39. Ibid., 3:152f.

40. Ibid., 3:153.

41. Ibid.

42. Ibid.

43. Ibid.

44. Ibid., 3:153f.

45. Ibid., 3:154.

46. Bacon, *The Refutation of Philosophies,* in Farrington, *The Philosophy of Francis Bacon,* 108.

47. Bacon, *New Atlantis, Works,* 3:155.

48. Ibid.

49. Ibid., 3:127.

50. Ibid., 3:156.

51. Ibid.

52. Ibid., 3:156–64.

53. Ibid., 3:159.

54. Ibid., 3:160.

55. Ibid., 3:161.

56. Ibid., 3:164.

57. Ibid., 3:165.

58. Ibid.

59. Ibid.

60. Ibid., 3:165f.

61. Bacon, *The Masculine Birth of Time,* in Farrington, *The Philosophy of Francis Bacon,* 72.

62. Bacon, *New Atlantis, Works,* 3:166.

63. Ibid.

64. Ibid.

65. See for example, J. Weinberger, "Science and Rule in Bacon's Utopia: An Introduction to the Reading of the *New Atlantis," American Political Science Review* 70: 865–85.

66. Ibid., 865.

67. Robert K. Merton, *Science, Technology and Society in Seventeenth Century England* (New Jersey: Humanities Press; Sussex: Harvester Press, 1978), "Preface: 1970," ix.

68. Michel Foucault, "Truth and Power," *Power/Knowledge: Selected Interviews & Other Writings, 1972–1977,* edited by Colin Gordon (New York: Pantheon Books, 1980), 109f.

Selected Bibliography

Allen, J. W. *English Political Thought, 1603–1660.* Vol. 1, *1603–44.* London: Methuen & Co., 1938.

Anderson, Fulton H. *The Philosophy of Francis Bacon.* Chicago: University of Chicago Press, 1948.

_____. *Francis Bacon, His Career and Thought.* Los Angeles: University of Southern California Press, 1962.

Bacon, Francis. *The Works of Francis Bacon,* edited by James Spedding, Robert Leslie Ellis, Douglas Denon Heath. London: Longmans & Co. et al., 1857–90.

Barnouw, Jeffrey. "Active Experience vs. Wish-Fulfilment in Francis Bacon's Moral Psychology of Science," *The Philosophical Forum* 9 (1977): 78–99.

_____. "The Separation of Reason and Faith in Bacon and Hobbes, and Leibniz's *Theodicy*," *Journal of the History of Ideas* 42 (1981): 607–28.

Ben-David, Joseph. *The Scientist's Role in Society: A Comparative Study.* Foundations of Modern Sociology Series. Englewood Cliffs, New Jersey: Prentice-Hall, 1971.

Berns, Laurence. "Francis Bacon and the Conquest of Nature," *Interpretation: A Journal of Political Philosophy* 7 (1978): 1–26.

Bierman, Judah. "Science and Society in the *New Atlantis* and Other Renaissance Utopias," *PMLA* 78 (1963): 492–500.

_____. "New Atlantis Revisited," *Studies in the Literary Imagination* 4 (1971): 121–41.

Bowen, Catherine Drinker. *Francis Bacon, The Temper of a Man.* Boston: Little, Brown, 1963.

Broad, C. D. *The Philosophy of Francis Bacon.* Cambridge: Cambridge University Press, 1926.

Brown, Theodore M. "The Rise of Baconianism in 17th-Century England: A Perspective on Science and Society during the Scientific Revolution." In *Science and History: Studies in Honor of Edward Rosen,* 501–22. Studia Copernicana 16. Wroclaw: Ossolineum, 1978.

Bullough, Geoffrey. "Bacon and the Defence of Learning." Reprinted in Brian Vickers (ed.). *Essential Articles for the Study of Francis Bacon,* 93–113. Hamden, Connecticut: Archon Books, 1968.

Cameron, Evan. "Francis Bacon and the Pragmatic Theory of Forms," *The Philosophical Forum* 5 (1974): 592–610.

Cohen, L. Jonathan. "Some Historical Remarks on the Baconian Conception of Probability," *Journal of the History of Ideas* 41 (1980): 219–31.

Crane, Ronald S. "The Relation of Bacon's *Essays* to His Program for the Advancement of Learning." Reprinted in Brian Vickers (ed.). *Essential Articles for the Study of Francis Bacon,* 272–92. Hamden, Connecticut: Archon Books, 1968.

Crowther, J. G. *Francis Bacon, The First Statesman of Science.* London: Cresset Press, 1960.

Dean, Leonard F. "Sir Francis Bacon's Theory of Civil History-Writing." Reprinted in Brian Vickers (ed.). *Essential Articles for the Study of Francis Bacon,* 211–35. Hamden, Connecticut: Archon Books, 1968.

Durel-Leon, Henri. "De l'idée de progrès chez Bacon dans cinq oeuvres de la maturité," *Echanges: Actes du Congress de Strasbourg,* Études Anglaises, No. 81, 7–15. Paris: Didier, [n.d.].

Epstein, Joel J. *Francis Bacon: A Political Biography.* Athens, Ohio: Ohio University Press, 1977.

Esler, Anthony. *The Aspiring Mind of the Elizabethan Younger Generation.* Durham, North Carolina: Duke University Press, 1966.

Farrington, Benjamin. *Francis Bacon, Philosopher of Industrial Science.* New York: H. Schuman, 1949.

———. "On Misunderstanding the Philosophy of Francis Bacon." In *Science, Medicine, and History, Essays . . . in Honour of Charles Singer,* 1:439–50. Edited by E. A Underwood. 2 vols. London: Oxford University Press, 1953.

———. *The Philosophy of Francis Bacon.* Chicago: University of Chicago Press, 1966.

———. "Francis Bacon after His Fall," *Studies in the Literary Imagination* 4 (1971): 143–58.

Fattori, Marta. "Des Natures Simples chez Francis Bacon." Translated by Michele Fourment. *Recherches sur le VIIeme Siècle,* 5 (1982): 67–75.

Ferguson, Arthur B. "The Non-Political Past in Bacon's Theory of History," *The Journal of British Studies* 14 (1974): 4–20.

Fussner, F. Smith. *The Historical Revolution.* London: Routledge and Kegan Paul, 1962.

Gardiner, S. R. "Francis Bacon," *Dictionary of National Biography,* 1:800–816. Oxford: Oxford University Press, 1959–60.

George, C. M. "The 'Learned English Writer' in *Of Reformation,*" *Milton Newsletter* 3: 54–55.

Gilbert, Neal W. *Renaissance Concepts of Method.* New York: Columbia University Press, 1960.

Gooch, G. P. *Political Thought in England from Bacon to Halifax.* London: Williams and Norgate, 1923.

Greenleaf, W. H. *Order, Empiricism and Politics: Two Traditions of English Political Thought, 1500–1700.* London: Published for the University of Hull by the Oxford University Press, 1964.

Grossart, Alexander Balloch. "Ann Bacon," *Dictionary of National Biography,* 1:795–96. Oxford: Oxford University Press, 1959–60.

Hall, Marie Boas. "Bacon and Gilbert," *Journal of the History of Ideas* 12 (1951): 466–67.

_____. "In Defense of Bacon's Views on the Reform of Science," *The Personalist* 44 (1963): 437–53.

Hattaway, Michael. "Bacon and 'Knowledge Broken': Limits for a Scientific Method," *Journal of the History of Ideas* 39 (1978): 183–97.

Hesse, Mary. "Francis Bacon's Philosophy of Science." Reprinted in Brian Vickers (ed.). *Essential Articles for the Study of Francis Bacon,* 141–52. Hampden, Connecticut: Archon Books, 1968.

Hexter, J. H. *Reappraisals in History: New Views on History and Society in Early Modern Europe,* 2d. ed. Chicago and London: University of Chicago Press, 1979.

Hill, Christopher. *Intellectual Origins of the English Revolution.* Oxford: Clarendon Press, 1965.

Hodges, Devon Leigh. "Anatomy as Science," *Assays: Critical Approaches to Medieval and Renaissance Texts* 1 (1981): 73–89.

Jardine, Lisa. *Francis Bacon: Discovery and the Art of Discourse.* London; New York: Cambridge University Press, 1974.

Johnson, Robert C. "Francis Bacon and Lionel Cranfield," *Huntington Library Quarterly* 23 (August 1960): 301–20.

Jones, Richard Foster. *Ancients and Moderns: A Study of the Rise of the Scientific Movement in Seventeenth Century England.* Berkeley and Los Angeles: University of California Press, 1965.

Jones, Whitney R. D. *The Tudor Commonwealth, 1529–1559.* London: University of London, The Athelone Press, 1970.

Keller, Evelyn Fox. "Baconian Science: A Hermaphroditic Birth," *The Philosophical Forum* 11 (1980): 299–308.

Kelly, Aileen. "Alexander Herzen and Francis Bacon," *Journal of the History of Ideas* 41 (1980): 635–62.

Knappen, M. M. *Tudor Puritanism: A Chapter in the History of Idealism.* Chicago and London: University of Chicago Press, Phoenix Books, 1966.

Kocher, Paul H. "Francis Bacon and His Father," *Huntington Library Quarterly* 21 (1958): 133–58.

_____. "Francis Bacon on the Science of Jurisprudence." Reprinted in Brian Vickers (ed.). *Essential Articles for the Study of Francis Bacon,* 3–26. Hamden, Connecticut: Archon Books, 1968.

Koyre, Alexandre. *From the Closed World to the Infinite Universe.* Baltimore: Johns Hopkins Press, 1968.

Larsen, Robert E. "The Aristotelianism of Bacon's *Novum Organum,*" *Journal of the History of Ideas* 23 (1962): 435–50.

Lemmi, Charles W. *The Classic Deities in Bacon: A Study of Mythological Symbolism.* Baltimore: Johns Hopkins Press, 1933.

Levy, F. J. *Tudor Historical Thought.* San Marino, California: The Huntington Library, 1967.

_____, (ed.). *The History of the Reign of King Henry VII by Francis Bacon.* Indianapolis, New York: Bobbs-Merrill, 1972.

Linden, Stanton J. "Francis Bacon and Alchemy: The Reformation of Vulcan," *Journal of the History of Ideas* 35 (1974): 547–60.

Macaulay, Thomas Babington. *Critical and Historical Essays Contributed to the Edinburgh Review.* London: Longman, Brown, Green, and Longmans, 1843.

Marwil, Jonathan. *Trials of Counsel: Francis Bacon in 1621.* Detroit: Wayne State University Press, 1976.

Mazzeo, Joseph Anthony. *Renaissance and Revolution: The Remaking of European Thought.* New York: Pantheon Books, 1965.

McCreary, Eugene P. "Bacon's Theory of Imagination Reconsidered," *The Huntington Library Quarterly* 36 (1973): 317–26.

McLuhan, Marshall. "Francis Bacon: Ancient or Modern?" *Renaissance and Reformation* 10 (1974): 93–98.

McNamee, Maurice B. "Bacon's Inductive Method and Humanistic Grammar," *Studies in the Literary Imagination* 4 (1971): 81–106.

Morris, Christopher. *Political Thought in England, Tyndale to Hooker.* London: Geoffrey Cumberlege, Oxford University Press, 1953.

Morrison, James C. "Philosophy and History in Bacon," *Journal of the History of Ideas* 38 (1977): 585–606.

Moser, Fernando de Mello. "The Island and the Vision: English Renaissance Approaches to the Problem of Perfection," *Studia Anglica Posnaniensia* 11 (1980): 155–62.

Mulryan, John. "The Occult Tradition and English Renaissance Literature," *Bucknell Review* 20 (1972): 53–72.

Multhauf, Robert P. "Copernicus and Bacon as Renovators of Science." In *Science and History: Studies in Honor of Edward Rosen,* 489–99. Studia Copernicana, 16. Wroclaw: The Polish Academy of Sciences Press, 1978.

Nadel, George H. "History as Psychology in Francis Bacon's Theory of History." Reprinted in Brian Vickers (ed.). *Essential Articles for the Study of Francis Bacon,* 236–49. Hamden, Connecticut: Archon Books, 1968.

Neale, J. E. *Elizabeth I and Her Parliaments, 1584–1601.* New York: W. W. Norton, 1966.

Paterson, Antoinette Mann. *Francis Bacon and Socialized Science.* Springfield, Illinois: Charles C. Thomas, 1973.

Patrick, J. Max. "Hawk versus Dove: Francis Bacon's Advocacy of a Holy War by James I against the Turks," *Studies in the Literary Imagination* 4 (1971): 159–71.

Prior, Moody. "Bacon's Man of Science." Reprinted in Brian Vickers (ed.). *Essential Articles for the Study of Francis Bacon,* 140–63. Hamden, Connecticut: Archon Books, 1968.

Quinton, Anthony. *Francis Bacon.* Oxford: Oxford University Press, 1980.

Ravetz, J. R. "Francis Bacon and the Reform of Philosophy." In Allen. G. Debus (ed.). *Science, Medicine and Society in the Renaissance: Essays to Honor Walter Pagel,* 2:97–119. 2 vols. New York: Science History Publications, 1972.

Rees, Graham. "Francis Bacon's Semi-Paracelsian Cosmology," *Ambix* 22 (1975): 81–101.

_____. "Francis Bacon's Semi-Paracelsian Cosmology and the Great Instaura-
tion," *Ambix* 22 (1975): 161–73.

_____. "The Fate of Bacon's Cosmology in the 17th Century," *Ambix* 24 (1977):
27–28.

_____. "Matter Theory: A Unifying Factor in Bacon's Natural Philosophy?"
Ambix 24 (1977): 110–25.

_____. "Francis Bacon on Verticity and the Bowels of the Earth," *Ambix* 26
(1979): 202–11.

_____. "An Unpublished Manuscript of Francis Bacon: Sylva Sylvarum Drafts
and Other Working Notes, *Annals of Science* 38 (1981): 377–412.

Renaldo, John J. "Bacon's Empiricism, Boyle's Science, and the Jesuit Response
in Italy," *Journal of the History of Ideas* 37 (1976): 689–95.

Rossi, Paolo. *Francis Bacon: From Magic to Science.* Tr. Sacha Rabinovitch.
London: Routledge and Kegan Paul, 1968.

Sessions, William. "Francis Bacon and the Negative Instance," *Renaissance Papers,* 1970: 1–9.

_____, (ed.). "The Legacy of Francis Bacon." A special issue of *Studies in the
Literary Imagination* 4 (1971).

Shapiro, Barbara. *Probability and Certainty in Seventeenth-Century England: A
Study of the Relationships between Natural Science, Religion, History,
Law, and Literature.* Princeton, New Jersey: Princeton University Press,
1983.

Skinner, Quentin. *The Foundations of Modern Political Thought.* 2 vols. Cambridge: Cambridge University Press, 1978.

Sprat, Thomas. *The History of the Royal-Society of London, For the Improving
of Natural Knowledge.* London: Printed by T. R. for J. Martyn, 1667.

Starkey, Thomas. *A Dialogue Between Reginald Pole & Thomas Lupset,* edited
by Kathleen M. Burton. London: Chatto & Windus, 1948.

Steadman, John M. "Beyond Hercules: Bacon and the Scientist as Hero," *Studies in the Literary Imagination* 4 (1971): 3–47.

Stephens, James. *Francis Bacon and the Style of Science.* Chicago: University of
Chicago Press, 1975.

Tillman, James S. "Bacon's Georgics of Science," *Papers on Language & Literature* 11 (1975): 357–66.

Tittler, Robert. *Nicholas Bacon: The Making of a Tudor Statesman.* Athens:
Ohio University Press, 1976.

Vickers, Brian. *Francis Bacon and Renaissance Prose.* Cambridge: Cambridge
University Press, 1968.

_____. *Essential Articles for the Study of Francis Bacon.* Hamden, Connecti-
cut: Archon Books, 1968.

_____. "Bacon's Use of Theatrical Imagery," *Studies in the Literary Imagina-
tion* 4 (1971): 189–226.

Wallace, Karl R. *Francis Bacon on Communication and Rhetoric.* Chapel Hill:
University of North Carolina Press, 1943.

_____. *Francis Bacon on the Nature of Man; The Faculties of Man's Soul:*

Understanding, Reason, Imagination, Memory, Will, and Appetite. Urbana: University of Illinois Press, 1967.

————. "Discussion in Parliament and Francis Bacon." Reprinted in Brian Vickers (ed.). *Essential Articles for the Study of Francis Bacon,* 195–210. Hamden, Connecticut: Archon Books, 1968.

Warhaft, Sidney. "Bacon and the Renaissance Ideal of Self-Knowledge," *The Personalist,* 44 (1963): 454–71.

Webster, Charles. *The Great Instauration: Science, Medicine and Reform, 1626–1660.* New York: Holmes & Meier, 1975.

Weinberger, J. "Science and Rule in Bacon's Utopia," *American Political Science Review* 70 (1976), 865–85.

Wheeler, Thomas V. "Sir Francis Bacon's Historical Imagination," *Tennessee Studies in Literature* 14 (1969): 111–18.

Whitaker, Virgil K. "Francis Bacon's Intellectual Milieu." Reprinted in Brian Vickers (ed.). *Essential Articles for the Study of Francis Bacon,* 28–50. Hamden, Connecticut: Archon Books, 1968.

————. "Francesco Patrizi and Francis Bacon," *Studies in the Literary Imagination* 4 (1971): 107–20.

White, Howard B. *Peace Among the Willows.* The Hague: Martinus Nijhoff, 1968.

————. *Antiquity Forgot: Essays on Shakespeare, Bacon, and Rembrandt.* The Hague; Boston: Martinus Nijhoff, 1978.

Wiener, Harvey S. " 'Science or Providence': Toward Knowledge in Bacon's *New Atlantis,*" *Enlightenment Essays* 3 (1972): 85–92.

————. "Bacon and Poetry: A View of the *New Atlantis,*" *Anglia: Zeitschrift fuer Englische Philologie* 94 (1976): 69–85.

Zappen, James P. "Francis Bacon and the Rhetoric of Science," *College Composition and Communication,* 26 (1975): 244–47.

Zetterberg, J. Peter. "Echoes of Nature in Salomon's House,: *Journal of the History of Ideas* 43 (1982): 179–93.

Index